Lecture Notes in Computer Science　14417

Founding Editors

Gerhard Goos
Juris Hartmanis

Editorial Board Members

The series Lecture Notes in Computer Science (LNCS), including its subseries Lecture Notes in Artificial Intelligence (LNAI) and Lecture Notes in Bioinformatics (LNBI), has established itself as a medium for the publication of new developments in computer science and information technology research, teaching, and education.

LNCS enjoys close cooperation with the computer science R & D community, the series counts many renowned academics among its volume editors and paper authors, and collaborates with prestigious societies. Its mission is to serve this international community by providing an invaluable service, mainly focused on the publication of conference and workshop proceedings and postproceedings. LNCS commenced publication in 1973.

Pari Delir Haghighi · Ismail Khalil ·
Gabriele Kotsis · Ngurah Agus Sanjaya ER
Editors

Advances in Mobile Computing and Multimedia Intelligence

21st International Conference, MoMM 2023
Denpasar, Bali, Indonesia, December 4–6, 2023
Proceedings

Springer

Editors
Pari Delir Haghighi
Monash University
Melbourne, VIC, Australia

Gabriele Kotsis
Johannes Kepler University Linz
Linz, Austria

Ismail Khalil
Johannes Kepler University Linz
Linz, Austria

Ngurah Agus Sanjaya ER
Udayana University
Denpasar, Indonesia

ISSN 0302-9743   ISSN 1611-3349 (electronic)
Lecture Notes in Computer Science
ISBN 978-3-031-48347-9   ISBN 978-3-031-48348-6 (eBook)
https://doi.org/10.1007/978-3-031-48348-6

This Springer imprint is published by the registered company Springer Nature Switzerland AG
The registered company address is: Gewerbestrasse 11, 6330 Cham, Switzerland

Paper in this product is recyclable.

Preface

This volume includes the papers presented at the 21st International Conference on Advances in Mobile Computing & Multimedia Intelligence (MoMM 2023), which was held in person from the 4th to the 6th of December 2023, in conjunction with the 25th International Conference on Information Integration and Web Intelligence (iiWAS 2023) in Bali, Indonesia. The conference was conducted virtually for three years (2020–2022), and we were delighted to hold it in person in Bali this year.

This year we received 37 papers from 12 different countries about a wide range of research topics including IoT, mobile security, AI applications, digital health, and mobile sensing. The papers were thoroughly reviewed by at least two reviewers in terms of originality, contribution and relevance. 10 papers were accepted as full papers and 5 papers were accepted as short papers, making the acceptance rate of full papers 27%. Accepted papers present novel solutions to deal with real-world problems of mobile healthcare, mobile security and authentication, and image and video processing.

The accepted papers are published by Springer in their Lecture Notes in Computer Science (LNCS). This distinguished conference proceedings series is submitted for indexing in the Conference Proceedings Citation Index (CPCI), part of Clarivate Analytics' Web of Science; Scopus; EI Engineering Index; Google Scholar; DBLP; etc.

This year, we were honored to have two distinguished keynote speakers, René Mayrhofer from Johannes Kepler University Linz, Austria and Maureen Tanner from University of Cape Town, South Africa. We also had our World ABC (AI-Big Data Convergence) Forum, which consisted this year of a tutorial on Demystifying Large Language Models and Generative Pretrained Transformer hosted by Won Kim from Gachon University, South Korea, and a panel on the future of LLMs which featured experts from a variety of fields, including academia, industry, and government, who shared their insights and perspectives on the future of LLMs and discussed the challenges and opportunities that lie ahead.

We would like to extend our heartfelt thanks to all the participants, dedicated authors, program committee members, keynote speakers, session chairs, organizing and steering committee members, and Udayana University for their generous support, unwavering commitment and hard work in making the conference a successful and memorable event. We are highly confident that the MoMM conference series will thrive as a distinguished international platform for sharing innovative ideas and the latest research findings, thanks to the ongoing and generous support of its participants and contributors.

December 2023

Pari Delir Haghighi
Gabriele Kotsis
Ismail Khalil
Ngurah Agus Sanjaya ER

Organization

Program Committee Chair

Pari Delir Haghighi   Monash University, Australia

Steering Committee

Gabriele Kotsis   Johannes Kepler University Linz, Austria
Ismail Khalil   Johannes Kepler University Linz, Austria
Eric Pardede   La Trobe University, Australia
Dirk Draheim   Tallinn University of Technology, Estonia
Syopiansyah Jaya Putra   Universitas Islam Negeri, Indonesia

Organising Committee

Ngurah Agus Sanjaya ER   Udayana University, Indonesia
I Putu Agung Bayupati   Udayana University, Indonesia

Program Committee Members

Abdur Forkan   Swinburne University, Australia
Agustinus Borgy Waluyo   Monash University, Australia
Amin Beheshti   Macquarie University, Australia
Anas Dawod Alrefaee   Swinburne University of Technology, Australia
Andreas Schrader   University of Lübeck, Germany
Andrzej Romanowski   Łódź University of Technology, Poland
Antonio Liotta   Free University of Bozen-Bolzano, Italy
Carlos Calafate   Universitat Politècnica de València, Spain
Chang Wu Yu   Chung Hua University, Taiwan
Chien-Cheng Lee   Yuan Ze University, Taiwan
Chow-Sing Lin   National University of Tainan, Taiwan
Chun-Hsin Wu   National University of Kaohsiung, Taiwan
Clemens Holzmann   University of Applied Sciences Upper Austria, Austria
Driss El Ouadghiri   Moulay Ismail University, Morocco

Federico Montori	University of Bologna, Italy
Hong Va Leong	Hong Kong Polytechnic University, China
Luca Davoli	University of Parma, Italy
Markku Turunen	University of Tampere, Finland
Marco Martalò	University of Cagliari, Italy
Panayotis Fouliras	University of Macedonia, Greece
Paolo Bellavista	University of Bologna, Italy
Prem Prakash Jayaraman	Swinburne University of Technology, Australia
Rene Mayrhofer	Johannes Kepler University Linz, Austria
Sami Habib	Kuwait University, Kuwait
Sara Comai	Politecnico di Milano, Italy
Srikanth Thudumu	Deakin University, Australia
Svetlana Boudko	Norsk Regnesentral (Norwegian Computing Center), Norway
Tejal Shah	Newcastle University, UK
Tommi Mikkonen	University of Helsinki, Finland
Tsutomu Terada	Kobe University, Japan
Tzung-Pei Hong	National University of Kaohsiung, Taiwan
Tzung-Shi Chen	National University of Tainan, Taiwan
Vilmos Simon	Budapest University of Technology and Economics, Hungary
Wen-Yang Lin	National University of Kaohsiung, Taiwan
Wolfgang Schreiner	Johannes Kepler University Linz, Austria
You-Chiun Wang	National Sun Yat-sen University, Taiwan
Yusuke Gotoh	Okayama University, Japan
Yuxin Zhang	Monash University, Australia

External Reviewers

Andreas Riegler	University of Applied Sciences Campus Hagenberg, Austria
Krzysztof Romanowski	Łódź University of Technology, Poland
Muhammad Azfar Yaqub	Free University of Bozen-Bolzano, Italy
Przemysław Kucharski	Łódź University of Technology, Poland

Organizers

The Android Platform Security Model (and the Security Status of Actual Devices) (Abstract of Keynote Talk)

René Mayrhofer

Johannes Kepler University Linz, Austria

Abstract. This talk is about the Android platform with over 3 billion active devices - not even counting devices that are based on AOSP (the Android Open-Source Project code) but are not officially Android. Providing security guarantees in such a massive and diverse ecosystem with multiple stakeholders is a major challenge. This keynote will present the main aspects of the security model, system architecture, and mitigations and safeguards developed over more than 10 years. Some of the early design decisions shaped the platform from the start and still form the foundation for its current security posture, while many additional safeguards were added over time. More recently, an academic consortium has started building a public transparency database for collecting measurements about the security status of devices, both from special device farms under laboratory settings and from in-the-field devices through crowdsourcing. Using such data to check for compliance with the Android platform security model and potentially ranking devices based on their security attributes is another interesting challenge. In this keynote, we will also present the current state of this database and ideas for next steps.

Contents

Security in Mobile Environments

Anonymously Publishing Liveness Signals with Plausible Deniability 3
  Michael Sonntag, René Mayrhofer, and Stefan Rass

Analysis of Data Obtained from the Mobile Botnet 20
  Jaroslaw Kobiela and Piotr Urbaniec

On the Impact of FFP2 Face Masks on Speaker Verification for Mobile
Device Authentication 35
  David Sedlak and Rainhard Dieter Findling

Blockchain-Enhanced IoHT: A Patient-Centric Internet of Healthcare
Things Platform with Smart Contract-Driven Data Management 50
  N. H. Bang, T. D. Khoa, M. N. Triet, V. H. Khanh, H. G. Khiem,
  Q. T. Bao, N. T. Phuc, M. D. Hieu, V. C. P. Loc, T. L. Quy, N. T. Anh,
  Q. N. Hien, L. K. Bang, D. P. N. Trong, N. T. K. Ngan, H. Son,
  and H. H. Luong

Federated Learning for Collaborative Cybersecurity of Distributed
Healthcare 57
  Svetlana Boudko

Mobile Computing and Wireless Sensors

Does Use of Blink Interface Affect Number of Blinks When Reading
Paper Books? 65
  Junpei Uchida, Tsutomu Terada, and Masahiko Tsukamoto

A Method for Stimuli Control of Carbonated Beverages by Estimating
and Reducing Carbonation Level 77
  Yusuke Miyajima, Tsutomu Terada, and Masahiko Tsukamoto

A Knee Injury Prevention System by Continuous Knee Angle Recognition
Using Stretch Sensors 93
  Ayumi Ohnishi, Kota Kirinoe, Tsutomu Terada, and Masahiko Tsukamoto

Ubiquitous Mobile Application for Conducting Occupational Therapy
in Children with ADHD 104
  Jonnathan Berrezueta-Guzman, Melissa Montalvo, and Stephan Krusche

Wearable Device Supporting Light/Dark Adaptation   120
   Hiroki Sato, Ayumi Ohnishi, Tsutomu Terada, and Masahiko Tsukamoto

Image and Video Processing

Face to Face with Efficiency: Real-Time Face Recognition Pipelines
on Embedded Devices   129
   Philipp Hofer, Michael Roland, Philipp Schwarz, and René Mayrhofer

Multi-camera Live Video Streaming over Wireless Network   144
   Takashi Koyama and Yusuke Gotoh

Effects of Deep Generative AutoEncoder Based Image Compression
on Face Attribute Recognition: A Comprehensive Study   159
   Ahmed Baha Ben Jmaa and Dorsaf Sebai

Implementation of a Video Game Controlled by Pressing the Upper Arm
Using PPG Sensor   173
   Kazuki Yoshida, Goro Mizuno, Naoki Kurata, and Kazuya Murao

Immerscape: Supporting the Creation of Immersive Soundscapes by Users
in Cultural Heritage Contexts   179
   Carolina Ferreira, Sofia Cavaco, Armanda Rodrigues, and Nuno Correia

Author Index   187

Security in Mobile Environments

Anonymously Publishing Liveness Signals with Plausible Deniability

Michael Sonntag[1][✉] ⓘ, René Mayrhofer[1] ⓘ, and Stefan Rass[2] ⓘ

[1] Institute of Networks and Security, Johannes Kepler University Linz,
Altenbergerstr. 69, 4040 Linz, Austria
`{michael.sonntag,rene.mayrhofer}@ins.jku.at`
[2] LIT Secure and Correct Systems Lab, Johannes Kepler University Linz,
Altenbergerstr. 69, 4040 Linz, Austria
`stefan.rass@jku.at`

Abstract. Sometimes entities have to prove to others that they are still alive at a certain point in time, but with the added requirements of anonymity and plausible deniability; examples for this are whistleblowers or persons in dangerous situations. We propose a system to achieve this via hash chains and publishing liveness signals on Tor onion services. Even if one participant is discovered and (made to) cooperate, others still enjoy plausible deniability. To support arbitrary numbers of provers on a potentially limited list of online storage services, an additional "key" distinguishes multiple provers. This key should neither be static nor predictable to third parties, and provide forward secrecy. We propose both a derivation from user-memorable passwords and an initial pairing step to transfer unique key material between prover and verifier. In addition to describing the protocol, we provide an open source App implementation and evaluate its performance.

Keywords: liveness · plausible deniability · hash chain

1 Introduction

For their personal safety, whistleblowers[1] need to prove that they are still alive to, e.g., prevent a "security package" stashed with a third party from being published. Of course, this only works well if the third party (or parties — there may be multiple) remains unknown to any potential threats for the whistleblowers themselves. Also, as soon as whistleblowers have been apprehended, their devices

---

[1] In this paper we use the term "whistleblower" as a placeholder for any person — or potentially some process — who may be in possession of confidential material, publicly, politically, militarily, or legally exposed for any reason, or otherwise threatened in relation to them potentially releasing such information to the public. There are too many threat scenarios to list exhaustively, which is why we use the commonly known term whistleblower when implying the general threat model and, synonymously, the term "prover" when implying the protocol aspects without loss of generality.

© The Author(s), under exclusive license to Springer Nature Switzerland AG 2023
P. Delir Haghighi et al. (Eds.): MoMM 2023, LNCS 14417, pp. 3–19, 2023.
https://doi.org/10.1007/978-3-031-48348-6_1

will be investigated and all data extracted. This should not allow to a) identify the third party/parties and b) if these are discovered despite all precautions, they should be able to plausibly deny that they are acting as such third parties. The same applies in reverse: if a third party is somehow discovered, it should remain impossible to discover the whistleblower or prove that someone suspected as that person was connected to this person in any way. While, depending on the circumstances, mere suspicion of being any party (whistleblower or trusted third party) might be enough for dire consequences [13,20,24], at least no technical proof should be possible. We note explicitly that hiding the fact that a party has been interacting with our proposed service (e.g., but not limited to, having installed the mobile client app) is outside the scope of this paper.

Such a scheme requires the whistleblower ("*prover*") to transmit or publish some data ("*signal*"), from which one/several third parties ("*verifiers*") can conclude the prover was "alive and well" at a certain point in time (e.g. when the signal was published). To prevent correlation attacks, signals must be published and retrieved asynchronously, i.e., stored on some publicly accessible location (typically a website) by the prover, while verifiers ideally access this location as part of their standard activities (e.g. "visiting some website and viewing content"). While a storage server for verifying liveness can also store the "security package" (to be published if the verifier is considered "dead"), it obviously must be encrypted and solely verifiers should know the decryption key. The storage server should not simultaneously be a verifier, as then direct and synchronous communication between them would take place; also trust in this context is typically something between two persons and not a person and some (potentially very large) organization. Both sending and verifying signals should look innocent, i.e., observing their traffic should not allow anyone to conclude that they are party to such a scheme. While a prover is typically a single person, one prover might have several verifiers. These could be e.g. journalists, friends, or representatives of trustworthy foreign institutions — someone the prover trusts[2]. At some previous point a brief secure communication with them is needed (e.g. in person), but not anymore during the scheme. If one verifier is discovered, not only the prover but any other verifier should enjoy anonymity and plausible deniability (see [3] for definitions and kinds) even under the assumption of collusion of *all* other participants. Plausible deniability is not a legal term; it should be seen as the existence of other explanations, which are at least as likely as the actual one, shifting the burden of proof to the other party. As a minimum, any existing suspicion may not be increased through any traces which might be found with full access to all devices and their forensic examination (i.e. including investigations touching national security and so enjoying almost unlimited ressources).

To solve this problem, we propose a system based on Tor onion services [5] combined with hash chains for publishing such signals. The signal itself is solely a binary flag "I am alive" and has no other content (for a related approach for signals alone without a verifier secret/considering storage see [21]), so here we focus solely on the publishing/verification and the storage aspect of the problem.

---

[2] Should this trust be misplaced, deniability gets very important — only the statement/data of that person should be available to attackers, but no other evidence.

2 Related Work

The potential issue of whistleblower protection has already been used as the motivation for very different technical approaches. Time-lock puzzles [18] seem to have been one of the first proposals suggesting the use of trusted agents to help with timed information release. More recently, public ledgers were proposed as a storage mechanism that could release information if heartbeats are not regularly received (e.g., in CALYPSO [12]). Other solutions to assist whisteblowers are confidential (in the sense of protecting sender anonymity) document submission systems such as SecureDrop[3] [22], which is in use by major newspapers [7], or anonymous messaging systems like Ricochet [2], Cwtch [17], or others (that no longer seem to be under active development). Group authentication in such anonymous messaging settings is even more challenging [4,23].

Many of these rely on onion routing [6] to hide sender and receiver IP addresses, particularly on *Tor Onion* services [25,26], as we also propose here. We argue that the use of Tor onion services no longer constitutes a proof of suspicion towards potential whistleblowers, as even large-scale services like Facebook or X/Twitter now offer access via onion services to work around local network censorship/monitoring [1,27]. Also, e.g., Cloudflare offers to provide access to websites hosted by them via onion services: when users connect via Tor to "somedomain.com" hosted by Cloudflare (and this feature is enabled), they will be redirected internally to an onion service of this domain [19]. From the security/anonymity point of view this changes little, but performance increases and no external exit-node is involved. Tor users will then use onion services even if they don't know the actual onion URL, increasing their utilization. A custom HTTP header was defined to "redirect" normal traffic to an onion address (which is much harder to remember) [11] too, for sites hosted in any other manner. When selecting anonymizing techniques, any method with a small number of users acts as a signal just through its network traffic patterns, independently of the content transported through it. Therefore, onion services seem to be the best compromise for a widely deployed and usable system with reasonable anonymity guarantees, even though onion service use can be measured at least statistically [10].

Recent research [8] describes how a deniable protocol can be subverted via remote attestation: through performing the local part of the protocol in a Trusted Execution Environment (TEE), a non-repudiable transcript can be generated in an undetectable way, so a party can later prove to third persons that the (then no longer undeniable) protocol was actually performed by them. However, this is not applicable to our proposal. We assume that an attacker can "convince" one (known) party/parties in some manner to cooperate, and therefore "trusts" them anyway. So moving the calculation of parts of our protocol into a TEE to attest that it actually took place as claimed has no influence on the deniability of the other party: the sender does not know whether the recipient even retrieved the signal and so could only prove that they sent a signal — providing no data on any potential verifier. On the other hand, the recipient can only prove that

---

[3] Available online at https://securedrop.org/.

someone sent a valid signal and they received/verified it, but not who did this. For an attacker this would only make sense if he could modify the hardware of a party undetectedly, first having identified them. However, in that case software modification (trojanizing their device) would be sufficient and produce exactly the same information: confirmation that the local activity took place, but no additional information about the other side.

In this paper, we focus specifically on preventing de-anonymization of either a whistleblower (prover) or people communicating with them (verifiers) regarding their "liveness". That is, actual (confidential, integrity-assured, and potentially authenticated) document or message transmission is out of scope here. However, we focus on the deniability aspect of locally detectable signals under the assumption that end-user devices of provers or verifiers are captured, which in turn is out of scope of many of the anonymous messaging or document submission services mentioned. Our goal is to provide plausible deniability of involvement in a specific whistleblower process as a certain party (prover or verifier) even for a person whose device is forensically analysed. Therefore, our scope is especially on the sending and receiving of liveness signals as one component of a whistleblowing process and a tool for assisting in the protection of whistleblowers.

3   Possible Alternative Approaches

An alternative solution to the one proposed here could be "classified ads": on some public site (e.g. X/Twitter, Facebook) a code is posted by the prover, telling verifiers that she/he is still alive. But this approach has several shortcomings: you need to register to be able to post (which typically means a valid E-Mail address and some E-Mail communication for account verification; today often a phone number too) and logging in to send. Depending on the service logins may be required for checking the existence of a post. Finding them might mean deliberately searching for them (= entering keywords). States can easily block or (selectively) delay access to such services generally or for individual users. Removal by the website (e.g., "only text messages, no binary codes", complaints/takedown notices) are an increasing difficulty. Any "technical" signal like a hash value is obvious as such, easily discovered automatically, and directly tied to a sender, while "normal" text would either have to be repeated for every signal instance (=suspicious) or require a complex scheme/external storage for changing content. Also, the complete message history with start and end date is (usually publicly, but at least for the service provider) available and easily archived by third parties for later verification too. In contrast, the presence of a Tor browser, or e.g., Tails Linux (no installation needed), is much more open to interpretation and while potentially suspicious for certain regimes, typically not in itself illegal and not useful to identify past usage patterns or behavior in any case.

Signing a public message by any other person like a recent newspaper article (could even be randomly selected as long as the source is provided) requires either a real public key (i.e., identifying the prover) or agreeing with each prover on a separate keypair. Remembering these is difficult and storing them is also potentially suspicious. Additionally, it immediately discloses the existence of the scheme and requires larger storage (for providing the source as well as a unique extract of the message beside the signature). This also doesn't solve the problem of the identical storage locations for each such message.

Such a scheme must be solely asynchronous communication or correlation attacks are possible, not only for verifying existing suspicions but with large-scale monitoring for identifying a — potentially small — subset of candidates for further investigation too. Therefore, approaches like double ratchet protocols [15] are unsuitable, as here no return channel exists. All logical communication must be solely one-directional from the prover to the verifier. Technically, the prover contacts the storage location to submit data, and at some later time verifiers individually contact the same storage location to retrieve it. Any return communication enhances the dangers of discovering an involved person.

4   Proposed Solutions

We propose two solutions, the main one described first and in detail, the possible alternative (albeit with certain shortcomings) briefly. The signal for this protocol is assumed to be short, like a single data block of 32–64 bytes, i.e., a hash value.

4.1   Main Solution

To prevent correlation attacks, signals are stored on third-party Tor onion services. This ensures transport encryption as well as meta data hiding (at least for address information if not for statistical traffic analysis) for prover and verifier when submitting/verifying a signal. If other activities, like web browsing via Tor (preferably on onion sites), are performed simultaneously, this effectively hides participation in such a protocol from on-path adversaries, as both submitting and checking a signal consist only of two (obtain&receive input for proof of work, submit result of challenge&submit/receive signal) short requests and responses.

Because it might be possible to distinguish normal Tor traffic from onion service access [14], it is beneficial that signal storage servers at the same time offer non-related (e.g. web) services through the same endpoint. While other activities should be performed there, their exact nature and duration is irrelevant: it is solely important that accessing that onion service does not solely consist of sending/verifying a signal. Then the traffic will not be easily recognizable as traffic related to this protocol. If both sides are known (prover or verifier and storage server), correlation is possible (which works reliably even for Tor [16]), but then the additional activity again prevents identifying the actions performed there as part of a liveness scheme — only of accessing this specific onion service.

A storage server can be run by anyone as a public service; a signal itself consist of only few bytes, so very few resources are needed. Additionally, their actions are extremely simple: submitting a value for storage or retrieving a specific value. The only useful attacks are DoS (deleting/modifying signals, thereby rendering responses invalid) and helping in correlation attacks (disclosing exactly when a signal is submitted/queried for or sending too large replies). If the person performs other activities via Tor on other sites simultaneously, the latter should not matter. Note that two signals/queries cannot be identified to come from the same party. As no payment is involved in the protocol, hosting such servers must be performed as a public service. However, because the demand on the server is likely minimal (see Sect. 4.1), this can be easily added to other public onion services, simultaneously taking care of publicizing/obtaining such an onion URL.

To facilitate selection of individual signals, they are associated with a "key" changing on every signal, i.e. specifically not a static or unique "prover ID". The storage server requires some proof of work (PoW) for submitting or retrieving a signal, e.g. performing some calculation that requires several seconds on a fast computer. This reduces the danger of DoS attacks through submitting huge numbers of signals, continuously retrieving them, or attempting to traverse the key space. A relatively small PoW comparable to intentionally slow derivation functions like Argon2 (used for verifying passwords) is sufficient here to balance DoS attacks on signal servers with the load on clients (in addition to the cryptographic requirements for onion connections; when performing other activities on the storage server as suggested even a 30 s delay for very slow computers would be irrelevant). As this is a challenge/response protocol, even very strong computational ressources are of limited use: enforcing creation of a new Tor circuit for every interaction is possible and proves an additional hurdle solely for attackers. In Sect. 4.1 we give an approximation of the load a single attacker can put on a storage server: very little, so even thousands of simultaneous attacks are of limited impact (e.g. 1000 attackers only produce 15 GB storage demand and negligible computational load - challenge generation/verification is trivial). In case a key is requested for which no data was stored, random data is generated by the server, stored (= same response on subsequent queries), and returned. Therefore, anyone querying cannot determine whether a signal had been submitted under that key or not. No identification is needed for submitting a signal, only completing the PoW. Signals are automatically deleted after an appropriate period, e.g., a day or a week (delay set by server for everyone to limit its storage load). Deleting them after the first query is not done, as an adversary might then discover whether a signal was queried for or not (and multiple verifiers for a single prover would not work).

As the signal itself is part of the hash chain, the verifier can be sure it was created by someone knowing the shared secret — i.e. the prover. Note that because of the direction of the chain, the verifier cannot calculate the "next" signal from the data they know, so impersonation by a (second) verifier is impossible.

Using multiple storage servers (= multiple onion URLs) enhances resilience. While a signal could be stored on each of them under the same key, it is advisable to use different data (and therefore different keys) on each server, as otherwise querying all of them for a non-existing key will produce different (random) values, while an existing key would return the same value, disclosing whether a key is valid or not. The number of storage servers required is determined by the trust in their continued provision of this service and the duration envisaged for the liveness scheme (trustworthy servers + brief duration = one server). Note that servers cannot be added later except via an additional secure out-of-band data exchange. Spare servers, which are only used if the first one is unavailable for whatever reason, are possible: only their onion URL is required and no data needs to be shared with them (prover → server or verifier → server) or with the other parties (between prover and verifiers) regarding them. It is therefore possible to use servers from a public trusted list accessible to both; however, accessing the list is a potential sign of involvement.

The storage key is calculated based on a hash chain (see formal description below): the prover creates a start value and shares this and an additional secret with one or more trustworthy verifiers. This has to be done securely, but is a very brief and one-time-only activity before any part of the protocol takes places electronically and therefore potentially observable for attackers. If this shared secret is lost, there is no recovery mechanism — a new secret has to be agreed upon by prover and verifier. Concatenating the start value and the secret and hashing it twice (in different configuration) produces the next key. This prevents third parties, which do not know this shared secret, from determining the next location under which a signal from the same prover will be stored, respectively looked for, as well as replay attacks.

After successfully verifying a signal, locally stored data is overwritten by new values, preventing adversaries from obtaining information on previous signals. The new key data is the result after only a single hashing, so that knowing a signal key (or simply storing them all and later trying brute-force) does not allow "calculating" forward even if the shared secret is obtained by an adversary (to avoid recreating later elements in the chain, the shared secret is appended for the key data and prepended for the actual key). This approach allows a verifier to also calculate future keys, even if a (range of) signal(s) was missed. Verification should consider as many keys as could have been generated up to the current time (and lost intermediate values) - or until the prover is considered "dead".

The current key data both parties store is random data from the point of view of adversaries as it is produced as the output of a hash function[4]: all binary values are valid in-/outputs, so it can be easily encrypted with any local value too. For this we suggest a human-brain only secret (=password) converted via a Password-Based Key Derivation Function (PBKDF, e.g. Argon2) and XORed with the key data. In this way, both prover and verifier have to remember a single shared secret/password and an individual own secret/password not disclosed to anyone else at any time. Note that disclosing an incorrect password - and its derived data - cannot be distinguished from those based on the correct one.

The (encrypted) key data stored by the verifier is the base data for the next key (note that this is not the key as such, as this will be hashed once before being used; see above), which is different at both parties exactly because of

---

[4] We currently rely on standard, non-random-oracle hash functions for building the hash chains of location keys and signals, and therefore do not aim for proofs under the random oracle model for properties of these chains.

this encryption. The prover does not store this value; it is calculated only when sending a signal. While the encryption key is the same length as the data, it includes the verifier's secret value so it changes on every signal too.

Because of these two elements we argue (without formal proof) that this fulfills IND-CCA2 as well as being indistinguishable from random noise as no other data encrypted with the same key is available to an adversary and XOR-encryption with a key used only once is similar to a one-time pad. The only difference is that the key in this scheme is the result of a hash function and therefore not truly random — but depending on the hash algorithm unpredictable enough without the input data. Any reasonably fast one-way derivation is suitable, especially cryptographic hash functions. As key and verification data are a single hash value each (e.g. 32 bytes), they can be explained as various other data because they look purely random and can so easily be incorporated in arbitrary steganographic schemes. Examples for this are e.g., internal checksums of (deliberately) damaged pictures (so no checksum verification is possible anyway), keys from other applications, or simply data left over on the disk from previous files. As the prover can designate any two similarly changing values as his (claimed as such) verification data (or randmly generate such), the data of both parties looks exactly the same (same count, length, properties). Therefore a prover can successfully claim to merely be a verifier.

Signal Calculation Algorithm

Signal$_0$ "Random" data of length of hash function output. Random initialization vector or e.g. H(ProverSecret | SharedSecret) (Fig. 1: S_0; PS ProverSecret, SS SharedSecret)

Signal$_i$ $=$ H(Signal$_{i-1}$ | SharedSecret) (Fig. 1: S_i)

Key Calculation Algorithm

KeyData$_N$ "Random" data of length of hash function output. This is beyond the "end" of the chain of signals, i.e. a continuation (Fig. 1: $KD_N = S_N$)

KeyData$_i$ $=$ H(KeyData$_{i+1}$ | SharedSecret) Data for deriving the next key (Fig. 1: KD_i)

Key$_i$ $=$ H(SharedSecret | KeyData$_i$) Key for publishing the signal (Fig. 1: K_i)

KeyData is used in reverse order, i.e. the first signal (value Signal$_{N-1}$) uses KeyData$_{N-1}$ resp. Key$_{N-1}$. The last possible signal uses Key$_0$ with value Signal$_0$.

Verification Algorithm For its stored data, a Verifier takes S_N and SS (exchanged with Prover) and calculates these values by adding its own secret data:

VerificationData$_{N-1}$ $=$ H(Signal$_N$ | VerifierSecret) (Fig. 2: V_i; VS Verifier-Secret)

KeyData$_{N-1}$^{Enc} $=$ H(Signal$_N$ | SharedSecret) $\oplus$ Argon2(Verifier Secret | VerificationData$_{N-1}$) (Fig. 2: KD$_{N-1}$)

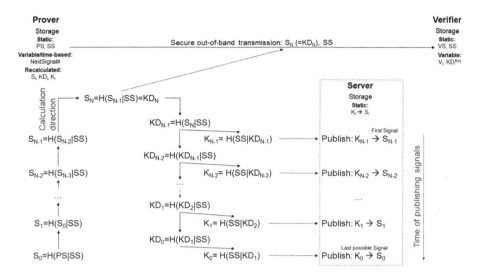

Fig. 1. Graphical description of the protocol - Prover part.

Verifying signal i ([1...N] in temporally ascending sequence) works as follows:

KeyData$_{N-i}$ = KeyData$_{N-i}{}^{Enc} \oplus$ Argon2(VerifierSecret | VerificationData$_{N-i}$)

Key$_{N-i}$ = H(SharedSecret | KeyData$_{N-i}$)

Success? H(H(Signal$_{N-i}$ | SharedSecret) | VerifierSecret) $==$ Verification Data$_{N-i}$

If "Success": Calculate VerificationData$_{N-i-1}$=H(Signal$_{N-i}$ | VerifierSecret) and store it. Conclude prover to be "alive". Calculate and store KeyData$_{N-i-1}{}^{Enc}$= H(KeyData$_{N-i}$ | SharedSecret) $\oplus$ Argon2(VerifierSecret | VerificationData$_{N-i-1}$)

If "Fail": Don't update KeyData$_{N-i-1}{}^{Enc}$. VerificationData$_{N-i-1}$ cannot be calculated anyway, as Signal$_{N-i}$ is unknown. Try again later with identical (retrieval problem) or on the next timeslot (incorrect result) updated data: KeyData$_{N-i-1}$=H(KeyData$_{N-i}$ | SharedSecret) and Key$_{N-i-1}$ = H(SharedSecret | KeyData$_{N-i-1}$). Compare then H(H(H(Signal$_{N-i-1}$ | SharedSecret) | SharedSecret) | VerifierSecret) to the previous VerificationData$_{N-i}$. If unsuccessful after a verifier-determined number of tries, conclude the prover to be "dead".

Data Stored by Prover

- Onion address(es) of storage server(s) (string or binary value of public key - hidden or encrypted similar to the current key generation data as described below; or as well-known, remembered, or bookmarked "harmless" service)
- Shared secret (human memory only). See Fig. 1: *SS*.
- Prover secret (human memory only) for signal/key generation. Figure 1: *PS*.

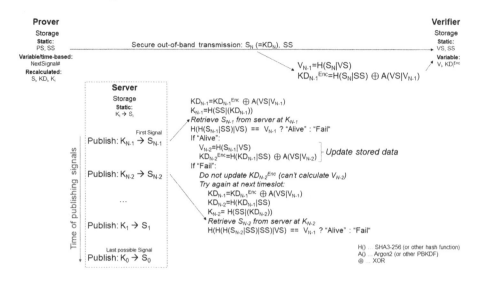

Fig. 2. Graphical description of the protocol - Verifier part.

– The number of the next signal (or some method of deriving it, e.g. through some starting point in time and the current date/time).

Data Stored by Verifier

– Onion address(es) of storage server(s) (same as above)
– Shared secret (human memory only; same as above). See Fig. 2: SS.
– Verifier secret (human memory only; similar to above). See Fig. 2: VS.
– Current key generation data. Encrypted via XOR with data derived from verifier secret and verification data during storage and ratcheted forward after each sending. See Fig. 2: KD_i resp. KD_i^{Enc}.
– Verification data for verifying the next signal value. Hash of current signal and verifier secret. See Fig. 2: V_i.

Data Stored by Onion Service Operator

– Map[key → signal]: Stored for a fixed duration, e.g., one day/week. For non-existing keys, random data is generated upon the first query and stored with the same retention period minus a random reduction to prevent detection of this fact.[5] Size per signal: $2 * 64$ Bytes + storage overhead. Assuming a

---

[5] This combination of requirements on the storage server make it act as a random oracle with time-outs or, in another interpretation, a series of random oracles defined by overlapping epochs. Such a random oracle service might be helpful for other cryptographic protocols whose security properties depend on a random oracle instead of standard hash functions for some building blocks. By re-using our proposed storage service for such other purposes, plausible deniability in communicating with this service could be significantly improved.

10-second PoW and one week retention period, a single computer solely sending random data can produce 60,480 signals; assuming 256 Byte for storage (=100%/128 bytes overhead) this translates to 14.8 MB storage wasted by a single malicious host. The probability of randomly generating exactly the next key is extremely low (using 1,000 PCs: 60,480,000 tries of a possible 2^{256} for a 256 bit hash; approx. $1:5.22 * 10^{-70}$); the prover would then be unable to store the signal, but it is extremely unlikely this will affect the next key again. When tolerating at least one missing signal no problem occurs.
- Secret data for generating/validating proof-of-work challenges.
- Temporary session data for a duration slightly longer than the maximum delay for completing the proof-of-work.

Length of Data to be Remembered For both prover and verifier two data elements should be stored solely in memory. But how long do these need to be (as humans are notoriously bad at remembering long random data)? The algorithm doesn't require a specific length, as they either serve as (part of) input to a hash function or are (preferably) used with a PBKDF. Consequently, any format/length is fine, as long as it is hard to discover via brute force attacks. They are equivalent to passwords, with all their problems and advantages: a short uncommon string is sufficient, as is a longer phrase of common words.

4.2 Alternative Solution

An alternative solution is to not store a fixed onion URL and employ varying keys, but rather generate a new onion URL — and therefore onion service — for each signal to replace the key. This allows to trivially swap storage servers: every hoster of the previous scheme can easily provide arbitrary additional tiny onion services with reasonable overhead [9]. Hosting an onion service for others is in this case harmless: it solely provides a single short static value upon every possible request (no other content, no input parsing, etc.). Using hierarchical encryption, from an initial private key and incorporating some secret data more private keys can be derived similar to a hash chain. Interestingly it is also possible with knowing solely the public key (and the secret data) to derive the matching public keys too. This technique is already used in onion services (v3) to mask the data sent to the hidden service directory (blinded keys [25]). However, each private key would have to be disclosed to the storage server as it is needed for operating the onion service. So the storage server cannot calculate the next keypair(s), the shared secret must be integrated in the key derivation (similar to deriving the keys from the keydata chain). This shared secret must be protected individually by each party (see above), as discovering it stored at both locations removes plausible deniability. As it is needed in cleartext for the calculations, hashing it for storage is impossible; but encryption works.

A deficiency of this approach is that, when performing hierarchical key derivation with Elliptic-Curve (EC) cryptography, the private key can be selected arbitrarily, but not the public key. So encrypting the private key by XOR with a random/secret value is possible and it still remains a "valid" private key. This is necessary for plausible deniability: disclosing an incorrect secret value still produces a valid private key (just without any other party). Because if private key and shared secret are stored in clear or disclosed by the prover — and so obtained by an adversary — the matching public key (and all future derived keypairs) can trivially be computed. If such a public key is found by an adversary at a suspect, the verifier role can no longer be denied. Unfortunately, masking similar to the prover is impossible for the verifier, as unlike the private key the public key for an EC cryptosystem *can* be verified: not all possible values are valid public keys. So a transformation is needed taking a valid public key and encrypting it so that it can be decrypted with two different arbitrary data (e.g. two passwords) resulting in two valid public keys (the second used for deniability). This could be achieved via deniable encryption and an arbitrary other public key as decoy. However, this still requires the decoy to point to a working onion service or be immediately recognizable as such. So the storage location would have to know that decoy private key, too. To be indistinguishable from the real key, it must be changed according to an identical schedule, so the verifier would have to act as a fake prover in this regard and initiate the decoy onion service creation. Still, prover and verifier are not as symmetric as a prover now stores one private key, and a verifier two public ones: a prover cannot as easily claim to be a verifier, as the private key will typically not validate successfully as a public key either.[6]

Another issue is that, if the prover is discovered and cooperates, future onion URLs can be calculated and hosted by the adversary as opposed by third parties in the previous scheme. The adversary can then much more easily (knowing the onion URLs of the third-party storage servers in the first scheme still requires discovering their physical locations before monitoring is possible) check whether someone attempts to verify liveness ($\rightarrow$ did the prover lie?) and obtains control over the process ($\rightarrow$ correlation attacks against suspected verifiers). Discovering the verifier does not allow such attacks, as while the public key alone does allow to pre-calculate the onion addresses, these will not be active earlier and, because of lack of the private key, cannot be impersonated or located in advance.

5   Limitations and Discussion

5.1   Limitations

Some limitations of this approach exist. Namely, the presence of the software needed for the scheme is a sign someone participates in it. This could be resolved by including it in a "standard installation", i.e., lots of persons possessing this software, but only few actually using it. Dedicated secure messaging apps like Signal seem like an optimal avenue to include such additional functions by default for the benefit of endangered minorities. The code required is minimal, so usability would be the main concern. Forensic investigations may provide traces,

---

[6] So two public key decoys are needed, for which the prover must initiate onion creation too, and the verifier needs an arbitrary fake private key.

whether some executable was run or not, so direct inclusion is preferable over adding it as "extension" or "module". Moving the software online is a bad idea, as this requires disclosing the secret (=human memory only) data to another party. However, providing it on a webpage ($\rightarrow$ no local software installation), e.g. as JavaScript, to be executed locally would work. This needs trust in the hoster and the transmission path that the downloaded program does not perform any other activities like sending data/keys to anyone. Securing the transmission is easy ($\rightarrow$ TLS), leaving how to recognize and trust the site. Manual verification of the software against a well-known hash value is possible, but not user-friendly, as is verifying some custom added signature. Storing the data in browser local storage immediately discloses participation in the scheme, as then there is no reasonable alternative explanation. The obvious approach, hosting it on the onion service used to store signals, is not necessarily secure: as a hoster providing storage few attacks are "interesting" (see above) and little trust in it is needed. Potentially trusting them with the keys and all private information is a much larger question. But approaches like binary transparency for web server content may be a future mitigation. Local caching after verification is the equivalent of a local installation and is detrimental to deniability. So if no local installation is acceptable, some trusted website (to avoid raising suspicion an onion service, not the public Internet) for hosting the software is required.

Another limitation is that all parties need to store the onion URL(s) of the storage server(s) (identical for each pair of prover/verifier), and because of the length/format this can hardly be done in human memory. If an onion URL solely provides a liveness service as described here, discovering the URL abolishes plausible deniability of participating in such a scheme. If an onion service provides other widely-used services, e.g., a normal webserver with legal and widely interesting content, the presence is much less of an evidence and could then even be stored as a bookmark. Candidates for including liveness storage services are e.g. secure drop sites that are already available as onion services at major news outlets (potentially problematic: also "undesirable" sites for adversaries interested in unmasking provers) or even public services like news outlets or social networks.

5.2 Plausible Deniability Achieved?

We now look at various scenarios to determine whether plausible deniability actually exists under the proposed scheme. We assume one party is fully cooperative (because of bribes, torture etc.) so the adversary obtains access to all their locally stored data, and either provides correct secrets from memory — or lies. Can such a lie be detected, and what does this imply for the other party/parties?

- Prover is "cooperative" and provides all secrets correctly, including memorized ones: The adversary obtains access to the initialization data and can calculate all keys for the future with the shared secret. But none of this data is found at a suspected verifier, as there the key data is encrypted with a secret solely known to this verifier, and the shared secret is stored solely in human memory.

The last key data of the suspected verifier can therefore be anything else or relate to a different prover. Lying about the verifier key or the shared secret produces keys indistinguishable from the ones used in the past and that can also be retrieved (as they are considered "valid" by the respective server(s)), but which cannot be successfully verified as a signal. So either the (fake) prover is no longer active, the verifier lied, or the data found is not related to such a scheme at all. Which case it is cannot be decided based on available data and all options are at least possible. As old key generation values cannot be generated (preimage attacks on the hash are assumed to be impractical) and are not stored, it cannot be proven that no previous values were valid keys or validated successfully. Even if all (globally observed) old keys and signals are known (e.g., stored for future validation; storage server cooperates/is the adversary), these cannot be used to generate later keys, preventing the adversary from proving no "old" but valid signals ever existed. As future keys are known through the prover, correlation attacks might be possible regarding suspected verifiers, but as the communication is asynchronous this requires locating the onion server, as without access to it, it is impossible to determine whether this server is accessed.

– Prover is "cooperative" but lies about the shared and/or prover secret: The adversary can calculate all (wrong) keys for the future, but nobody is going to check them — but this cannot be detected by an adversary. If this can be verified (the adversary controls the storage service or it cooperates), the prover can no longer deny that they are lying, but only if done quickly; otherwise, verifiers might already have concluded the prover as no longer active and do not check any longer.

– Verifier is "cooperative" and provides all secrets correctly: This is symmetric to the prover. Future keys can be calculated, but this data is not found at a suspected prover. However, working together with the storage service — after it being located — would allow correlation attacks (but nothing else).

– Verifier is "cooperative" but lies about the shared or verifier secret: The adversary can calculate (incorrect) future keys and query for them, but none can be verified successfully. Whether the prover is no longer active, stopped publishing signals for other reasons, or the verifier lied cannot be discerned.

– If a prover is found and all physically stored data is available, they can still claim to merely be a verifier: any arbitrary data can be designated as the variable verification and key data a verifier stores. The only limitation of plausible deniability is that no future "signal" can be successfully validated, so the (imaginary) "prover" is considered no longer active. Note that old keys/signals cannot be generated from this data in any case, so any past data stored by an adversary cannot be used for validation.

– If a verifier is found and all physically stored data is available, they can claim to be a prover (if desirable): they can designate the current key generation data as the initial data, producing a correct but unused hash chain. That there is no verifier validating these is again impossible to determine without timely collusion of the storage server. The only limitation is that the verification

data may not be discernible as such and can be explained as unrelated —
which should be possible for all the data.

5.3   Performance Evaluation

Using a prototype implementation of the protocol in Java, we measure the practical runtime overhead of creating and verifying signals on the client respectively
server sides. Both were executed on a (today comparatively slow) PC with Core
i5-2400 CPU (3.1 GHz) running Windows 10. We ignore the webserver here, as
that would require a PoW for the client, skewing the results enormously.

We measure execution speed after warm-up of the Java runtime by execut-
ing at least 10 similar operations (calculating the first signal with 1,000,000
potential signals as well as verifying) in the same instance before starting the
measurements, which are executed 100 times for averaging measurement noise
on the test systems. Calculating the initialization data (i.e., calculating the full
signal chain up plus a single additional hash to obtain the initialization data to
be shared with the verifier) takes on average 1.4 s. Verifying a signal requires
approx. 9 ms (most of this probably test overhead, as very few hashes need to be
calculated). Producing the last signal takes a bit longer, as the hash chain must
be calculated up to the first signal, and then down again to obtain the last key
data: 2.6 s. This seems reasonable, especially when considering that few application will require a million potential signals. Reducing this to 10,000 signals, the
duration drops to 13/27 ms for generation and 8 ms for validation (=unchanged;
independent of potential signal count), which should not be problematic even
for slow computers.

5.4   Prototype App Implementation

A prototypical implementation of the whole end-to-end user interaction process
in the form of an Android app accessing the fully implemented prototype webserver is available as open source at https://github.com/rmayr/livenesssignal-
android. The app implements both prover and verifier roles and only stores data
as described in the protocol above permanently on-device, protected with the
local app password. Passwords need to be entered on every invocation of the app
(sending or checking) and are not stored permanently.

To test the app and allow other researchers easy experimentation, a first
instance of our prototype webserver for hosting signals is available at http://
fng5mhuck2n7l4we2egjnbp6l4cofw46wjyvi7t6s37uhwbcanmylyqd.onion/liveness This
instance can be used by the general public, but may be subject to future restrictions depending on resource considerations. However, as described above, in the
absence of explicit DoS attacks, typical use of such a service should only result in
insignificant system load in the sense of computation, storage, and data transfer
requirements.

6   Conclusion

We provide a system for publishing liveness signals with plausible deniability: even if some participant of such a scheme is discovered, others can still plausibly deny their involvement or claim the opposite role. Two drawbacks are that possession of the software necessary for the scheme might provide a hint to participation, and that a third party is needed to host/publish signals. These are issues of our prototype implementation and could be overcome by a) integrating our liveness verification protocol into well-known apps or as a web page and b) hosting of storage servers by well-known web hosts. The system is easy to implement, fast, and fulfills all our requirements for anonymity and security.

Acknowledgments. This work has been carried out within the scope of Digidow, the Christian Doppler Laboratory for Private Digital Authentication in the Physical World. We gratefully acknowledge financial support by the Austrian Federal Ministry for Digital and Economic Affairs, the National Foundation for Research, Technology and Development and the Christian Doppler Research Association, 3 Banken IT GmbH, ekey biometric systems GmbH, Kepler Universitätsklinikum GmbH, NXP Semiconductors Austria GmbH, and Österreichische Staatsdruckerei GmbH.

References

1. Muffett, A.: On behalf of @Twitter, I am delighted to announce their new @TorProject onion service. https://twitter.com/AlecMuffett/status/1501282223009542151
2. Brooks, J.: Ricochet. https://ricochet.im/
3. Celi, S., Symeonidis, I.: The current state of denial. In: Privacy Enhancing Technologies Symposium (2020). https://petsymposium.org/2020/files/hotpets/The_current_state_of_denial.pdf
4. Corrigan-Gibbs, H., Ford, B.: Dissent: accountable anonymous group messaging. In: Proceedings of the 17th ACM Conference on Computer and Communications Security, pp. 340–350. CCS 2010. Association for Computing Machinery, New York (2010). https://doi.org/10.1145/1866307.1866346
5. Dingledine, R.: Next generation tor onion services. DEF CON **25** (2017)
6. Goldschlag, D., Reed, M., Syverson, P.: Onion routing. Commun. ACM **42**(2), 39–41 (1999)
7. Guardian, T.: The Guardian SecureDrop. https://www.theguardian.com/securedrop
8. Gunn, L.J., Parra, R.V., Asokan, N.: Circumventing cryptographic deniability with remote attestation. In: Proceedings on Privacy Enhancing Technologies **2019**(3), 350–369 (2019). https://doi.org/10.2478/popets-2019-0051
9. Höller, T., Raab, T., Roland, M., Mayrhofer, R.: On the feasibility of short-lived dynamic onion services. In: 2021 IEEE Security and Privacy Workshops (SPW), pp. 25–30. IEEE (May 2021). https://doi.org/10.1109/SPW53761.2021.0001
10. Höller, T., Roland, M., Mayrhofer, R.: On the state of V3 onion services. In: Proceedings of the ACM SIGCOMM 2021 Workshop on Free and Open Communications on the Internet (FOCI 2021), pp. 50–56. ACM (Aug 2021). https://doi.org/10.1145/3473604.3474565

11. Kadianakis, G.: Onion-location. https://gitweb.torproject.org/tor-browser-spec. git/tree/proposals/100-onion-location-header.txt
12. Kokoris-Kogias, E., Alp, E.C., Gasser, L., Jovanovic, P., Syta, E., Ford, B.: Calypso: private data management for decentralized ledgers. Cryptology ePrint Archive, Report 2018/209 (2018). https://ia.cr/2018/209
13. Kumagai, J.: The whistle-blower's dilemma. IEEE Spectrum (2004). https:// spectrum.ieee.org/the-whistleblowers-dilemma
14. Kwon, A., AlSabah, M., Lazar, D., Dacier, M., Devadas, S.: Circuit fingerprinting attacks: Passive deanonymization of tor hidden services. In: 24th USENIX Security Symposium (USENIX Security 2015), pp. 287–302. USENIX Association, Washington (Aug 2015), https://www.usenix.org/conference/usenixsecurity15/technical-sessions/presentation/kwon
15. Marlinspike, M.: The double ratchet algorithm. https://signal.org/docs/specifications/doubleratchet/
16. Nasr, M., Bahramali, A., Houmansadr, A.: DeepCorr: strong flow correlation attacks on tor using deep learning. In: Proceedings of the 2018 ACM SIGSAC Conference on Computer and Communications Security. ACM (Jan 2018). https://doi.org/10.1145/3243734.3243824
17. Open Privacy Research Society: cwtch. https://cwtch.im/
18. Rivest, R.L., Shamir, A., Wagner, D.A.: Time-lock puzzles and timed-release crypto. Tech. rep. (1996)
19. Sayrafi, M.: Introducing the cloudflare onion service. https://blog.cloudflare.com/cloudflare-onion-service/ (Sep 2018)
20. Snowden, E.: Permanent Record. Pan Macmillan (Sept 2019)
21. Sonntag, M.: Anonymous proof of liveness. In: Proceedings of IDIMT-2021. Trauner Verlag (2021)
22. Swartz, A.: Securedrop. https://github.com/freedomofpress/securedrop
23. Syta, E., Peterson, B., Wolinsky, D.I., Fischer, M., Ford, B.: Deniable anonymous group authentication. Tech. Rep. YALEU/DCS/TR-1486, Yale University (February 2014)
24. Tate, J.: Bradley Manning sentenced to 35 years in WikiLeaks case. Washington Post, online archived at. https://web.archive.org/web/20130825043050/http://articles.washingtonpost.com/2013-08-21/world/41431547_1_bradley-manning-david-coombs-pretrial-confinement (Aug 2013)
25. The Tor Project: Tor Rendezvous Specification - Version 3. https://github.com/torproject/torspec/blob/master/rend-spec-v3.txt
26. Tor Project, I.: The Tor project. https://www.torproject.org/ (2021)
27. Hoffman, W.: Facebook's Dark Web. Onion Site Reaches 1 Million Monthly Tor Users. https://www.inverse.com/article/14672-facebook-s-dark-web-onion-site-reaches-1-million-monthly-tor-users

Analysis of Data Obtained from the Mobile Botnet

Jaroslaw Kobiela$^{(\boxtimes)}$ (ID) and Piotr Urbaniec (ID)

Institute of Computer Science, University of Opole, Opole, Poland
{jaroslaw.kobiela,urbanip}@uni.opole.pl

Abstract. As the use of mobile devices increases, the security risks associated with them also steadily increase. One of the most serious threats is the presence of mobile botnets, which are a group of devices controlled by cybercriminals to launch attacks or data theft. Identifying infected devices is a key step in counteracting these hazards. This article presents an analysis of the data collected in the experiment using a mobile botnet application. We focused on the analysis of the generated network traffic and events registered by mobile devices. As our results show, such data analysis and searching for patterns left by malicious software in today's reality can no longer remain an efficient tool for the detection of such threats. The results highlight the need for further research and improvement of techniques for the detection of mobile botnet members to improve the efficiency and accuracy of their identification. This article also describes possible reasons for the lack of unambiguous results and presents proposals for further research.

Keywords: security · mobile botnet · bot · botmaster · botnet detection

1 Introduction

Mobile devices contain extensive personal information not accessible from regular computers [1].

The term 'mobile botnet' refers to a group of compromised smartphones controlled remotely by botmasters (bot-headers) via Command & Control (C&C) channels. Smartphones are used by billions of end users, who often store huge amounts of sensitive personal data on them and perform online payments. Thus, mobile botnets pose a serious threat to end-users and cellular networks. It is therefore important to research how mobile botnets operate and consequently find ways to detect them [2, 3].

Mobile botnets differ from other threats in that they communicate dynamically with their operators, called botmasters [4, 5]. They use communication based on HTTP (Hypertext Transfer Protocol), IRC (Internet Relay Chat). Some botnets also utilize P2P (peer-to-peer) communication architectures, which are more complex, making botnet detection more difficult than with centralized architectures. Moreover, mobile botnets have additional features when compared with PC botnets, such as portability, 24/7 Internet connection, access to the most credible information, function of sending and receiving text and MMS messages, and the option of dialling telephone numbers

P. Delir Haghighi et al. (Eds.): MoMM 2023, LNCS 14417, pp. 20–34, 2023.
https://doi.org/10.1007/978-3-031-48348-6_2

[6, 7]. A malicious application is installed on a susceptible host that can perform various operations for the benefit of the end user according to the botmaster's instructions. The most popular vectors of attack are websites, drive-by-download, spam messages, viral mechanisms, etc. A botnet is one of the most effective methods in which a mobile device can be used for malicious operations against organizations or individuals. [8]. It can also be used by botmasters for identity theft, launching DDoS (Denial of Service) attacks, information phishing, fraud, or sending spam, mainly for financial gain [9, 10].

2   Mobile Botnet Architecture

Mobile botnets have the same architecture as computer botnets, that is, they can be centralized, decentralized, and hybrid.

Centralized Botnet Architecture. In the case of a centralized architecture, all bots report to the central Command & Control server to establish a communication channel. The botmaster controls and supervises all the bots in a botnet from a single server. Communication with bots is continuous, enabling the easy management of botnets. In addition, this architecture uses two types of topologies, star and hierarchical, and two types of protocols, IRC and HTTP. Advantages include short response time, easy means of communication, and direct feedback. As for the disadvantages, failure of the C&C server renders the entire botnet inoperable, and detection of the botmaster is easier than in other architectures [8, 9, 11].

DeCentralized Botnet Architecture. There is no specific C&C server in this architecture, and all bots operate as C&C servers and clients simultaneously. It is based on Peer-to-Peer (P2P) protocols which are more complex, making botnet detection more difficult than in other architectures [8, 12].

Hybrid Botnet Architecture. This is a combination of centralized and decentralized architectures. It includes two bot types: slaves and clients. The monitoring and detection of botnets in a hybrid architecture is more difficult than that in other architectures [8].

3   Stages of the Mobile Botnet Life Cycle

The lifecycle of a mobile botnet can be divided into three main stages: (1) infection and spread, (2) performing operations and communication, and (3) performing tasks and attacks requested by the botmaster [4, 13].

(1) Infection and spreading are affected by a number of techniques used (e.g., malicious email attachments, infected URLs, SMS/MMS messages, or Bluetooth) to attack new devices and make them botnet members without users' knowledge. Botmasters use smartphones as less-monitored devices with high-speed connections to spread their bots.
(2) Operations and communication occur when bots interact with the C&C servers to receive new commands or updates from the botmaster.
(3) Performing tasks and attacks requested by the botmaster means that mobile botnets can be used as platforms for carrying out any type of malicious operation on mobile devices and networks.

4   Mobile Botnet Detection – Related Work

Botnets are referred to as 'silent threats' because bots do not make unusual or suspicious use of the device's battery, processor, memory, or other resources on infected devices, which would make their presence known [4]. Examples include AnserverBot, Droid-Dream, Geinimi, and DroidKungFu, which use the HTTP protocol to hide their activities amidst normal network traffic by communicating with C&C servers [14].

Various detection techniques have been proposed for detecting botnets. To better understand this issue, current detection techniques can be divided into static, dynamic, and hybrid analysis [15]. Static analysis uses reverse engineering to investigate the application source code to extract its characteristics. Reverse engineering is used in static analysis to investigate source code and specific files, such as a manifest file Android-Manifest.xml, which requires appropriate access permissions [1, 6, 16]. In contrast, dynamic analysis involves techniques that include launching an application with malicious code in a controlled laboratory environment (also known as a sandbox) to observe the malicious behaviour of malware [1, 6, 17]. The third type of analysis, referred to as hybrid, combines static and dynamic techniques. Much better results can be achieved by combining static and dynamic analysis [18].

Mobile botnets are usually detected by identifying their characteristic features. Then, machine learning algorithms, such as decision tree, Random Forest, KNN (K-Nearest Neighbor), SVM (Support Vector Machines), etc., are utilized, using features to train the detection system and ultimately to identify botnets in the network. However, the selected features can only be useful if any of the functions reveal important links between the botmaster and bots, and when the correlation between them is high [19, 20]. Another feature could be the periodic behaviour of HTTP bots. Unfortunately, many regular applications use auto-refresh (e.g., Gmail) or location services that exhibit the same pattern as botnets. Thus, such a solution may not be very effective, especially because bots can easily generate random delays and a number of messages to avoid their detection [14, 21].

It is clear that current research on mobile botnet detection requires continuous improvement owing to the evolution of malware. As mentioned at the beginning of this chapter, until recently, the only feature that allowed the detection of anomalies was the abnormal drain of the battery of the device. Currently, this can no longer serve as an indication of infection.

In our research, we combined the analysis of network traffic with that of mobile device logs, making it a basis for determining the possibility of identifying hazards.

As mentioned earlier, most of the existing research on detecting mobile botnets has relied on the analysis of extensive data sets. Such an approach allows for the observation of broader botnet identification patterns, increasing the chances of detecting infections. However, it requires significant time investment and the capability for monitoring over an extended period.

What is lacking, however, is research on detecting mobile botnets based on much more limited data, which can be obtained in a short time frame—within minutes. Hence, our research focuses on methods for identifying botnet behaviours that could be used in the future to detect the presence of a botnet based on data obtained from a single, short-term scan.

5   Test Environment

We set up a test environment with our own C&C server to analyse the mobile botnet behaviour. To do so, we used a Spy-Droid server available in GitHub repositories [22]. It is characterized by high functionality; it enables, among others, downloading print screens, remote activation of the camera and microphone, retrieval of contacts, call history, sending text messages from the infected device, and many more. The C&C server was installed on a physical device (laptop) with installed Apache2 and other add-ons required for server operation. The server operated at IP address 192.168.0.25 on port 22533 (http://192.168.0.25:22533). The botnet's client application was installed on two physical devices from renowned manufacturers and one virtual device. The botnet client communicated with the server using port 22222. During the tests, commands were sent from the C&C server to individual bots (e.g., retrieving contacts, GPS location, call history, and sending texts).

Wireshark software was used to record network traffic, configured to capture full packets (not just headers) of all traffic in the local test network. For collecting system logs from mobile devices, LogCat and MatLog apps were used, allowing logs to be saved to a TXT file. The apps were granted ROOT permissions to access the full log buffers. The permission granted allows access to logs at the root user level: *adb shell pm grant com.dp.logcatapp android.permission.READ_LOGS*. Logs were recorded throughout the duration of the experiment.

The recording of network traffic and system logs was carried out by repeatedly initiating botnet communication with the C&C server. This scope of data was considered sufficient for a preliminary analysis of botnet detection capabilities. However, for further research, it is advisable to consider collecting data over a longer time frame, which will allow for the observation of a broader communication pattern in the botnet. Figure 1 shows the architecture of the test environment.

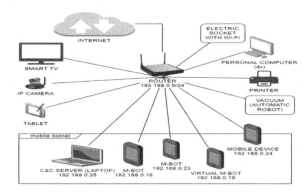

Fig. 1. Test environment

The test environment should mimic real conditions to the greatest extent. Therefore, in addition to computers, our network also includes IoT devices, such as smart TV, IP cameras, and robot vacuums. This allowed us to collect data corresponding to events in a real environment.

Our research includes an attempt to identify a distinguishing indicator for mobile botnet detection. Matters outside our scope of interest included the following: (1) the origin of device infection, that is, whether susceptibility to any application or system was exploited, or whether it was intentional or unintentional user activity; (2) how the malware obtained the required permissions in the system; (3) the architecture of the mobile botnet was also of no interest, as our task was not to locate the C&C server, but only to identify the infection based on the transmitted data.

During the tests, we simulated the normal use of infected devices, that is, launching various applications, browsing websites, and installing new software.

The experiment conducted by the authors highlights the difficulties in detecting mobile botnets based on a single scan of the device and its immediate network environment. The goal was to determine whether data collected in a relatively short period of time could be sufficient for detecting a botnet infection on a mobile device. Given the limitations of this approach, complex network traffic analyses over a longer time frame and application code analyses were not applicable. The results of the experiment underscored the challenges in detecting mobile botnets based on such limited data, serving as a starting point for further research on improving detection methods.

5.1 Network Traffic Analysis

Each type of mobile application has its own traffic pattern. For example, messaging applications tend to transmit a small amount of traffic with a small frame size. Streaming applications, however, receive large volumes of traffic with large frame sizes. Statistical traffic information, such as frame size distribution, frame count, and traffic volume, can be used to represent application traffic patterns. User behaviour profiling was performed to distinguish between regular and abnormal activities. Information leaks, such as device information, authentication data in HTTP headers, and network characteristics, including connection duration, TCP frame size, and a number of GET/POST parameters, are also used [13].

We used the following steps to monitor network traffic in the test environment to identify suspicious traffic: (1) we collected all network traffic on our network; (2) we identified attributes for analysis, such as source and destination IP, source and destination port, timestamp, and payload; (3) we looked for regular patterns and documented network behaviour during the attack; and (4) we evaluated the results.

Knowing the IP address of the C&C server and the IP addresses of the infected mobile devices, we were able to analyse the traffic which took place between these devices and see how it 'blends in' with the rest – regular network traffic.

If many requests for a large number of IP addresses are observed, it is likely that network identification will be performed. The filter for the ICMP protocol (ping) did not exhibit such a phenomenon. The number of requests was only 150 out of nearly 670,000 requests.

It is also possible to use tcp.flags.syn $==$ 1 and tcp.flags.ack $==$ 0 and tcp.window_size $>$ 1024 filter, with SYN flag set, ACK flag not set, and a window size exceeding 1024 bytes. A large number of such frames in a short time would most likely indicate that the network ports were scanned (e.g., using nmap). Again, no such behaviour was observed in the network. Frames account for only 0.1% of the recorded network traffic.

Multiple retransmissions and interruptions in network communication (missing frames) may indicate probable Denial of Service attacks. The filter used in Wireshark is tcp.analysis.lost_segment or tcp.analysis.retransmission. The detected frames accounted for 5% of all the recorded network traffic.

Statistical analysis of the network traffic, which included 666,069 collected frames, revealed that nearly 96% of all traffic was generated by two protocols: TCP and TLSv1.2. The overall distribution of protocols is presented in Table 1. The average frame length was 960 bytes, with a standard deviation of 698 bytes, the minimum frame length was 34 bytes and the maximum was 1514 bytes.

Table 1. Percentage share of protocols in recorded network traffic

Protocol	%	Protocol	%	Protocol	%
TCP	80.278	SNMP	0.054	Ieee1905	0.005
TLSv1.2	15.513	NBNS	0.036	LLDP	0.004
ARP	1.527	IGMPv3	0.033	ICMPv6	0.002
TLSv1.3	1.371	GQUIC	0.028	DHCP	0.002
DNS	0.381	QUIC	0.027	OCSP	0.001
SSDP	0.138	SSL	0.026	HTTP/XML	0.001
MDNS	0.123	LLMNR	0.024	NTP	0.000
RTPproxy	0.064	ICMP	0.022	NAT-PMP	0.000
IGMPv2	0.057	SSLv2	0.007		

We also analysed the length of the frames across the recorded network traffic, as shown in Fig. 2.

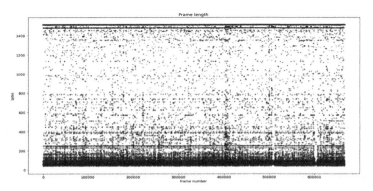

Fig. 2. Frame length

Numerous small frames (<100 bytes) and numerous large frames (>1400 bytes) could be observed. A series of frames of other sizes (approximately 400 bytes, 800 bytes, etc.) are also clearly visible. However, the distribution of the data did not indicate any anomalies. Therefore, in the next step, we verified how the frame length changed in relation to specific ports. Knowing that the server used port 22533 and the client used port 22222, it was possible to observe a random distribution of frame lengths when examining them for both the destination port (Fig. 3) and the source port (Fig. 4).

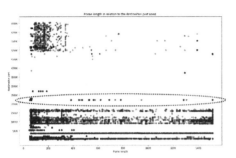   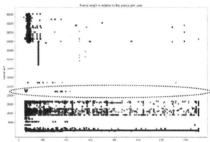

Fig. 3. Frame length in relation to the destination port used

Fig. 4. Frame length in relation to the source port used

The analysis of network traffic did not identify any elements indicating anomalies that could reveal a botnet infection. The number of frames generated from and to the botnet members (as seen in Table 2) raised no suspicion, and it could easily blend in with the rest of the network traffic.

Table 2. Number of registered frames

	Number of frames (total: 666,069)	
	Source	Destination
192.168.0.25 (C&C)	873	1,736
192.168.0.18 (mbot)	14	42
192.168.0.19 (mbot)	14	42
192.168.0.23(mbot)	14	42
192.168.0.24 (NOT bot)	112	42

In addition, frame analysis showed that information from the infected device was sent to the C&C server as plain text. Thus, it was easy to read information that had been stolen (Fig. 5).

The information presented above indicates that identifying the members of a mobile botnet based on network traffic analysis is extremely difficult and requires further in-depth analysis.

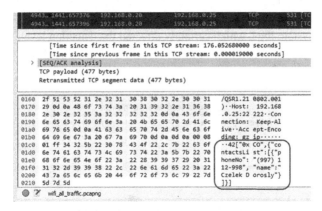

Fig. 5. Plain text message to C&C server

5.2 Analysis of the Events Recorded by the Device

Analysis of the Type and Number of Logs

Mobile devices require detection mechanisms that are not limited by their nature of mobile devices. Android has a logging system that allows output messages to be collected, filtered, viewed, and debugged using the Logcat command. Logcat allows logs to be collected from different parts of the system, showing them as a three-part message, i.e.: (1) tag: a priority tag represented by letters – 'D' for debug, 'E' for error, 'I' for info, 'W' for warn, and 'V' for verbose; (2) message tag – showing the origin of the message; and (3) log message – shows the actual message [23]. To achieve this, we used the apps available on Google Play, LogCat, and MatLog. Their main purpose was to record logs in a file so that they could be analysed and searched for traces of bot activity. The number of logs collected is listed in Table 3.

Table 3. Logs on mbot device

Event	Quantity	%
(D)ebug	167,589	85.2%
(V)erbose	14,675	7.5%
(I)nfo	10,696	5.4%
(E)rror	2,638	1.3%
(W)arning	1,002	0.5%
SUM:	196,600	100.0%

The largest group of events consists of debugging events. This indicated that a large volume of diagnostic information was collected to identify errors or problems. In contrast, a few warning and error events indicated stable system operation and the absence of any serious errors or failures. Verbose and info events accounted for a small percentage of all events and were not significant from a system analysis point of view. When analysing the device logs as part of a botnet, we found no noticeable number of errors recorded in the system logs, which certainly affected the detection level.

The next step was to analyse the number of registered events in the system logs over time, as shown in Fig. 6.

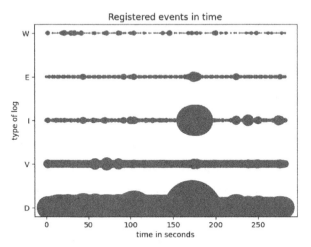

Fig. 6. Registered events in time

An increased number of logged events between the 150 and 200-s mark could be observed, which might suggest that the system or applications were operating more intensively than usual during that period. However, this did not necessarily indicate that there were problems, especially as the C&C server's communication with the device occurred at random intervals throughout the recording period. Although there was an apparent increase in error events, they were not significant and did not cause any noticeable performance problems for the user.

Analysis of the Processes Registered in the Device Logs
The analysis of the processes activated over time (Fig. 7) also showed no anomalies.

The apparently large number of processes that appeared only a few times and then no longer occurred may indicate that these were individual tasks that were executed and completed. There were no processes that repeatedly occurred and grew in frequency over time (such tendencies could cast suspicion on the process). None of the processes exhibited excessive activity. Knowing that the botnet client was connected to the C&C server (IP:192.168.0.25) on port 22222 (the 14716 process is highlighted in a bold box in the diagram), we extracted the process and noted all references to the server (lighter), and then we imposed those references on the indicated port (darker), as shown in Fig. 8.

What is noticeable here is the degree of regularity in the establishment of the connection to the server, which may indicate that data were automatically sent to the server, even though communication was initiated at random intervals from the server.

One approach for selecting suspicious processes from among those operating in the system that the authors found applicable was the "multi-stage process set narrowing

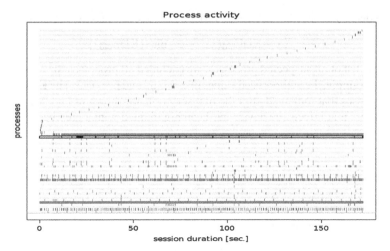

Fig. 7. Number of events over time

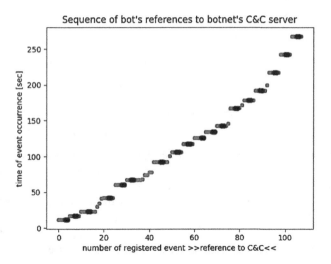

Fig. 8. Sequence of bot's references to the botnet's C&C server

method," which involved eliminating processes in successive stages on the basis of successive characteristics.

Here, we present a possible course for such elimination using a specific example. We start by collecting the activities of all processes operating in the system in the specified time frame $[0, T]$.

Stage 1: Screening out processes that occur ephemerally. Suppose we denote the random variable as the time (from the observed interval) of the occurrence of the activity of process p_{id} as X_{pid}. For each p_{id} process, we determined the KDE_{pid} function, which is a kernel density estimator of the X_{pid} variable. Let $L_{pid} = \max(S) - \min(S)$, where:

$$S = \{x : \text{KDE}_{pid}(x) > \alpha \cdot \max(\text{KDE}_{pid})\}. \tag{1}$$

From the list of all suspected processes, we excluded all processes for which L_{pid} / T $< \beta$. In this example, the authors used values of $\alpha = 0.02$ and $\beta = 0.75$. The KDE_{pid} charts for the processes that remained after the first selection are shown in Fig. 9 (the chart of the bot process that infects the device has been highlighted with a grey background).

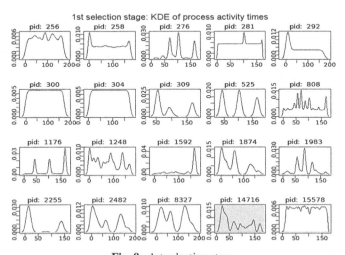

Fig. 9. 1st selection stage

The parameters α and β were selected through experimental calibration to emphasize processes with long-lasting and stable operation times, which are characteristic of botnet time activity structure. Similarly, the parameters γ and δ, implemented in the second and third stages of the selection process, were carefully optimized for the precise identification of processes exhibiting attributes typical of mobile botnets. The overall methodology of experimental parameter selection aimed to optimize the effectiveness of botnet process selection while minimizing the number of false-positive detections related to processes not associated with botnets.

Even a cursory analysis of the figure shows why, in the authors' opinion, the use of KDE_{pid} is a good method to support intuitive heuristics for classifying typical process behaviours over time. It provides a good starting point for differentiating bot activity from that of other processes and for comparing the activity of different bots. The proper selection of parameters used in the structure of KDE_{pid} makes it possible to highlight or suppress the different features of these behaviours. The adoption of $\alpha = 0.02$ and $\beta = 0.75$ in this particular case is interpreted as follows: α is a threshold value, allowing to select the 'core' of the process activity in the tested interval; and β parameter allows the detection of processes of an appropriate length in time which is one of the factors of the increased activity.

Stage 2 – Screening out processes with flat histograms of the differences in the times of the subsequent activities from the set obtained in the first stage. Let $t_0, t_1, \ldots, t_m$ be the recorded activity times of a given process that has passed stage 1. We created a histogram of a set of numbers of the form $t_k - t_{k-1}$, for $k = 1, 2, ..., m$, with 10 equal class intervals. Let fmax denote the highest value (highest bar) occurring in the histogram. From the set of suspected processes, we excluded those for which $f_{max} / m < \gamma$. In this case, the authors applied the values $\gamma = 0.6$. Histograms of the processes that passed the second selection stage are shown in (Fig. 10). Operations at this stage (and selection of the γ parameter) aim to detect the processes that are characterized by an increased regularity of activities over time.

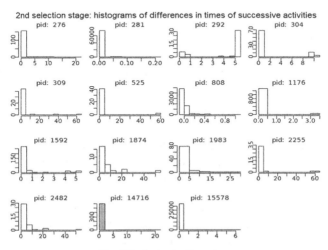

Fig. 10. 2nd selection stage

Stage 3 – Screening out processes with low kurtosis of the differences in the times of the subsequent activities from the set obtained in the second stage. Kurtosis was determined for each process as follows:

$$K = \mu_4/\sigma^4, \tag{2}$$

where μ_4 is the fourth central moment and σ is the standard deviation specified for the set of numbers $t_k - t_{k-1}$ (designation as in the description of stage 2). We eliminated all processes for which $K < \delta$. In this case, the authors applied the values of $\delta = 30$. The logarithms (to make the tails more visible) of the histograms of the two processes that passed the three-stage screening are shown in (Fig. 11). An intuitive interpretation of the activities of this stage is as follows: we want to eliminate the processes in which the only characteristic is "pulsation in time" as the bot, apart from cyclic activation in time, will also perform other operations of more heterogenous distribution in time which will correspond to the just increased weight of distribution tails.

The analysis of the last drawing suggests that if the resulting is still too numerous, then at the subsequent stage of elimination, the weight factors of the value dispersion in the tail could be taken into consideration.

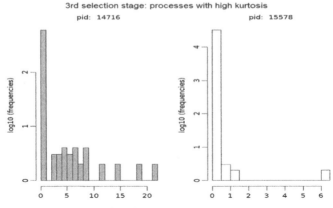

Fig. 11. 3rd selection stage

6   Conclusions and Future Work

This article describes the analysis of system logs on mobile devices and network traffic to potentially detect mobile botnets. Our research is based on various data analysis techniques. The results show that network traffic and system logs may be useful for identifying infected devices.

However, these experiments presented some challenges. The system logs recorded on the mobile device were not as detailed as those collected on a personal computer. Additionally, botnet applications use a minimal amount of data, making it significantly more difficult to detect their activities.

Mobile botnets can be diverse and use a variety of techniques, such as hiding in system processes or changing their behaviour in real time. Therefore, the analysis of network traffic and mobile device logs can only be effective when used in conjunction with other tools and methods such as machine learning or anomaly detection. Therefore, we will expand these techniques to include them in further studies.

The obtained results indicate that the analysis of a single scan of the device and its immediate network environment provides limited information about potential botnet infections. It can be surmised that the applied methods of network traffic analysis and system logs were insufficient due to the narrow scope of data included in a single scan. Perhaps the botnet generated too little traffic to be easily identified against the 'noise' of total network traffic. Additionally, system logs may not have recorded sufficiently detailed information about the processes occurring on the device to enable the detection of botnet activity traces.

The experiment's results clearly show that detecting mobile botnets based solely on the analysis of limited data obtained in a short period is currently very challenging. This points to the need for exploring new, more effective detection methods that utilize a broader range of data over a longer time span. A promising direction appears to be the combination of traffic and log analysis with machine learning techniques, which would allow for the detection of more subtle behavioural anomalies that may be indicators of the presence of a botnet.

Acknowledgments. This work was supported by the Polish National Centre of Research and Development under the CyberSecIdent Programme within CYBERSECIDENT/489912/ IV/NCBR/2021 project.

References

1. Anwar, S., Zain, J.M., Inayat, Z., Haq, R.U., Karim, A., Jabir, A.N.: A static approach towards mobile botnet detection. In: 2016 3rd International Conference on Electronic Design, ICED 2016, pp. 563–567 (2017). https://doi.org/10.1109/ICED.2016.7804708
2. Xiang, C., Binxing, F., Lihua, Y., Xiaoyi, L., Tianning, Z.: AndBot: towards advanced mobile botnets. In: LEET 2011 - 4th USENIX Workshop on Large-Scale Exploits and Emergent Threats: Botnets, spyware, Worms, and More, August 2011
3. Bernardeschi, C., Mercaldo, F., Nardone, V., Santone, A.: Exploiting model checking for mobile botnet detection. Procedia Comput. Sci. **159**, 963–972 (2019). https://doi.org/10.1016/ j.procs.2019.09.263
4. Eslahi, M., Rostami, M.R., Hashim, H., Tahir, N.M., Naseri, M.V.: A data collection approach for mobile botnet analysis and detection. In: IEEE Symposium on Wireless Technology and Applications, ISWTA, pp. 199–204 (2014). https://doi.org/10.1109/ISWTA.2014.6981187
5. Wazzan, M., Algazzawi, D., Bamasaq, O., Albeshri, A., Cheng, L.: Internet of things botnet detection approaches: analysis and recommendations for future research. Appl. Sci. **11**(12), 5713 (2021). https://doi.org/10.3390/app11125713
6. Anwar, S., Zolkipli, M.F., Mezhuyev, V., Inayat, Z.: A smart framework for mobile botnet detection using static analysis. KSII Trans. Internet Inf. Syst. **14**(6), 2591–2611 (2020). https:// doi.org/10.3837/tiis.2020.06.015
7. Yusof, M., Saudi, M.M., Ridzuan, F.: A new android botnet classification for GPS exploitation based on permission and API calls. In: Duy, V., Dao, T., Zelinka, I., Kim, S., Phuong, T. (eds.) AETA 2017. LNEE, vol. 465, pp. 27–37 (2018). https://doi.org/10.1007/978-3-319-69814-4_3
8. Anwar, S., Zolkipli, M.F., Inayat, Z., Odili, J., Ali, M., Zain, J.M.: Android botnets: a serious threat to android devices. Pertanika J. Sci. Technol. (2018)
9. Kaur, N., Singh, M.: Botnet and botnet detection techniques in cyber realm. In: Proceedings of the International Conference on Inventive Computation Technologies, ICICT 2016, vol. 2016 (2016). https://doi.org/10.1109/INVENTIVE.2016.7830080
10. Rovetta, S., Suchacka, G., Masulli, F.: Bot recognition in a web store: an approach based on unsupervised learning. J. Netw. Comput. Appl. **157**, 102577 (2020). https://doi.org/10.1016/ j.jnca.2020.102577
11. Rovetta, S., Cabri, A., Masulli, F., Suchacka, G.: Bot or not? A case study on bot recognition from web session logs. In: Esposito, A., Faundez-Zanuy, M., Morabito, F.C., Pasero, E. (eds.) Quantifying and Processing Biomedical and Behavioral Signals. SIST, vol. 103, pp. 197–206. Springer, Cham (2019). https://doi.org/10.1007/978-3-319-95095-2_19
12. Šimon, M., Huraj, L., Hosťovecký, M.: A mobile botnet model based on P2P grid. In: Kravets, A., Shcherbakov, M., Kultsova, M., Groumpos, P. (eds.) Creativity in Intelligent Technologies and Data Science. CCIS, vol. 754, pp. 604–615. Springer, Cham (2017). https://doi.org/10. 1007/978-3-319-65551-2_44
13. Mongkolluksamee, S., Visoottiviseth, V., Fukuda, K.: Robust peer to peer mobile botnet detection by using communication patterns. In: Asian Internet Engineering Conference, AINTEC 2018, pp. 38–45 (2018). https://doi.org/10.1145/3289166.3289172

14. Eslahi, M., Yousefi, M., Naseri, M.V., Yussof, Y.M., Tahir, N.M., Hashim, H.: Cooperative network behaviour analysis model for mobile Botnet detection. In: ISCAIE 2016 - 2016 IEEE Symposium on Computer Applications and Industrial Electronics, pp. 107–112 (2016). https://doi.org/10.1109/ISCAIE.2016.7575046

15. Yusof, M., Mohd Saudi, M., Ridzuan, F.: Mobile botnet classification by using hybrid analysis. IJET **7**(4.15), 103 (2018). https://doi.org/10.14419/ijet.v7i4.15.21429

16. Yusof, M., Saudi, M.M., Ridzuan, F.: A new android botnet classification for GPS exploitation based on permission and API calls. In: Duy, V., Dao, T., Zelinka, I., Kim, S., Phuong, T. (eds.) AETA 2017 - Recent Advances in Electrical Engineering and Related Sciences: Theory and Application. LNEE, vol. 465, pp. 27–37. Springer, Cham (2018). https://doi.org/10.1007/978-3-319-69814-4_3

17. Yan, P., Yan, Z.: A survey on dynamic mobile malware detection. Software Qual. J. **26**(3), 891–919 (2018). https://doi.org/10.1007/s11219-017-9368-4

18. Karim, A., Chang, V., Firdaus, A.: Android botnets: a proof-of-concept using hybrid analysis approach. J. Organ. End User Comput. **32**(3), 50–67 (2020). https://doi.org/10.4018/JOEUC.2020070105

19. Moodi, M., Ghazvini, M., Moodi, H.: A hybrid intelligent approach to detect android botnet using smart self-adaptive learning-based PSO-SVM. Knowl. Based Syst. **222**, 106988 (2021). https://doi.org/10.1016/j.knosys.2021.106988

20. Hamzenejadi, S., Ghazvini, M., Hosseini, S.: Mobile botnet detection: a comprehensive survey. Int. J. Inf. Secur. **22**(1), 137–175 (2023). https://doi.org/10.1007/s10207-022-00624-4

21. Velasco-Mata, J., González-Castro, V., Fidalgo, E., Alegre, E.: Real-time botnet detection on large network bandwidths using machine learning. Sci. Rep. **13**(1), 4282 (2023). https://doi.org/10.1038/s41598-023-31260-0

22. Dhakal, D.:coderdipesh/spydroid. https://github.com/coderdipesh/spydroid

23. Girei, D.A., Ali Shah, M., Shahid, M.B.: An enhanced botnet detection technique for mobile devices using log analysis. In: 2016 22nd International Conference on Automation and Computing, ICAC 2016: Tackling the New Challenges in Automation and Computing, pp. 450–455 (2016). https://doi.org/10.1109/IConAC.2016.7604961

On the Impact of FFP2 Face Masks on Speaker Verification for Mobile Device Authentication

David Sedlak[1]([✉])[ID] and Rainhard Dieter Findling[1,2][ID]

[1] University of Applied Sciences Upper Austria, Wels, Austria
david.sedlak@live.at
[2] Google, Hamburg, Germany

Abstract. Voice-based authentication can allow for straightforward and unobtrusive authentication with mobile devices. With COVID-19, wearing face masks has become common in many parts of the world. While prior research has shown that face masks act like low pass filters, the impact of face masks on voice-based authentication with mobile devices is still unclear. In this paper we analyze the impact of FFP2 masks on voice authentication for mobile devices in realistic scenarios. We evaluate a pretrained EPACA-TDDN speaker verification model with a self-recorded database of 450 mobile voice authentication utterances from 30 speakers, with a total length of 29 min. Results indicate that wearing FFP2 face masks has a slight but significant impact on speaker verification scores. Results also indicate that in authentication scenarios they lead to a slight increase of the FNR, and in comparison smaller decrease of the FPR, and in direct comparison, to a slight increase of the EER.

Keywords: speaker verification · mobile authentication · face masks

1 Introduction

Mobile devices provide users with many services for their everyday life. As a result, those devices process and store personal and sensitive data that needs to be protected from unauthorized local access. To provide this protection different authentication methods exist that allow users to authenticate to their mobile devices, each with their individual advantages and drawbacks. Knowledge-based methods, such as a PIN or password, allow users to easily change the authentication secret, but suffer from limited usability and shoulder surfing attacks. Biometrics-based methods are easy to use, but once the biometrics are compromised, users cannot easily change them. How helpful biometrics-based approaches, such as face, fingerprint, voice, or gait pattern verification are for users to authenticate to their mobile device depends on the situation in which they authenticate [14,19].

With COVID-19, frequently used combinations of biometrics-based mobile device authentication approaches, such as face and fingerprint verification, face new challenges. COVID-19 has made wearing face masks more common around

P. Delir Haghighi et al. (Eds.): MoMM 2023, LNCS 14417, pp. 35–49, 2023.
https://doi.org/10.1007/978-3-031-48348-6_3

the world. This is a challenge for face verification to authenticate to mobile devices, as the face is partially covered by the mask, hence partially shielded from assessment [10]. In addition to wearing face masks, in winter situations, users might also wear gloves. Gloves make it more difficult for users to use fingerprint verification to authenticate to their mobile devices, as they might shield the fingerprints from assessment.

Complementary mobile authentication approaches that work as a drop-in replacement in such situations would help to keep authentication to mobile devices straightforward and unobtrusive. Speaker-verification-based authentication to mobile devices might be such an approach. It could be used by users who wear both a face mask and gloves. One potential drawback of using speaker verification with face masks is that the face mask might negatively affect the speaker verification. Prior research has shown that face masks attenuate high frequencies [1,3,5] and diminish speech intelligibility for human listeners when noise is present [17,18]. The impact that this might have on automatic speaker verification for mobile device authentication has not yet been assessed. Assessing this impact seems important as a basis to better support users who wear face masks in future mobile voice authentication. Note that voice-based authentication is often employed because of its ease of use and high user acceptance, not because of its authentication accuracy [14]. Hence, if face masks were to further diminish the verification accuracy, then this could have a negative impact on its applicability to mobile device authentication.

In this paper, we investigate the impact that face masks have on speaker verification to authenticate to mobile devices. We focus on the following research question: How much do FFP2 masks impact speaker verification in a realistic mobile device authentication scenario? To answer this research question we compare the speaker verification results of using face mask data and non-face mask data with a well-known speaker verification approach for authentication to mobile devices. As a speaker verification approach we use a pretrained EPACA-TDNN model, which provides state-of-the-art accuracy in in-the-wild scenarios [4,13]. We focus on FFP2 masks as they are a commonly used type of face mask in the European Union, as many European Union countries made it mandatory to wear this type of mask in public places during the COVID-19 pandemic[1], and as FFP2 masks are similar to the N95, K95, and KN95 mask types that are widely used in other parts of the world. To the best of our knowledge, currently there is no mobile speaker verification database that contains voice utterance data of the same speakers with and without FFP2 masks. In this paper, we record such a database and use it for our evaluation. In real-world usage of mobile devices, it is common to have uncontrolled background noise. Previous research indicates that the negative impact of face masks on speech intelligibility by human listeners increases with the background noise level [17,18]. To our knowledge, it has not yet been investigated if this also applies to automatic speaker verification. We account for this by allowing environmental background noise in our evaluation data. In summary, the key contributions of this paper are:

---

[1] https://www.ecdc.europa.eu/en/publications-data/using-face-masks-community-reducing-covid-19-transmission (Jul 2022).

- We record a mobile device speaker verification database that contains 450 mobile device voice authentication utterances from 30 speakers, with and without FFP2 face masks, with a total length of 29 min.
- We measure the impact of FFP2 face masks on speaker verification for mobile device authentication by applying this data to an EPACA-TDNN model.

2   Related Work

We review prior research on the audio attenuation of face masks, on the impact of face masks on human speech recognition, and on speech and speaker recognition with face masks. The impact of face masks on audio features and speech recognition by human listeners has been targeted mainly in the field of medical research. In comparison, research on the impact of face masks on automatic speaker verification is more limited.

2.1   Impact of Face Masks on Audio Features

Multiple prior studies came to the conclusion that face masks act like low-pass filters on sound [1,3,5]. The filter strength varies with mask type. N95 masks have similar properties to FFP2 masks[2], but are more thoroughly researched than FFP2 masks. Poerschmann et al. [12] found similar impact of FFP2 and N95 masks on sound and spectral energy. FFP2 and N95 masks had an attenuation of up to 15 dB. Frequencies below 1 kHz are hardly affected. This study was conducted with a mouth simulator to approximate features of the human voice. By using an artificial voice the study avoided the Lombard effect, which describes a human behaviour of increasing the voice amplitude when other noises are present [20], which in turn can influence speech samples for speech and speaker recognition evaluations in real-world conditions.

Other studies have conducted similar experiments with N95 masks [1,3,5]. They utilized a variety of mask types and compared them with artificial voice generators. Peak attenuation for N95 masks varied between 12–14 dB, with the notable exception of Corey et al. [3], who measured a peak attenuation of 6 dB. In addition to artificial voice generation, [3] also evaluated the impact with human speakers, where masks turned out to have similar impact. For all mask types, the attenuation is significantly higher in frequency above 3 kHz, which is why face masks act as low-pass filters to the speaker's voice.

2.2   Impact of Face Masks on Speech Recognition by Humans

Harmonic-to-noise ratio (HNR) and cepstral peak prominence smoothed (CPPS) can be used as metrics to measure voice quality. Nguyen et al. [11] compared the voice quality of multiple mask types to non-masks situations. While CPPS stayed

---

[2] https://www.ecdc.europa.eu/en/publications-data/using-face-masks-community-reducing-covid-19-transmission (Jul 2022).

the same, HNR improved when wearing a mask from a mean of 25.0 dB without face masks to 27.3 with surgical masks, and to 28.4 dB with KN95 masks. As a possible explanation, the study reasons the test subjects could have adapted their phonation style, as this was not controlled for in their study. Magee et al. [8] used similar methods, but could detect no impact of face masks on HNR and CPPS, and concluded that voice quality remains largely unaffected.

Smiljanic et al. [17] analyzed the impact of surgical masks on speech intelligibility. Speakers recorded samples in 3 conditions: without masks, with masks while speaking normally, and with masks while speaking clearly. 4 levels of noise in form of talker babble were added: no-noisy, +5 dB signal-to-noise ratio (SNR), 0 dB SNR, and −5 dB SNR. The speech intelligibility was determined by the accuracy of the transcriptions, produced by human listeners. The results have shown that intelligibility decreased the most when wearing masks and speaking normally. This effect is amplified by the noise level, where lower noise led to higher intelligibility. Speaking clearly with masks increased the intelligibility in all situations, over speaking with no mask. The applicability of these findings to FFP2 masks is limited as surgical masks have a lower attenuation than FFP2 masks.

Toscano et al. [18] analyzed human speech recognition with and without face masks in increasingly noisy environments. The study used disposable surgical masks, fitted/center-seam cloth masks, pleated cloth masks, and N95 respirator masks. Two speakers recorded utterances with these masks in low SNR (+3 dB) and in high SNR (+13 dB) environments. 200 human listeners then transcribed these recordings, which was the basis for the evaluation. The human speech recognition accuracy was similar between noise-free and noisy environments, but in noisy environments, when the speaker wore a face mask, the accuracy was up to 18% worse, compared to utterances where speakers were not wearing face masks.

Schwartz et al. [16] compared the effects of including frequencies up to 3 kHz and up to 10 kHz in speaker recognition performed by humans in noisy conditions. 10 speakers participated in two experiments. The first experiment focused on producing specific vowel sounds, the second on reading out the Rainbow Passage. Noise was artificially added in 3 levels: +5 dB, 0 dB, and −5 dB SNR. Increasing the bandwidth to 10 kHz increased identification accuracy by 6–10%. The results of the experiments show that identification for male participants was significantly higher than for female participants in both experiments. Further decreasing the SNR more strongly impacted utterances with frequencies up to 3 kHz, implying that high frequency energy is beneficial for speaker recognition performed by humans when noise is present.

In summary, previous research indicates that the Lombard effect can compensate the impact of face masks or even improve the audio quality when no noise is present [8,11]. It also shows that the negative impact of face masks on intelligibility and speaker recognition performed by humans increases when other noise is present [17,18]. As these studies used artificial noise, the participants could only adapt their phonation style to the face masks, not to the environmental noise.

2.3   Automatic Speech and Speaker Recognition with Face Masks

Gutz et al. [6] evaluated if the performance of automatic speech recognition systems is impacted by KN95 masks. The study had 19 healthy adults as participants. The participants recorded data in 5 different conditions: no masks, with masks, with masks and clear speech, with mask and loud speech, and with mask and slow speech. The study used Google Cloud Speech to transcribe the spoken content and measured the word error rate (WER) to evaluate the performance. The utterances with no masks had the highest WER with 7.34% compared to 2.73–5.12% when wearing masks. Utterances recorded with masks and clear or loud speech had a significant positive effect on the WER compared to the utterances with no masks. The study also presents evidence that suggests that the data was impacted by the Lombard effect. However, no effect size was reported. Because this study used speech recognition, its findings have limited applicability to speaker verification, which does not necessarily depend on the same underlying information of an utterance to perform verification.

Bogdanel et al. [2] analysed the impact of surgical masks and FFP2 masks on forensic speaker identification. This model was evaluated on a data set from 30 speakers. While recording the utterances, interference was minimized and the speakers were required to maintain their habitual voice. For both mask types a negative impact on forensic speaker identification was observed. Even though FFP2 masks have a greater attenuation than surgical masks, the study found evidence that the negative impact from surgical masks was greater than of FFP2 masks. The study further analyzed the average intensity of an utterance and found an average increase of 1.06 dB when wearing FFP2 masks over not wearing a mask, and an increase of 1.6 dB over wearing surgical masks. Although speaker identification and verification are related, the results of this study still have limited applicability to speaker verification, as identification and verification do not necessarily rely on the same underlying information.

Saeidi et al. [15] investigated the impact of different face covers on speaker verification. For their evaluation, they recorded data of 8 different participants with 5 different face cover conditions: without face cover, with a motorcycle helmet, a hood, a scarf, a rubber mask, and a surgeon mask. Each speaker recorded about 1.5 h of content in total. They extracted Mel frequency cepstral coefficient (MFCC) features from the utterances and used i-vectors and PLDA for classification. In their experiments, the absolute precision dropped by 1.0% from utterances recorded with no masks to utterances recorded with surgeon masks. It seems likely that FFP2 masks would show a greater effect size than surgical masks due to their higher audio attenuation. However, it is unclear if those findings, which are based on less recent features and speaker verification models and on a different mask type, would translate to a modern speaker verification approach like EPACA-TDDN and to FFP2 masks.

Khan et al. [7] analyzed the impact of cloth masks, N95 masks, and surgical masks on automatic speaker verification. They used a 20-speaker data set recorded in indoor and outdoor environments. For their recording, they used different microphones, including microphones from mobile devices. The study proposed a novel speaker verification approach with ternary deviated overlapping patterns, gammatone cepstral coefficient, and MFCC for feature extraction. A linear regression model was used to detect if an utterance was recorded with face masks, and peak norm filter was applied to counteract the attenuation of the masks. The classification was done with an ensemble classifier. Their experiments showed an error rate of 0.01 with data recorded without face masks, while data recorded with N95, surgical masks, and cloth masks had an error rate of 0.06, 0.05, and 0.07, respectively.

In summary, previous research on automatic speech recognition with face masks indicates that face masks can have a positive effect on accuracy when speaking loudly or clearly. This can likely be attributed to the Lombard effect. Previous research also indicates that some speaker recognition approaches show decreased accuracy when wearing different types of face masks, in both non-noisy and noisy situations. It is unclear if those findings translate to modern state-of-the-art speaker verification approaches and FFP2 masks.

In conclusion, prior research has shown that face masks act as a low-pass filter to human speech, which leads to information loss of speech utterances. In turn, this leads to lowered speech intelligibility and can negatively impact human and automated speech and speaker recognition. It has been shown that this negative impact tends to be stronger in the presence of background noise, but also that the Lombard effect can lead to better results over non-mask and non-noise situations. Those aspects have been investigated in isolation, however it is still unclear if or how strongly they would translate to FFP2 masks used with modern speaker recognition models, like a ECAPA-TDDN, in a mobile device authentication scenario with short challenge-based voice utterances.

3   Mobile Device Voice Authentication Approach

In this section, we discuss the mobile voice authentication approach which we use as a basis for our evaluation in the next section. We describe the approach from the user perspective as well as the mobile device voice authentication recording application we use to gather data.

3.1   Authentication Approach

From the user perspective, the mobile voice authentication approach we employ consists of two main parts: enrollment and authentication (Fig. 1). At first, the user enrolls on their mobile device. The mobile device shows an enrollment phrase on its display that the user speaks aloud (1). It then records the voice utterance (2) and uses it as an enrollment sample for the speaker verification model. Later, the user attempts to authenticate to the device to unlock it. The

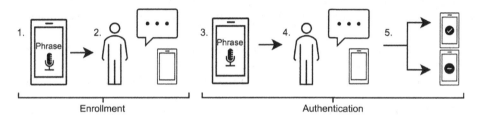

Fig. 1. The user perspective on enrollment and authentication with our mobile device voice authentication approach.

mobile device again shows a phrase on its display that the user speaks aloud (3). That phrase acts as an authentication challenge. The mobile device records the voice utterance (4) and uses the speaker verification model with the enrolled phrase and the authentication phrase to compute a speaker verification score $[0, 1]$. Only if the score is higher than a predefined authentication threshold the approach determines that this is the authorized user and unlocks the mobile device.

For speaker verification we use a pretrained ECAPA-TDNN model [4,13]. We use this model for its state-of-the-art performance in in-the-wild speaker verification scenarios [9]. We also use this model as it is publicly available in a pretrained state through the SpeechBrain [13] framework, which allows for good experiment reproducibility and comparisons of authentication accuracy across experiments.

Both the enrollment and authentication phrases are from a large word pool. During authentication, the phrase shown on the device display acts as an authentication challenge that is different for each authentication attempt. This mitigates replay attacks, in which attackers would record the user during authentication and replay the authentication utterance to the mobile device later – which would expect the same authentication phrase as it did in the previous attempt – to unlock it.

3.2   Voice Authentication Recording Application

For step (1) to (4) we developed an Android application. The application displays the phrases for enrollment and authentication on its display, records the user's voice utterances, and exports the recorded data. We aggregate the data recorded with this application to create the database that we use for step (5) with the speaker verification model in our evaluation (Sect. 4).

4   Evaluation

This section covers the recording and processing of our voice authentication utterance database, with and without face masks, and how we use this database in our evaluation to measure the impact of face masks on mobile voice authentication.

To answer the research question of this paper, we formulate the following hypothesis: FFP2 face masks have a significant impact on speaker verification in realistic voice-based authentication to mobile devices. This translates to the null-hypothesis that FFP2 masks do not have such significant impact. Hence, utterances with and without face masks would stem from the same distribution, and that there would be no significant difference in voice authentication results with and without FFP2 masks. We gather a database that contains mobile voice authentication utterances of the same speakers with and without FFP2 face masks. We then test the hypothesis by evaluating our mobile authentication approach with this database and measuring any potentially existing differences between wearing and not wearing FFP2 face masks.

4.1 Data Recording Considerations

Our evaluation database should contain samples that reflect realistic mobile voice authentication conditions, and allow to measure the impact that FFP2 masks might have. To address those needs, we consider the following aspects for the recording of our database:

Authentication phrases: voice utterances in our database should represent phrases to enroll and authenticate to mobile devices via voice authentication. We address this by each phrase consisting of four words randomly chosen from a predefined word pool. We chose four words so that authentication is fast (the resulting voice utterances have a length of 2–8 s). The static word pool consists of 3000 words that were randomly chosen from the English language.

Environmental noise: voice utterances can contain uncontrolled background noise in realistic mobile voice authentication scenarios. We account for this by not controlling for background noise in our data recording. Participants were able to record voice authentication utterance samples in situations of their own choosing. As a result, there are voice utterance samples in our database that contain background music, wind, conversations of people talking to each other, and other forms of background noise.

Speech: how users would speak an authentication phrase would depend on the situation they are in. We account for this by not controlling the situation in which users authenticate. Participants were not restricted in their choice of situation in which to record authentication phrases. Participants also did not receive instructions on how loudly or clearly they should speak authentication phrases in relation to the environment they are in. As a result, there are voice utterance samples in our database where participants spoke normally, as well as samples where participants spoke more loudly or more clearly, e.g. when being in a noisy environment, or when speaking to someone on the phone.

Recording device: in realistic mobile voice authentication scenarios users would authenticate to their own off-the-shelf mobile device. We account for this by allowing participants to record voice authentication utterances on their own mobile devices via the Android application we developed for this purpose. To allow for a wide range of devices, the application is compatible with Android 7.0+ (covers 94.8% of the Android market share[3]).

4.2 Data Recording

Participants were made aware of the goals of this research, had the recording application installed on their mobile device and explained to them by a researcher, and were instructed to use the application as if it were part of their process to unlock their mobile device.

Each of 30 speakers contributed 15 voice authentication utterances to our database. Each speaker contributed 5 utterances without face mask for enrollment, 5 for authentication with face masks, and 5 for authentication without face masks. This results in a total of 450 utterances with a total length of 29 min. The mean duration per utterance is 3.86 s (SD: 1.16). The mean participant age is 28.1 years (SD: 10.6). 8/30 participants identify as female, 22/30 participants identify as male. 8/30 participants speak English and 22/30 participants speak German in their daily work environment.

4.3 Evaluation Procedure

For our evaluation we split our database into 3 data sets. Each data set contains 5 utterances from each of the 30 speakers, hence 150 utterances in total:

– Enrollment: we use this set to simulate users enrolling. Contains utterances without face masks.
– Authentication without face masks: we use this set to simulate users authenticating who do not wear face masks.
– Authentications with face masks: we use this set to simulate users authenticating who wear face masks.

We simulate enrollment of a user to their mobile device with one of their utterances from the enrollment data set. We then simulate the authorized user attempting to authenticate to their device with one of their utterances from one of the authentication data set (same speaker verification). We also simulate other users attempting to authenticate to the device via one of their respective utterances from one of the authentication data sets (different speaker verification). Note that the latter only simulates a zero-effort attack, in which the attacker (the unauthorized user) accidentally tries to authenticate to the wrong device. This does not simulate attackers with realistic adversarial capabilities, such as the capability to record the authorized user's voice through some means, to train a speech generation model from the recording, and to use this model to try to pass the voice authentication challenge of the device.

---

[3] Android version market share: https://gs.statcounter.com/android-version-market-share/mobile (Jul 2022).

Table 1. T-test results for speaker verification scores with and without face masks being sampled from the same underlying distribution.

	t-statistic	p-value
same speaker	3.1069	0.0019
different speaker	−2.4483	0.0143

We repeat this for all possible permutations. This results in a total of 1500 authentication attempts of authorized users to their mobile devices (50 per enrolled user), and to a total of 43500 authentication attempts of users trying to authenticate to the device of another user (1450 per enrolled user). 50% of those authentication attempts are made with face masks, 50% without (22500 authentication attempts each).

Each authentication attempt results in one speaker verification score. This score indicates the similarity of the speaker of the authentication voice utterance to the speaker of the enrolled voice utterance, where a higher score means a higher similarity. This yields 45000 verification scores in total, 22500 each for authentication attempts with and without face masks.

5   Results and Discussion

5.1   Verification Score Distribution

Our null hypothesis is that face masks have no impact on speaker verification for mobile device voice authentication. Hence, the verification scores we obtained in our evaluation for authentication attempts with and without face masks are sampled from the same underlying distribution. We test this null hypothesis with a paired Student's t-test ($\alpha = 0.05$). The test yields a p-value of 0.0019 for same speaker verification, and of 0.0143 for different speaker verification (Table 1). This confirms a significant difference between verification scores with and without FFP2 face masks for both same and different speaker verification scenarios. We can therefore reject our null hypothesis for both same and different speaker verification scenarios, and conclude that FFP2 face masks have a significant impact on speaker verification in realistic mobile voice authentication scenarios.

5.2   Mobile Authentication Results

We first analyze the raw speaker verification scores. The distributions of those scores with and without FFP2 face masks, for same and different speaker verification, indicate that both same and different speaker verification are negatively impacted by face masks (Fig. 2). The mean same speaker verification score decreases by 0.0185, from 0.5498 without faces masks to 0.5313 with face masks (Table 2). The mean different speaker verification score increases by 0.0024, from 0.1184 without face masks to 0.1209 with face masks. From this, we conclude

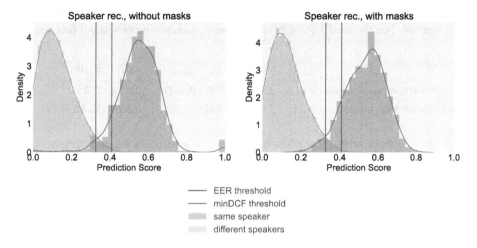

Fig. 2. Speaker verification score distributions for same and different speaker verification, with and without face masks.

Table 2. Mean and standard deviation of prediction scores.

	same speaker		different speaker	
	score mean	score SD	score mean	score SD
without face masks	0.5498	0.1155	0.1184	0.0964
with faces masks	0.5313	0.1027	0.1209	0.0943

that wearing FFP2 face masks leads to a loss of speaker information that has negative impact on both same and different speaker verification for mobile voice authentication.

We then obtain mobile voice authentication results by applying an authentication threshold to the speaker verification scores. For same speaker verification, applying this threshold yields true positives if the score is above the threshold, hence indicating a sample is correctly recognized as coming from the same speaker, and false negatives if the score is below the threshold, hence indicating a sample is incorrectly recognized as coming from different speakers. For different speaker verification this yields true negatives if the score is below the threshold, hence indicating a sample is correctly recognized as coming from different speakers, and false positives if the score is above the threshold, hence indicating a sample is incorrectly recognized as coming from the same speaker. From those we then compute the corresponding false positive rate (FPR) and false negative rate (FNR) per scenario. Note that these values correspond to zero-effort attacks in which the unauthorized user accidentally tries to authenticate to the wrong device, and not attackers with realistic adversarial capabilities who would try on purpose to maliciously pass the mobile device voice authentication.

At first, we use the equal error rate (EER) from scores without face masks as an authentication decision threshold and apply it to both scores with and without

Table 3. Authentication error rates. The authentication decision threshold is the EER (left) and based on the minDCF (right) for authentication attempts without face masks.

	EER	FPR	FNR	minDCF	FPR	FNR
without face masks	2.81%	2.81%	2.81%	0.1441	0.35%	7.70%
with face masks	N/A	2.53%	3.40%	N/A	0.30%	13.03%

Table 4. Reference error rates when basing the authentication decision threshold on the EER (left) and the minDCF (right) of authentication attempts with face masks.

	EER	FPR	FNR	minDCF	FPR	FNR
with face masks	2.96%	2.96%	2.96%	0.1772	0.32%	11.55%

face masks. Due to this choice of threshold, the FPR and FNR will be equal for authentication without face masks. With this threshold, the FPR decreases by 0.28%, from 2.81% without wearing masks to 2.53% when wearing masks (Table 3). The FNR increases by 0.59%, from 2.81% without wearing masks to 3.4% when wearing masks. This indicates a slightly lower chance to successfully authenticate as an authorized user when wearing a face mask, as well as a slightly lower chance for non-authorized users to successfully pass the authentication when wearing a face mask. Note that the impact on the former is noteworthy larger than on the latter, which indicates an overall slightly negative effect from wearing face masks. For reference, when comparing the EER of authentication attempts without face masks to the EER of authentication attempts with face masks, the EER increases by 0.15%, from 2.81% without masks to 2.96% with masks (Table 4). This too indicates that wearing FFP2 face masks has a slight negative impact on the correctness of the authentication decision.

We then exchange the EER authentication threshold with a minDCF-based authentication threshold. The minDCF allows to consider a class imbalance and to weigh the costs of false positives and false negatives accordingly. Hence, when using the minDCF, the threshold is set where weighted costs are minimized. We again set the threshold according to the minDCF of the verification scores without face masks for both distributions (Table 3). With equal minDCF weights for false positives and false negatives, we observe a decrease of the FPR by 0.05%, from 0.35% without wearing masks to 0.30% when wearing masks. The FNR increased by 5.96%, from 7.7% without wearing masks to 13.03% when wearing masks. Note that the impact on the latter is noteworthily larger than the former. Overall this also indicates that wearing FFP2 face masks has a slight negative impact on the authentication decision correctness.

The comparison of the ROC curves for authentication attempts without and with FFP2 face masks (Fig. 3) confirms that face masks in general have a slight negative impact for configurations with similar costs for FPR and FNR. Given that we observe a negative impact on the authentication results when wearing

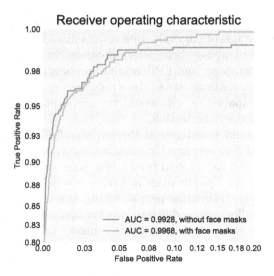

Fig. 3. Receiver operating characteristic curve of verifications with face masks and without.

FFP2 masks, we can also conclude that the Lombard effect is not sufficient to compensate for the loss of information caused by wearing FFP2 masks in mobile authentication scenarios.

6   Conclusion

In this paper we investigated the impact of FFP2 masks on mobile voice authentication in realistic scenarios. We recorded a 30-speaker database composed of short voice-authentication utterances with and without FFP2 masks. With this data, we conducted an experiment that simulated a voice-based authentication process to a mobile device. For speaker verification in the authentication process we used an ECAPA-TDNN speaker verification model [4]. We conducted a hypothesis test to answer the question if wearing FFP2 masks has a significant impact on speaker verification scores, and were able to confirm such a significant impact. We also observed that wearing a face mask slightly decreased the mean verification score for same speaker verification, and slightly increased it for different speaker verification. When applying an authentication threshold to the verification scores we observe a slight decrease of the FPR (-0.28%), and in comparison larger increase of the FNR ($+0.59\%$). When comparing the EER between authentication attempts without and with face masks directly we too observe a slight error increase ($+0.15\%$) from wearing face masks. Overall, we can conclude that FFP2 masks can have slight but significant impact on mobile voice authentication, on both different speaker authentication and same speaker authentication. From this impact we can also conclude that the Lombard effect of users who voice-authenticate to their mobile device while wearing an FFP2 face mask seems insufficient to counterbalance the voice attenuation caused by the face mask. Limitations of our evaluation results include young male speakers with German as native language being overrepresented in the participants of our speaker verification database, and FPR results representing unauthorized users who accidentally try to authenticate to the wrong device, and not attackers with realistic adversarial capabilities who would try on purpose to maliciously pass the mobile device voice authentication.

Future research could investigate if the impact of FFP2 masks on mobile voice authentication differs over specific authentication situations of interest, e.g. while being in a car with background from traffic noise or from other passengers talking, or while being in a public place indoors and outdoors, with background noise from wind or again from other people talking. It could also investigate how strongly the impact differs across different speaker verification approaches – and if there are approaches on which wearing face masks has no or only marginal negative impact, to better support users wearing face masks in mobile voice authentication of the future.

References

1. Balamurali, B.T., Enyi, T., Clarke, C.J., Harn, S.Y., Chen, J.M.: Acoustic effect of face mask design and material choice. Acoust. Aust. **49**(3), 505–512 (2021)
2. Bogdanel, G., Belghazi-Mohamed, N., Gómez-Moreno, H., Lafuente-Arroyo, S.: Study on the effect of face masks on forensic speaker recognition. In: Alcaraz, C., Chen, L., Li, S., Samarati, P. (eds.) Information and Communications Security, pp. 608–621. Springer, Cham (2022). https://doi.org/10.1007/978-3-031-15777-6_33
3. Corey, R.M., Jones, U., Singer, A.C.: Comparison of the acoustic effects of face masks on speech. Hear. J. **74**(1), 36–38 (2021)
4. Desplanques, B., Thienpondt, J., Demuynck, K.: ECAPA-TDNN: emphasized channel attention, propagation and aggregation in TDNN based speaker verification. In: Interspeech 2020. ISCA (2020)
5. Goldin, A., Weinstein, B., Shiman, N., et al.: How do medical masks degrade speech perception. Hear. Rev. **27**(5), 8–9 (2020)
6. Gutz, S., Rowe, H., Green, J.: Speaking with a KN95 face mask: ASR performance and speaker compensation. Interspeech **2021**, 4798–4802 (2021)
7. Khan, A., et al.: Toward realigning automatic speaker verification in the era of covid-19. Sensors **22**(7), 2638 (2022)
8. Magee, M., et al.: Effects of face masks on acoustic analysis and speech perception: implications for peri-pandemic protocols. J. Acoust. Soc. Am. **148**(6), 3562–3568 (2020)
9. Nagrani, A., et al.: VoxSRC 2020: the second VoxCeleb speaker recognition challenge. arXiv:2012.06867
10. Ngan, M., Grother, P., Hanaoka, K.: Ongoing face recognition vendor test (FRVT) part 6A: face recognition accuracy with masks using pre- COVID-19 algorithms (2020)
11. Nguyen, D.D., et al.: Acoustic voice characteristics with and without wearing a facemask. Sci. Rep. **11**(1), 5651 (2021)
12. Pörschmann, C., Lübeck, T., Arend, J.M.: Impact of face masks on voice radiation. J. Acoust. Soc. Am. **148**(6), 3663–3670 (2020)

13. Ravanelli, M., et al.: SpeechBrain: a general-purpose speech toolkit (2021). arXiv:2106.04624
14. Rui, Z., Yan, Z.: A survey on biometric authentication: toward secure and privacy-preserving identification. IEEE Access **7**, 5994–6009 (2019)
15. Saeidi, R., Niemi, T., Karppelin, H., Pohjalainen, J., Kinnunen, T.H., Alku, P.: Speaker recognition for speech under face cover. In: Interspeech 2015 (2015)
16. Schwartz, J.C., Whyte, A.T., Al-Nuaimi, M., Donai, J.J.: Effects of signal bandwidth and noise on individual speaker identification. J. Acoust. Soc. Am. **144**(5), EL447–EL452 (2018)
17. Smiljanic, R., Keerstock, S., Meemann, K., Ransom, S.M.: Face masks and speaking style affect audio-visual word recognition and memory of native and non-native speech. J. Acoust. Soc. Am. **149**(6), 4013–4023 (2021)
18. Toscano, J.C., Toscano, C.M.: Effects of face masks on speech recognition in multi-talker babble noise. PLoS ONE **16**(2), 1–12 (2021)
19. Wang, C., Wang, Y., Chen, Y., Liu, H., Liu, J.: User authentication on mobile devices: approaches, threats and trends. Comput. Netw. **170**, 107118 (2020)
20. Zollinger, S.A., Brumm, H.: The Lombard effect. Curr. Biol. **21**(16), R614–R615 (2011)

Blockchain-Enhanced IoHT: A Patient-Centric Internet of Healthcare Things Platform with Smart Contract-Driven Data Management

N. H. Bang[1]([⊠]), T. D. Khoa[1], M. N. Triet[1], V. H. Khanh[1], H. G. Khiem[1],
Q. T. Bao[1], N. T. Phuc[1], M. D. Hieu[1], V. C. P. Loc[1], T. L. Quy[1], N. T. Anh[1],
Q. N. Hien[1], L. K. Bang[1], D. P. N. Trong[1], N. T. K. Ngan[2], H. Son[3],
and H. H. Luong[1]([⊠])

[1] FPT University, Can Tho city, Vietnam
bangnhce160624@fpt.edu.vn, huonghoangluong@gmail.com
[2] FPT Polytecnic, Can Tho city, Vietnam
[3] RMIT University, Ho Chi Minh city, Vietnam

Abstract. The Internet of Things (IoT) has seen rapid adoption across various sectors, with healthcare being one of the most significant. The IoHT-MBA platform, an Internet of Healthcare Things (IoHT) system based on microservice and brokerless architecture, has proven to be highly effective in addressing critical challenges such as data collection, user and device management, and remote device control. However, to further enhance patient data privacy and control, an additional layer of decentralization and self-sovereign data management is necessary. In this work, we introduce a blockchain-enhanced IoHT-MBA platform - a new system that incorporates a distributed ledger technology, specifically Hyperledger Fabric, to provide a secure, transparent, and patient-controlled data management system. Patients can manage their edge local devices at the edge layer, contributing to a distributed storage service. All requests for user data must comply with the patient's privacy conditions, defined through smart contracts, adding an extra layer of security and transparency. We further evaluate our platform using the microservice and brokerless architecture theories (Round Trip Time and Broken Connection Test Cases), in addition to data creation tests in Hyperledger Caliper, demonstrating the robustness and efficiency of our blockchain-enhanced system.

Keywords: Internet of Health Things (IoHT) · Microservice · Brokerless · Single Sign-On · Blockchain · Smart Contract · Distributed Ledger · Hyperledger Fabric · Hyperledger Caliper · Edge Computing · Patient-Centric

P. Delir Haghighi et al. (Eds.): MoMM 2023, LNCS 14417, pp. 50–56, 2023.
https://doi.org/10.1007/978-3-031-48348-6_4

1   Introduction

In the healthcare sector, the traditional systems for managing patient data and emergency cases have shown considerable limitations [3,6]. The urgent need for a secure, reliable, and efficient system for healthcare data management has led to the exploration of blockchain technologies for managing various healthcare operations [4].

The Internet of Things (IoT) has expanded its horizon to a myriad of applications such as smart cities, healthcare, supply chains, industry, agriculture, and more. On the other hand, Blockchain, a decentralized and secure ledger system, presents a promising solution to many of these challenges.

In this paper, we propose a novel approach that combines the power of blockchain technologies with IoT called Blockchain-Enhanced IoHT: A Patient-Centric Internet of Healthcare Things Platform with Smart Contract-Driven Data Management. Our system addresses the key challenges in existing IoT platforms by providing a secure, reliable, and efficient solution for healthcare data management. Our proposed platform leverages the blockchain to create a secure and traceable record of patient data. It enables a brokerless and microservice architecture, ensuring fault tolerance, horizontal scaling, and system availability. The system offers a comprehensive management model of the components involved in the platform, based on the Role-base Access Control (RBAC) architecture combined with hierarchical user management.

2   Related Work

Several works have proposed various architectures for data collection from medical devices. For instance, Maktoubian et al. [5] introduced an architecture that combines the MQTT protocol and Kafka Message Queue. While the use of Kafka offers secure data transmission, the MQTT protocol and brokering architecture have recognized drawbacks such as potential single point failure and uncertainties regarding the optimal Quality-of-Service (QoS) levels [7,8]. Moreover, the security measures in their system are not explicitly addressed.

Jita et al. [2] built an in-home medical care system using a scalable microservice architecture and blockchain for enhanced security. However, the system uses the Zetta IoT Platform, which relies on the HTTP and RESTful protocols, less suitable for low-end devices [1].

Le et al. [4] have also developed a system for managing medical waste using blockchain. Their work emphasizes the importance of sharing and securely managing information related to medical equipment and supplies.

These works highlight the potential of blockchain technology in enhancing data security, privacy, and patient-centricity in healthcare systems. Our work extends these efforts by proposing a blockchain-enhanced IoHT platform that integrates microservice and brokerless architecture for enhanced scalability, efficiency, and patient data control.

3   System Architecture

3.1   Overview Architecture

The proposed blockchain-enhanced IoHT-MBA platform adopts a multi-tiered architecture, consisting of the edge layer, the blockchain layer, and the cloud layer.

At the edge layer, we have the patient's local devices including smartphones, sensors, and other IoT devices. Each device is embedded with a light client of the blockchain, enabling it to communicate with the blockchain layer. The data collected by these devices is stored locally, enhancing data privacy and security.

The blockchain layer is the core of the patient-centric data management system. We utilize the Hyperledger Fabric, a permissioned blockchain. The blockchain stores only the aggregated health data and all transactions related to data access and sharing. Each transaction on the blockchain is validated and recorded across multiple nodes, ensuring data integrity and traceability. Smart contracts are used to automate the execution of agreements related to data sharing. These contracts are coded with the patient's privacy conditions and are executed whenever there is a request for data access or sharing. This ensures that the patient's privacy preferences are always honored.

The cloud layer is responsible for providing various services to the users of the platform, such as data analytics, health monitoring, and alert services.

With this architecture, the proposed platform provides a secure, decentralized, and patient-centric data management system for healthcare IoT. The following sections will detail the implementation and evaluation of the platform.

3.2   Detail Architecture

The utilization of microservices and brokerless architecture is a key aspect of our system design that offers several benefits. In particular, microservices architecture refers to the development of applications as a suite of small, independent services. In the context of our IoHT platform, different services such as data collection, user management, device management, and alerting services can be implemented as separate microservices. Brokerless architecture, on the other hand, eliminates the need for a central broker or server, which can be a single point of failure and can limit scalability. In our brokerless architecture, each node or device can communicate directly with each other, enhancing the system's reliability, efficiency, and scalability. This is particularly beneficial in a healthcare environment where the availability and timeliness of data are crucial.

Edge Computing Architecture. The edge computing process in our Blockchain-Enhanced IoHT platform comprises two primary layers: the Things layer and the Client layer (see Fig. 1).

Things Layer. The Things layer is composed of various medical devices owned by the patient. Each of these devices is equipped with sensors to monitor various health parameters and collect critical health data. These devices implement two independent services: a data collection service and a control service.

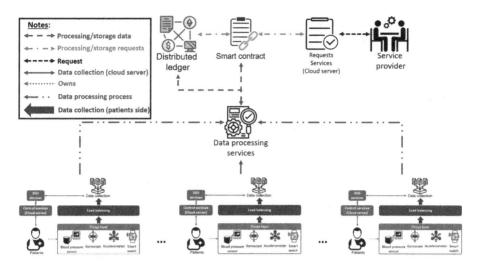

Fig. 1. Blockchain-Enhanced IoHT platform based on Microservice and Brokerless architecture

Client Layer. The Client layer, represented by the patient, interacts with the medical devices in the Things layer. This layer plays a crucial role in ensuring patient-centric data management, as it allows the patient to exercise control over their health data, ensuring that their privacy preferences are honored. By integrating edge computing in our platform, we can process data closer to the source, reducing latency and improving real-time data processing capabilities.

Blockchain-Enhanced IoHT Architecture. The Blockchain-Enhanced IoHT platform's architecture is designed in Fig. 1. This architecture comprises several interconnected components, each playing a critical role in ensuring data privacy and control.

Data Processing Services: Once health data has been collected from the patient's devices at the edge, it is transferred to the data processing services for further processing. Instead of storing raw, detailed patient data in the blockchain, only aggregated data is stored.

Service Providers: Service providers could be healthcare professionals, healthcare institutions, researchers, or any other entities that require access to the health data for providing services.

Distributed Ledger and Smart Contracts: The aggregated data is then stored in a distributed ledger, a decentralized database that is maintained by various nodes in the blockchain network. Each entry in the ledger is validated by multiple nodes, ensuring data integrity and transparency.

The interaction between the distributed ledger and service providers is governed by smart contracts. These are self-executing contracts with the terms of the agreement directly written into lines of code.

4 Evaluation Scenarios

4.1 Performance Evaluation

Round Trip Time (RTT) is measured from the moment data is streamed from the IoT devices until it is received at the Message Queue. Additionally, the error rate, defined as the number of messages lost out of total messages, is assessed. The results are presented in Table 1.

Table 1. Round trip time results in the Four places

Location	Factor	1,000	5,000	10,000	50,000	100,000
North California	**RTT(s)**	3.23	13.78	27.42	131.16	259.11
	Error(%)	0	0	0	0	0
Stockholm	**RTT(s)**	3.41	13.98	25.86	129.14	259.43
	Error(%)	0	0	0	0	0
Ho Chi Minh city	**RTT(s)**	3.62	13.74	24.93	131.11	259.98
	Error(%)	0	0	0	0	0
Sydney	**RTT(s)**	3.21	14.02	26.08	129.98	258.06
	Error(%)	0	0	0	0	0

When the Blockchain-Enhanced IoHT platform is in use, the subscriber receives all messages that were published by the publisher, even those sent during the connection failure. This is made possible by the Kafka message queue, which stores all outgoing messages until they are successfully delivered, thereby

Table 2. Medical data creation performance in five increasing each 1,000 requests scenarios

Name	Success	Fail	Send Rate (TPS)	Max Latency (s)	Min Latency (s)	Avg Latency (s)	Throughput (TPS)
1,000 request	26,987	19,801	135.0	1,532.18	10.41	654.12	11.9
2,000 request	29,604	16,402	138.5	1,523.78	9.82	634.21	16.4
3,000 request	27,412	18,523	142.7	1,457.34	10.43	678.43	15.3
4,000 request	29,617	19,176	139.9	1,686.23	10.67	651.24	15.4
5,000 request	30,401	16,205	145.6	1,712.12	11.01	696.18	17.2

preventing any data loss during transmission. This maintains the integrity of the medical data and allows for accurate and comprehensive analysis, thereby improving patient care outcomes (Table 2).

4.2 Discussion

The evaluation of our proposed Blockchain-Enhanced IoHT system provides valuable insights into its performance and efficiency. The system's brokerless and microservice architecture, combined with a blockchain-based data management approach, demonstrates its potential to handle a significant number of data transactions while maintaining low latency and high throughput.

5 Conclusion

This paper proposed a blockchain-enhanced, patient-centric system, called Block- chain-Enhanced IoHT, which incorporates a microservice and brokerless architecture. This structure not only enhances the fault tolerance, scalability, and availability of the system but also allows for a more efficient and resilient healthcare data management system. The integration of blockchain technology ensures secure and traceable data sharing, addressing key challenges faced by conventional healthcare systems. The use of smart contracts further bolsters security measures, particularly in the interaction between patients and service providers. Furthermore, the evaluation of the Blockchain-Enhanced IoHT based on its architecture and the use of blockchain technology provided insights into its effectiveness in managing healthcare data. Future work should focus on further optimizing the system's performance, exploring ways to enhance the scalability and efficiency of the blockchain-based system.

Acknowledgement. We would like to extend our deepest gratitude to Engineer Le Thanh Tuan and Mr. Lam Nguyen Tran Thanh for their invaluable contribution and insight throughout the conceptualization, execution, and assessment of this project.

References

1. Bansal, M., et al.: Application layer protocols for internet of healthcare things (IoHT). In: 2020 Fourth International Conference on Inventive Systems and Control (ICISC), pp. 369–376. IEEE (2020)
2. Jita, H., Pieterse, V.: A framework to apply the internet of things for medical care in a home environment. In: Proceedings of the 2018 International Conference on Cloud Computing and Internet of Things, pp. 45–54 (2018)
3. Le, H.T., et al.: Patient-chain: patient-centered healthcare system a blockchain-based technology in dealing with emergencies. In: Shen, H., et al. (eds.) PDCAT 2021. LNCS, vol. 13148, pp. 576–583. Springer, Cham (2022). https://doi.org/10.1007/978-3-030-96772-7_54
4. Le, H.T., et al.: Medical-waste chain: a medical waste collection, classification and treatment management by blockchain technology. Computers **11**(7), 113 (2022)

5. Maktoubian, J., Ansari, K.: An IoT architecture for preventive maintenance of medical devices in healthcare organizations. Heal. Technol. **9**(3), 233–243 (2019)
6. Son, H.X., Le, T.H., Quynh, N.T.T., Huy, H.N.D., Duong-Trung, N., Luong, H.H.: Toward a blockchain-based technology in dealing with emergencies in patient-centered healthcare systems. In: Bouzefrane, S., Laurent, M., Boumerdassi, S., Renault, E. (eds.) MSPN 2020. LNCS, vol. 12605, pp. 44–56. Springer, Cham (2021). https://doi.org/10.1007/978-3-030-67550-9_4
7. Toldinas, J., Lozinskis, B., Baranauskas, E., Dobrovolskis, A.: MQTT quality of service versus energy consumption. In: 2019 23rd International Conference Electronics, pp. 1–4. IEEE (2019)
8. Yassein, M.B., Shatnawi, M.Q., Aljwarneh, S., Al-Hatmi, R.: Internet of things: survey and open issues of MQTT protocol. In: 2017 International Conference on Engineering & MIS (ICEMIS), pp. 1–6. IEEE (2017)

Federated Learning for Collaborative Cybersecurity of Distributed Healthcare

Svetlana Boudko[✉]

Norsk Regnesentral, Oslo, Norway
svetlana@nr.no

Abstract. Healthcare 4.0 is a new paradigm for providing healthcare services in highly distributed and complex settings. The distributed and heterogeneous nature of home-based medical devices, and their need to exchange data with external sources make Healthcare 4.0 solutions susceptible to cyberattacks and require decentralized solutions to protect sensitive local data. This work presents a collaborative approach to security incident detection for distributed healthcare utilizing federated learning. At this stage, the federated learning process has been facilitated and evaluated using simulation, training, and testing.

Keywords: Distributed healthcare · Federated learning · Cybersecurity · Collaborative protocols

1 Introduction

The Healthcare 4.0 concept is a new paradigm that provides services in a highly distributed and heterogeneous context covering hospitals, GP offices, nursing houses, and home care. These services require distributed infrastructure that integrates cloud solutions, edge computing, and various medical IoT devices. While improving the efficiency of patient care, it also expands the attack surface increasing safety risks for healthcare. Medical smart devices constantly process and communicate large amounts of sensitive patient data vulnerable to cyberattacks that can cause a violation of user privacy and threats to human life.

Conventional machine learning (ML) has been traditionally used for developing intrusion detection solutions. However, this approach implies that sensitive data are collected from network devices and sent to centralized entities for training machine learning models, thus violating privacy requirements. The latency cost of data transmission is also high, and, to be effective, these solutions need to comply with the diverse and distributed nature of Healthcare 4.0.

Given the background, this work studies the applicability of Federated Learning (FL) [11] to intrusion detection. FL was proposed by Google for collaborative training of machine learning models aiming to handle the exchange of privacy-sensitive information in distributed environments and to reduce data transmission costs. The main contribution of this work is an evaluation of a federated

P. Delir Haghighi et al. (Eds.): MoMM 2023, LNCS 14417, pp. 57–62, 2023.
https://doi.org/10.1007/978-3-031-48348-6_5

learning approach for collaborative and distributed training of security incident detection models. For this evaluation, an FL model training process is implemented using a convolutional neural network classifier.

2   Federated Learning

FL facilitates a collaborative decentralized model training process. This technique enables on-device training using local data without exposing these data to other devices or a central aggregator. The training process is an iteration process of several steps alternating between local updates and global aggregation. The aggregator trains the initial global model and sends this model to the end devices called *workers*. The workers train their models using local data and share the obtained model updates with the aggregator. The aggregator uses these updates to generate a new global model that is sent back to the workers to perform the next iteration step.

Different strategies have been proposed to facilitate the aggregation process, improve the convergence, and reduce communicational and computational expenses [1,10,14]. Federated Averaging is most commonly used due to its communication efficiency [10]. In this method, a subset of workers is selected to perform updates. The process alternates between multiple local stochastic gradient updates and exchanging their averaged weights for updates at the aggregator.

Several challenges are outlined in the literature concerning FL. Importantly, poisoning attacks can be launched by malicious workers to misclassify inputs. To tackle this problem, different defense techniques exist [3,6,16]. Further, locally generated data cannot be assumed independently and identically distributed (non-iid) increasing complexity in model training and aggregation. In this survey [9], the authors present data-based, model-based, algorithm-based, and framework-based techniques to address the non-iid problem. Although the local data are not shared with external parties, there are still privacy concerns since model updates can reveal sensitive information. Privacy-preserving technologies, e.g. homomorphic encryption, are applied to secure data protection.

3   Related Work

While a number of studies utilize conventional ML for intrusion detection in healthcare systems [5,7,8], the research conducted on intrusion detection using FL mostly focuses on general IoT systems.

A decentralized optimization framework [4] was implemented using the sparse Support Vector Machine (sSVM) classifier. It enables multiple data holders to collaborate and converge to a common predictive model in a decentralized manner. To solve large-scale sSVM problems, the authors developed an iterative cluster Primal-Dual Splitting (cPDS) algorithm with improved convergence.

FL was used for training a multi-task deep neural network utilized for anomaly detection, VPN traffic recognition, and traffic classification tasks [15].

The authors showed that the multi-task method effectively reduced training time compared to multiple single-task models.

In [13], the authors presented a federated learning-based intrusion detection system with feature selection technology. To achieve better intrusion detection accuracy, this study proposed a greedy algorithm for selecting optimal features that are used to generate global models.

The work in [12] utilized Long Short Term Memory Networks and Gated Recurrent Units to facilitate a federated learning-based process for anomaly detection in the IoT networks. The presented solution outperformed the non-FL version of intrusion detection algorithms while ensuring the privacy of user data.

In [2], the authors proposed a federated learning-based intrusion detection technique that uses decentralized data for performing training and inference procedures at the device's end. The device's data was not shared with any other external device, and the multi-view ensemble learning component was used to optimize the learning effectiveness.

FL is a relatively new research initiative, and, compared to conventional ML, its application to intrusion detection for healthcare systems is not thoroughly addressed. The feature selection is mostly limited to network parameters. Detecting security incidents in healthcare environments will also require features that characterize patient behavior and health data.

4   Evaluation and Experimental Setup

The motivation for this study was to set up an experimental validation framework for different FL scenarios and aggregation strategies. In these experiments, a varying number of workers cooperatively train an FL model. To better interpret the outcome of the experiments, the results are benchmarked against a centralized ML solution.

4.1   Experimental Setup

To evaluate the performance of the proposed approach, the publicly available Intrusion Detection Evaluation Dataset CIC IDS 2017 was used. The dataset was created by the Canadian Institute for Cybersecurity for testing anomaly-based intrusion detection techniques. It consists of data for benign traffic and the most up-to-date common attacks. The dataset was divided into training and testing sets using a 70:30 ratio respectively. To initiate the training process, a small subset was used for training the initial model that was sent to all participants. Further, the training set was split among the participating workers.

A Convolutional Neural Network classifier was trained using TensorFlow. The neural network contained the following layers: 1) a 1D CNN layer since the data are one-dimensional; 2) a pooling layer; 3) a flatten layer; 4) a dropout layer for regularization to prevent outfitting; 5) two dense layers with activation 'relu'. For optimization, the adam algorithm was applied, which is a version of stochastic gradient descent. The binary cross entropy loss function was used in these settings. The number of epochs was 30.

4.2   Experimental Results

Three experiments were performed, with the following numbers of workers: 5, 10, and 50 workers. For each experiment, the training dataset was equally divided among the workers. It implied that the workers in the succeeding experiment were using smaller datasets for each training session than the workers from the previous experiment. This provided an opportunity to observe how varying the size of training sets influences the convergence of the proposed solution. Each experiment consisted of 10 consequent training rounds, and the received weights were averaged and aggregated after each round.

To measure the performance, the classification accuracy rate was used. It defines the ratio of correctly predicted points to the total number of points. To benchmark the results, a neural network with the same settings as described above was trained and tested on the whole dataset. The results of the benchmark, the initial model, and the successive training rounds are depicted in Fig. 1. The accuracy result of the benchmark was approximately 0.998. The accuracy of the initial trained model was 0.386. While the accuracy of the first round was higher for the experiment with 5 workers, the convergence speeds are slightly different for the three curves. In the experiment with 50 workers, the curve converged faster with the highest final accuracy. The final results were 0.943, 0.947, 0.961 for 5, 10, and 50 workers respectively.

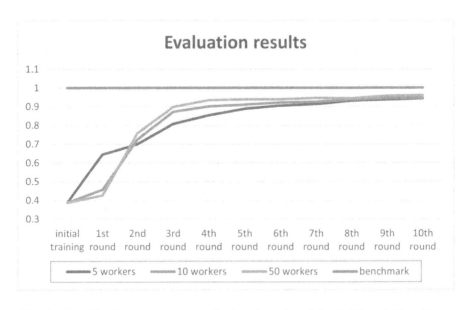

Fig. 1. Classification accuracy rates for benchmark and for 5, 10, and 50 workers

5   Conclusion and Future Work

The paper presents a federated learning-based collaborative approach to security incident detection in a distributed context. At this stage, the feasibility of the approach has been validated by simulations, training, and testing. The presented experimental setup will be further developed and used in future work to optimize and verify collaborative model training schemes and processes.

The next stages will involve: 1) producing datasets; 2) selecting and optimizing aggregation strategies; and 3) integrating data protection measures. Acquiring high-quality data is the most critical part of this work. A number of open intrusion detection datasets are available, however, these are based on network settings. Preparing datasets, defining and engineering features that are both network and health-data specific is planned using simulations and lab experiments. Feature fusion will help reduce dimensionality and obtain a concise representation of network parameters and patient information. Using real patient data is considered in compliance with current regulations.

Further, the work will focus on tuning local training, optimizing aggregation strategies, and addressing the effects of non-iid data with the help of data partitioning strategies. Other performance metrics, e.g., precision, recall, and F1 score, will be included as evaluation criteria. Using the new datasets, the aggregation strategies from the literature will be evaluated against criteria that include convergence rate and transmission cost. Modifications will be made if applicable. To ensure the confidentiality of local updates, it is important to select privacy-preserving methods with low computational and transmission overhead.

Acknowledgements. This work has been carried out in the context of the Center for Research-based Innovation NORCICS, grant number 310105/F40, and the research project Health Democratization, grant number 288856. The projects are funded by the Research Council of Norway.

References

1. Arivazhagan, M.G., Aggarwal, V., Singh, A.K., Choudhary, S.: Federated learning with personalization layers (2019)
2. Attota, D.C., Mothukuri, V., Parizi, R.M., Pouriyeh, S.: An ensemble multi-view federated learning intrusion detection for Iot. IEEE Access **9**, 117734–117745 (2021). https://doi.org/10.1109/ACCESS.2021.3107337
3. Bhagoji, A.N., Chakraborty, S., Mittal, P., Calo, S.: Analyzing federated learning through an adversarial lens. In: Chaudhuri, K., Salakhutdinov, R. (eds.) Proceedings of the 36th International Conference on Machine Learning. Proceedings of Machine Learning Research, vol. 97, pp. 634–643. PMLR (2019), https://proceedings.mlr.press/v97/bhagoji19a.html
4. Brisimi, T.S., Chen, R., Mela, T., Olshevsky, A., Paschalidis, I.C., Shi, W.: Federated learning of predictive models from federated electronic health records. Int. J. Med. Inform. **112**, 59–67 (2018). https://doi.org/10.1016/j.ijmedinf.2018.01.007, https://www.sciencedirect.com/science/article/pii/S138650561830008X

5. Hady, A.A., Ghubaish, A., Salman, T., Unal, D., Jain, R.: Intrusion detection system for healthcare systems using medical and network data: a comparison study. IEEE Access **8**, 106576–106584 (2020). https://doi.org/10.1109/ACCESS. 2020.3000421

6. Hitaj, B., Ateniese, G., Perez-Cruz, F.: Deep models under the gan: Information leakage from collaborative deep learning. In: Proceedings of the 2017 ACM SIGSAC Conference on Computer and Communications Security, pp. 603–618. CCS '17, Association for Computing Machinery, New York, NY, USA (2017). https://doi. org/10.1145/3133956.3134012

7. Jeyanthi, D.V., Indrani, B.: Iot-based intrusion detection system for healthcare using rnnbilstm deep learning strategy with custom features. Soft Comput. **27**(16), 11915–11930 (2023). https://doi.org/10.1007/s00500-023-08536-8

8. Lakhotia, P., Dwivedi, R., Sharma, D.K., Sharma, N.: Intrusion detection system for ioe-based medical networks. J. Database Manage. **34**(2), 1–18 (2023). https:// doi.org/10.4018/JDM.321465

9. Ma, X., Zhu, J., Lin, Z., Chen, S., Qin, Y.: A state-of-the-art survey on solving non-iid data in federated learning. Future Gen. Comput. Syst. **135**, 244–258 (2022). https://doi.org/10.1016/j.future.2022.05.003, https://www.sciencedirect. com/science/article/pii/S0167739X22001686

10. McMahan, H.B., Moore, E., Ramage, D., Arcas, B.A.: Federated learning of deep networks using model averaging (2016). http://arxiv.org/abs/1602.05629

11. McMahan, H.B., Moore, E., Ramage, D., Hampson, S., Arcas, B.A.: Communication-efficient learning of deep networks from decentralized data (2016)

12. Mothukuri, V., Khare, P., Parizi, R.M., Pouriyeh, S., Dehghantanha, A., Srivastava, G.: Federated-learning-based anomaly detection for Iot security attacks. IEEE Internet Things J. **9**(4), 2545–2554 (2022). https://doi.org/10.1109/JIOT.2021. 3077803

13. Qin, Y., Kondo, M.: Federated learning-based network intrusion detection with a feature selection approach. In: 2021 International Conference on Electrical, Communication, and Computer Engineering (ICECCE), pp. 1–6 (2021). https://doi. org/10.1109/ICECCE52056.2021.9514222

14. Wang, H., Yurochkin, M., Sun, Y., Papailiopoulos, D., Khazaeni, Y.: Federated learning with matched averaging. arXiv preprint arXiv:2002.06440 (2020)

15. Zhao, Y., Chen, J., Wu, D., Teng, J., Yu, S.: Multi-task network anomaly detection using federated learning. In: Proceedings of the Tenth International Symposium on Information and Communication Technology, pp. 273–279. SoICT 2019, Association for Computing Machinery, New York, NY, USA (2019). https://doi.org/ 10.1145/3368926.3369705

16. Zhu, L., Han, S.: Deep Leakage from Gradients, pp. 17–31. Springer International Publishing, Cham (2020). https://doi.org/10.1007/978-3-030-63076-8_2

Mobile Computing and Wireless Sensors

Does Use of Blink Interface Affect Number of Blinks When Reading Paper Books?

Junpei Uchida(ID), Tsutomu Terada(✉)(ID), and Masahiko Tsukamoto(ID)

Kobe University, Hyogo, Japan

junpei-uchida@stu.kobe-u.ac.jp, tsutomu@eedept.kobe-u.ac.jp,
tuka@kobe-u.ac.jp

Abstract. Blinking is essential in maintaining eye health. The lack of blinking may lead to dry eyes, which usually happens when reading paper books. The previous blink acceleration system prompted users to blink effectively, but mandatory blinking made users uncomfortable. If users stop using the blink acceleration system, the number of blinks will reduce. Therefore, we proposed a new blink acceleration system using classical conditioning to prompt to blink when reading paper books unconsciously. Specifically, the number of blinks would increase while reading paper books because of the association between page-turning action and blinking by using the system that assigns blinking to the page-turning action when reading e-books. As a result of our evaluation experiment, the number of blinks increased for some participants with our system. There is a possibility of increasing the number of blinks while reading paper books by periodically using the proposed blink acceleration system.

Keywords: Dry eye · Wearable computing · Classical conditioning

1 Introduction

In recent years, dry eye has become a common disease because of the rapidly increased number of patients. Eye fatigue, discomfort, and abnormal visual function caused by dry eye may reduce the quality of life and productivity [1]. Dry eye is a multifactorial disease, and one of the factors is the lack of blinking. Because the lack of blinking leads to insufficient tear fluid production, which damages the cornea and conjunctiva, the possibility of suffering from dry eye will increase.

The lack of blinking occurs in some situations requiring visual concentration, such as long-term computer work and reading [2,3]. A study shows that the decrease in blinking caused by reading is more severe than in other situations [4]. However, few studies proposed methods to trigger blinking while reading, and many have focused on triggering blinking at work. For example, a system that triggers blinking by blowing air around the eyes with a glasses-type

© The Author(s), under exclusive license to Springer Nature Switzerland AG 2023
P. Delir Haghighi et al. (Eds.): MoMM 2023, LNCS 14417, pp. 65–76, 2023.
https://doi.org/10.1007/978-3-031-48348-6_6

device equipped with an air puff has been proposed [6]. However, forcing users to blink by an external stimulus may cause users to be uncomfortable and prevent them from concentrating on the work. Likewise, users will hardly concentrate on reading books when they use the system. Therefore, this paper considered a non-mandatory method to prompt users to blink using classical conditioning. This method does not require users to wear any wearable devices or systems all the time to increase the number of blinks (ex., people will not have to wear any device when reading a paper book on the sofa).

Classical conditioning is a phenomenon for learning a certain behavior passively by presenting two stimuli together. Studies have confirmed that blinking could be associated with a sound by classical conditioning and triggered by the sound [7–9]. In other words, the sound induces blinking like a habit because of classical conditioning. Thus, we assumed that we could trigger blinking by a kind of action that usually happens in reading books.

Therefore, this paper proposed a method that induces users to blink while reading paper books by conditioning the blinking to a page-turning action while reading e-books with an eye-blink interface. The eye-blink interface is designed to prompt users to blink when turning a page on an e-book. According to classical conditioning, if blinking is associated with the page-turning action when users read e-books, they will blink when reading paper books. In this paper, we investigated the number of blinks during reading a paper book without an eye-blink interface after reading e-books with the interface for a certain period. Based on the changes in the number of blinks, we evaluated whether the proposed method is effective in prompting to blink.

The remainder of this paper is presented as follows. We introduce related works in Sect. 2 and the proposed method in Sect. 3. We describe the evaluation experiment in Sect. 4 and discuss its results in Sect. 5. Finally, we summarize this study in Sect. 6.

2 Related Work

2.1 Blink Acceleration System

The blink acceleration system is the system to increase the user's blink rate in some ways. Many studies have progressed on blink acceleration, especially for intensive tasks such as computer use. Miura et al. proposed a system to trigger blinking steadily by attaching an LED timer device to a laptop and lighting LEDs up regularly [5]. Crnovrsanin et al. proposed a system that accelerated blinking by flashing the PC screen, blurring the screen, flashing the window frame, and displaying a pop-up notification when blinking decreased while working on a computer [10]. Dementyev et al. proposed a system to trigger blinking using a glasses-type device by flashing LEDs, touching the eyes with a plastic chip, and blowing air [6].

These studies forced users to blink reflexively by providing external stimuli. However, forcing users to blink causes users to be uncomfortable and prevents users from concentrating on the work [11]. In addition, it is not easy to prompt to blink when the above systems are not used because only external stimuli from the systems could trigger blinking. Therefore, this study focused on triggering blinking in a way such as making blinking like a habit.

2.2 Classical Conditioning

Classical conditioning is a phenomenon in which an output response is triggered by an input stimulus when a conscious association is formed between the input stimulus and the output response [12–14]. Watson et al. confirmed that if infants were conditioned to be fearful by showing a visual stimulus in front of them, such as a white rat, and simultaneously playing a loud sound, infants would have developed fearful responses to the visual stimulus that they were not fearful initially [15]. Research has also been conducted to condition blinking as an output response. Mauk et al. triggered blinking on rabbits by a sound stimulus unrelated to blinking after prompting them to blink by air puffing while simultaneously playing the sound [7].

Futami et al. confirmed that presenting an auditory stimulus in the darts game could improve the score by conditioning auditory stimuli to successful experiences at the practice [16]. In the practice game, when the distance between the center of the board and the position of the targeted arrow thrown by the participant was within a threshold, a successful experience was judged, and a chime was played simultaneously. In a subsequent game, the score would be improved if the chime had been played immediately before the arrow was thrown. As for the blinking situation, if a new stimulus were repeatedly presented when the people blinked by a previously perceived stimulus, the association between blinking and the new stimulus would be linked, and then a new stimulus might trigger people blinking. Therefore, this study used a page-turning action as a new stimulus to trigger blinking during reading by conditioning blinking and the page-turning action.

3   Proposed Method

In this study, we proposed a method that conditions blinking and page-turning action when reading e-books with an eye-blink interface to prompt them to blink when reading paper books according to classical conditioning.

Figure 1 shows the procedure of classical conditioning by the proposed method. It consists of a learning phase and a practice phase. In the learning phase, we assigned blinking to turn pages while reading e-books with the eye-blink interface instead of clicking or swiping. In the practice phase, we conditioned blinking to the page-turning action without the eye-blink interface. Figure 2 shows an overview of the eye-blink interface, which consists of a blink operation device, an e-book application, and a PC. We used a glasses-type device called JINS MEME, which could detect blinks and eye movements, as the blink operation device. The e-book on the PC would be operated when the blink operation device detected eye movements and blinking.

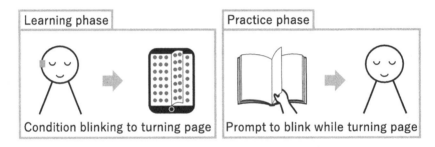

Fig. 1. Procedure of Conditioning

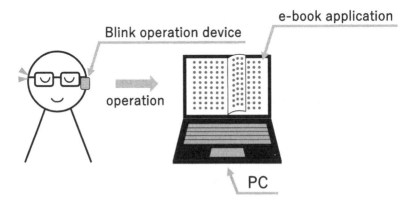

Fig. 2. Eye-Blink Interface

JINS MEME is a smart eyeglass with the same shape as ordinary eyeglasses. A built-in three-point eye-potential sensor in JINS MEME could measure blink intensity, speed, and eye movements in real-time. The sampling interval of the sensor data is 20 Hz. The blinking and eye movement data were measured by JINS MEME and transmitted to an e-book application on a PC based on Web-Socket transmission by JINS MEME Logger, which is a smartphone application working with JINS MEME. The first author developed the e-book application.

The blinking for the operation of the e-book application mentioned in the proposed method should be only accomplished by the user's eyes. It has to be an easy operation with few errors. Also, because a normal blink might occur to read e-books, we have to avoid a normal blink affecting the operation of the e-book application. Therefore, we designed that the page-turning action of the e-book only worked when users blinked immediately after turning a gaze to the right for a moment. The recognition method for blink operations is as follows. JINS MEME could detect two characteristics of blinks: blink speed and blink intensity. JINS MEME could detect four eye movements: up, down, left, and right. We referred to the rightward gaze shift data for the blink operation device and calculated its variance based on the current data set to the previous ten

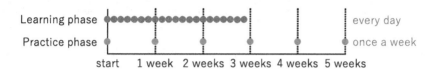

Fig. 3. Experiment Procedure

data sets. If the variance were larger than 0.5, the interface would know users were turning their gaze to the right for a moment. If users blinked within 5 s from that moment, the page-turning action would be recognized. The blink at this time is the same as a normal blink but can be distinguished by the eye movement immediately before the blink.

4 Evaluation Experiment

In this section, we evaluated the difference in the number of blinks while reading a paper book between reading an e-book with the eye-blink interface and without the eye-blink interface to confirm whether the proposed method could condition blinking to page-turning action and whether the conditioning mechanism is effective in prompting to blink while reading paper books.

4.1 Experiment Design

In our experiment, we designed the following two phases to investigate changes in the number of blinks of subjects with the eye-blink interface.

- Learning phase: Subjects read an e-book with the eye-blink interface
- Practice phase: Subjects read a paper book without the eye-blink interface

Figure 3 shows the experimental procedure. The learning phase and the practice phase were conducted in parallel. We investigated whether the daily use of the eye-blink interface in the learning phase triggered blinking while reading a paper book after the page-turning action and blinking were conditioned.

The OPI (Ocular Protection Index) is an indicator of the onset or worsening of dry eye symptoms, and it is calculated by the TFBUT (Tear Fluid Breakdown Time) on the ocular surface, and the average number of blinks in Eq. (1) [17].

$$OPI = \frac{TFBUT \times Number\ of\ Blinks\ [times/min]}{60} \tag{1}$$

If the OPI is less than 1, the tear fluid will be reduced, and the ocular surface will be exposed, which may lead to the onset of dry eye or worsening of symptoms. In this study, we set the TFBUT value to 10 s, a typical value for normal subjects. When the TFBUT is 10 s, according to Eq. (1), the average number of blinks per minute must be six or more if the OPI is equal to or higher than 1. Therefore, the standard value for evaluating the average number of blinks per minute is six in the following sections.

Table 1. Number of Blinks While Reading a Paper Book without the Eye-Blink Interface

Subjects	Blinks per min	Subjects	Blinks per min
N1-A	6.20	N1-F	7.07
N1-B	6.38	N1-G	22.67
N1-C	8.73	N1-H	10.43
N1-D	18.67	N1-I	8.07
N1-E	6.27	N1-J	3.47

(a) Group N1

(b) Group N2

Fig. 4. Learning Phase

4.2 Experiment Procedure

In the experiment, we divided the subjects into group N1, asked to use the eye-blink interface, and group N2, asked not to use the interface. Group N1 has ten male subjects, and group N2 has three male subjects in their 20 s. Before the start of the experiment, all subjects were asked to answer whether they had dry eyes or not. Then, group N1 was asked to read a paper book for 15 min without using the eye-blink interface and did not wear the blink operation device, and the number of blinks during that time was measured. Table 1 shows the number of blinks.

Learning Phase. In the learning phase, the subjects read an e-book with blinking operations for three weeks using the eye-blink interface to condition their blinking to page-turning action. Figure 4 shows the situation of reading an e-book. Group N1 wore the blink operation device, as shown in Fig. 4(a), and read an e-book with blinking operation for 30 min daily. Group N2 did not wear the blink operation device as shown in Fig. 4(b) and read an e-book with clicking operation on a PC for 30 min daily. After the reading task every day, subjects scored the discomfort level of the device on a 5-point Likert scale (1:comfort-5:discomfort). All subjects read the same book, and the experimental location was not specified.

(a) Group N1   (b) Group N2

Fig. 5. Practice Phase

Practice Phase. In the practice phase, we investigated the changes in the number of blinks during reading a paper book after reading an e-book with the eye-blink interface for a certain period. Figure 5 shows the reading situation with a paper book. Group N1 wore the blink operation device as shown in Fig. 5(a) and read a paper book for 15 min once a week, continuing for approximately five weeks, six times in total, without blinking operations. Group N2 did not wear the blink operation device, as shown in Fig. 5(b), and read a paper book for 15 min once a week, continuing for approximately five weeks, six times in total. In the days when both the learning and practice phases were conducted, the practice phase was conducted first. During the experiment, a camera recorded the subject's face and hand. The overall blink rate and the blink rate during page-turning action were manually counted according to the video. The number of blinks during the page-turning action was defined as the number of blinks from 3 s before the start of the action to 3 s after the end. After the reading task every week, subjects scored the discomfort level of the device on a 5-point Likert scale (1:comfort-5:discomfort). All subjects read a novel, and the experimental location was designated in the practice phase. The temperature and humidity at the experimental location were kept at $20 \pm 5°C$, $20 \pm 20\%$ using an air conditioner.

4.3   Results

The solid red line in Fig. 6 shows the average number of blinks per minute while reading a paper book without the eye-blink interface for group N1, which read an e-book using the eye-blink interface during the learning phase. The dotted line in Fig. 6 shows the standard blink rate, six times per minute. Comparing group N1 with N2, group N1 blinked more frequently because their blink rate was higher than the standard value. However, group N2 did not blink much because their blink rate was lower than the standard value. Thus, we considered that the eye-blink interface had increased the number of blinks while reading a paper book. The variance of the number of blinks in group N1 was much higher

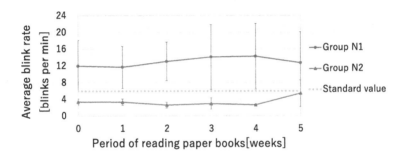

Fig. 6. Number of Blinks While Reading a Paper Book

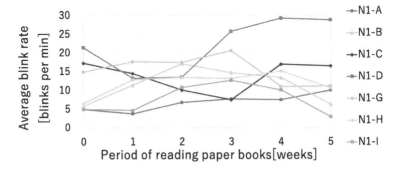

Fig. 7. Number of Blinks While Reading a Paper Book for Subjects with Increased Blink Rate

than in group N2. This result means that the effect of conditioning varied from user to user.

Figure 7 shows the average number of blinks per minute while reading a paper book for some subjects in group N1. The blink rate of the seven subjects increased during the experimental period. N1-A's (Subject A in group N1) blink rate gradually increased throughout the experiment. N1-B, N1-G, N1-H, and N1-I (Subject B, G, H, and I in group N1) showed an increasing trend of blinking from the beginning of the experiment and a decreasing trend after the second to fourth week. Subjects N1-A, N1-B, N1-H, and N1-I blinked more frequently than when reading with paper books without the eye-blink interface shown in Table 1. N1-C and N1-D (Subject C and D in group N1) showed a decreasing blink rate trend from the beginning of the experiment and an increasing trend after the second to third week. The two subjects blinked more frequently than when reading with paper books without the eye-blink interface shown in Table 1 after the second to fourth week. These results show that the eye-blink interface might prompt users to blink. Figure 8 shows the average number of blinks during the page-turning action. The number of blinks during the page-turning action was counted manually as the number of blinks from 3 s before the start of the action to 3 s after the end. The average number of blinks during the

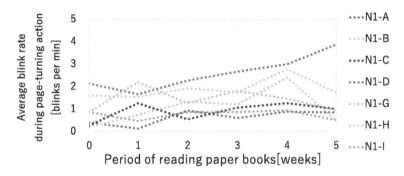

Fig. 8. Number of Blinks During the Page-Turning Action While Reading a Paper Book

page-turning action showed an increasing trend during the experimental period similarly. These results show that the seven subjects might have conditioned blinking to the page-turning action.

The average discomfort level of subjects in group N1 in the learning and practice phases was shown in Fig. 9(a) and Fig. 9(b). The discomfort level in the practice phase was lower than in the learning phase, and the discomfort level in the learning phase decreased over the third week. Until the subjects became accustomed to blink operation using the eye-blink interface, interface errors occurred, such as incorrectly recognizing or not being able to recognize blinks. In the learning phase, the false-positive detection of the eye-blink interface caused high levels of discomfort, especially in the first week, and reducing false positives would reduce discomfort. Therefore, the subjects could read e-books using the eye-blink interface with low discomfort once the subjects became accustomed to the blink operation.

5   Discussion

As discussed in Sect. 4.3, seven of the ten subjects in group N1 showed an increasing trend of blinking while reading a paper book. On the other hand, the other three subjects did not show an increasing trend of blinking during the experimental period. Figure 10 shows the average number of blinks per minute while reading a paper book for subjects in group N1 whose blink rate did not show increasing trends. The dotted line in Fig. 10 shows the average number of blinks during page-turning action. The average number of blinks and the average number of blinks during page-turning actions for the three subjects did not change significantly. The three subjects might not condition their blinking and page-turning actions well during the learning phase. After the experiment, we interviewed the three subjects, and they commented that the eye-blink interface had many false-positive detections during the learning phase, and they could not successfully complete the page-turning operation with the blinking. Therefore,

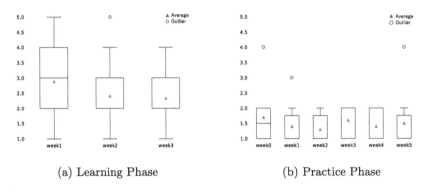

(a) Learning Phase   (b) Practice Phase

Fig. 9. Average Discomfort Level of Subjects in Group N1

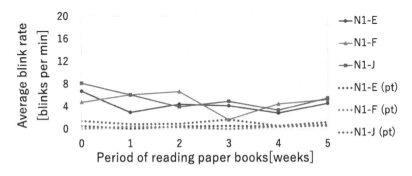

Fig. 10. Number of Blinks While Reading a Paper Book for Subjects with No Trend in Blink Rate

improving the detection accuracy of the eye-blink interface may enhance the conditioning of blink and page-turning actions.

Although the eye-blink interface proposed in this paper conditioned blink and page-turning actions for most subjects, the increased number of blinks may depend on the number of page-turning actions. The average number of page-turning actions per minute was 1.13 (SD = 0.40). In other words, the eye-blink interface could increase the number of blinks by approximately one per minute. Conditioning the blinking to another action frequently happening during reading, such as a line-breaking action rather than a page-turning action, may increase the number of blinks further.

6   Conclusion

This paper proposed a method that prompts users to blink in reading paper books by conditioning blinking to a page-turning action. We developed an eye-blink interface for learning to condition blinking to the page-turning action when reading e-books. We investigated the changes in the number of blinks when reading a paper book after reading an e-book with the eye-blink interface. The seven subjects showed an increasing trend of blinking while reading a paper book throughout the experimental period. We considered that our method gave a possibility that using the eye-blink interface while reading e-books could prompt one to blink while reading paper books.

Acknowledgements. This work was supported by JST CREST Grant Number JPMJCR18A3, Japan.

References

1. Yamada, M., Mizuno, Y., Shigeyasu, C.: Impact of dry eye on work productivity. ClinicoEconom. Outcomes Res. **4**(4), 307–312 (2012)
2. Ponder, E., Kennedy, W.P.: On the act of blinking. Q. J. Exp. Physiol. **18**(2), 89–110 (1927)
3. Orchard, L.N., Stern, J.A.: Blinks as an index of cognitive activity during reading. Integr. Physiol. Behav. Sci. **26**(2), 108–116 (1991). https://doi.org/10.1007/BF02691032
4. Bentivoglio, A.R., Bressman, S.B., Cassetta, E., Carretta, D., Tonali, P., Albanese, Dr.A.: Analysis of blink rate patterns in normal subjects. Off. J. Int. Parkinson Mov.Disord. Soc. **12**(6), 1028–1034 (2004)
5. Miura, D.L., Hazarbassanov, R.M., Yamasato, C.K.N., Silva, F.B., Godinho, C.J., Gomes, J.P.: Effect of a light-emitting timer device on the blink rate of non-dry eye individuals and dry eye patients. British J. Ophthalmol. **97**(8), 965–967 (2013)
6. Lois, N.O., John, A.S.: DualBlink: a wearable device to continuously detect, track, and actuate blinking for alleviating dry eyes and computer vision syndrome. In: Proceedings of the ACM on Interactive, Mobile, Wearable and Ubiquitous Technologies, IMWUT 2017, pp. 1–19 (2017)
7. Mauk, M.D., Steinmetz, J.E., Thompson, R.F.: Classical conditioning using stimulation of the inferior olive as the unconditioned stimulus. In: Proceedings of the National Academy of Sciences of the United States of America, pp. 5349–5353 (1986)
8. Sears, L.L., Finn, P.R., Steinmetz, J.E.: Abnormal classical eye-blink conditioning in autism. J. Autism Dev. Disord. **24**, 737–751 (1994). https://doi.org/10.1007/BF02172283
9. Clark, L.E., Squire, L.R.: Human eyeblink classical conditioning: effects of manipulating awareness of the stimulus contingencies. Psychol. Sci. **10**(1), 14–18 (1999). https://doi.org/10.1111/1467-9280.00099
10. Crnovrsanin, T., Wang, Y., Ma, K.L.: Stimulating a blink: reduction of eye fatigue with visual stimulus. Conf. Hum. Factors Comput. **31**(3), 2055–2064 (2014)
11. Portello, J.K., Rosenfield, M., Chu, C.A.: Blink rate incomplete blinks and computer vision syndrome. Optomeetry Vision Sci. **90**(5), 482–487 (2013)
12. Arcediano, F., Ortega, N., Matute, H.: A behavioral preparation for the study of human pavlovian conditioning. Q. J. Exp. Psychol. **49**(3), 270–283 (1996)
13. Aizenberg, M., Geffen, M.N.: Bidirectional effects of aversive learning on perceptual acuity are mediated by the sensory cotex. Nat. Neurosci. **16**(8), 994–996 (2013)
14. Neumann, D.L., Waters, A.M.: The use of an unpleasant sound as an unconditional stimulus in a human aversive pavlovian conditioning procedure. Biol. Psychol. **73**(2), 175–185 (2006). https://doi.org/10.1016/j.biopsycho.2006.03.004

15. Watson, J.B., Rayner, R.: Conditioned emotional reactions. J. Exp. Psychol. **3**(1), 1–14 (1920)
16. Futami, K., Terada, T., Tsukamoto, M.: Success imprinter: a method for controlling mental preparedness using psychological conditioned information. In: Proceedings of the 7th Augmented Human International Conference 2016, AH 2016, pp. 1–8 (2016)
17. George, W.O.III., Hagberg, K.W., Schindelar, M., Welch, D., Abelson, M. B.: The ocular protection index. J. Cornea External Disease **27**(5), 509–513 (2008)

A Method for Stimuli Control of Carbonated Beverages by Estimating and Reducing Carbonation Level

Yusuke Miyajima⬤, Tsutomu Terada$^{(\boxtimes)}$⬤, and Masahiko Tsukamoto⬤

Kobe University, 1-1, Rokkodai-cho, Nada-ku, Kobe, Japan
tsutomu@eedept.kobe-u.ac.jp

Abstract. Carbonated beverages provide a distinct sensory experience; some enjoy it while others dislike it. Consumers should be aware of the intensity of stimuli when drinking carbonated beverages already offered and be able to adjust it according to their preferences. However, no proposal is currently available to customize the stimulation intensity according to consumers' preferences before they drink it. In this study, we proposed a non-contact estimation function using a CO_2 sensor to estimate the stimulate intensity of carbonated beverages, along with an adjustment function using ultrasonic waves to reduce the intensity. Our method measures the carbonation level diffused from the surface of carbonated beverages with a CO_2 sensor and calculates feature values based on the time variation for machine learning. As a result of our experiment, both the estimation function and the adjustment function achieved the required levels of accuracy, allowing precise estimation and adjustment under diverse conditions.

Keywords: Carbonated beverages · Machine learning · Controlling stimili

1 Introduction

Carbonated beverages are served in many social occasions, such as banquets and parties. Demand for carbonated beverages is increasing regardless of gender or age [1]. In addition, health benefits from carbonated beverages have attracted attention in recent years. Compared to drinking water, carbonated water could produce a sense of satiety when being consumed and may prevent overeating at meals [2,3]. Furthermore, drinking carbonated beverages may assist in swallowing [4,5].

While some people like the stimuli of carbonated beverages, others find them unpleasant. Wendrick et al. evaluated which wines created with non-carbonated and five different carbonated stimuli intensities would make consumers purchase [6]. The result was that customers all preferred carbonated wines, but their preferences for the intensity of the stimulus were inconsistent, which suggested individual differences in the intensity of the stimulus from carbonated beverages. However, because the stimulation intensity of the carbonated beverages is

P. Delir Haghighi et al. (Eds.): MoMM 2023, LNCS 14417, pp. 77–92, 2023.
https://doi.org/10.1007/978-3-031-48348-6_7

only known after being drunk, customers usually wish to realize the intensity before drinking the carbonated beverages and to adjust the stimulation intensity according to their preferences.

The unique sensation of carbonated stimulation in drinking is caused by the generation of hydrogen ions from the carbon dioxide gas contained in carbonated beverages by an enzyme called carbonic anhydrase on the tongue's surface [7, 8]. Therefore, the stimulation intensity of carbonated beverages may be closely related to the carbonation level. Speers et al. evaluated whether an empirical approximation of beer's amount of carbon dioxide can be correctly calculated [9]. Although the approximate formula in the study can calculate the amount of carbon dioxide dissolved in beer, it is not applicable to other carbonated beverages because the approximate formula includes variables such as alcohol concentration.

In addition, a method for adjusting stimulus intensity, Kanayama et al. proposed a method of applying electrical stimulation to the drinker's tongue to adjust the stimulation intensity while drinking carbonated beverages [10]. Ranasinghe et al. claimed to control acidity by releasing an electric current to the human tongue [11]. The above methods would cause oral cavity pain due to electrical stimulation, which must be continuously enhanced to maintain the stimulation.

This study developed a system indirectly estimating the stimulation intensity of carbonated beverages and adjusting the stimulation smoothly according to users' requirements. In this paper, gas volume (GV), which represents the amount of carbon dioxide gas per liter of beverage [L], indicates the carbonated beverage stimulus. We estimated the carbonated beverage stimuli according to the carbon dioxide rising to the surface from carbonated beverages using a CO_2 sensor without contact, and reduced the carbonated beverages stimulus using ultrasonic waves. This paper evaluated the estimation accuracy of carbonated beverage stimuli of the proposed system and investigated whether the estimation error is acceptable when people drink the beverage adjusted by our system. We also evaluated the accuracy of the ultrasonic stimuli reduction of carbonated beverages.

This paper is organized as follows. Section 2 introduces related research, Sect. 3 describes the proposed system, Sect. 4 presents evaluation experiments using the proposed function and a discussion, and Sect. 5 concludes the discussion based on the experimental results and discussion. Finally, Sect. 6 concludes the paper.

2   Related Research

This section introduces research on the reason for stimulation, the measurement of stimulation, the problems of indirect estimation, and the methods of stimuli adjustment in carbonated beverages.

2.1 Stimuli of Carbonated Beverages

When carbonated beverages are consumed, distinctive oral cavity stimuli are produced. Komai et al. confirmed that the stimuli of carbonated beverages are received by the trigeminal nerves distributed on the tongue and in the oral cavity and are caused by the chemical stimuli of carbon dioxide gas dissolved in the beverage [7]. Simons et al. injected a chemical in to one side of the tongue as the catalyst to inhibit the conversion of carbon dioxide into the chemical that makes carbonated beverages stimulating and confirmed a significant reduction in the amount of subjectively perceived stimuli on the side where the chemical was applied [12]. Based on these previous studies, the perceived stimuli when drinking carbonated beverages change according to the carbonation level. Therefore, this study focuses on carbonation level as an indicator of carbonated beverage stimuli.

Quantitative measurement of the amount of carbon dioxide in liquids has been conducted. Liu et al. proposed a method to calculate the amount of carbon dioxide in seawater based on D.B.S/Henry's law [13]. Because the amount of carbon dioxide contained in the seawater was much smaller than that of carbonated beverages, and the experimental environment required a vacuum, large equipment, and contact with the seawater, the above method is not applicable to carbonated beverages. Therefore, this study examined a non-contact method to estimate carbonation level using a simple device.

2.2 Research on Indirect Estimation

Many studies estimated not easily directly measurable data from indirect correlation data. Whitehill et al. also noted that by applying machine learning to image data of a student's facial expression during a task, they were able to identify the student's willingness to perform the task with an accuracy comparable to that of human perception [14]. Banerjee et al. have built a system to estimate food nutrients and calorie content in real-time by measuring microwaves when food is microwaved [15]. A non-contact food quality estimation method using near-infrared for beer and chocolate and the concentration of alcohol in beer, has been proposed [16–18]. Liu et al. measured the odor of wine using MOS sensors and applied machine learning to construct a device to estimate the region of production, variety, year of production, and fermentation process [19]. Since many indirect estimation methods are used as described above, we believe that a machine learning-based estimation system can be applied to carbonated beverage stimulus estimation. In this study, we investigate a method for estimating carbonated beverage stimuli using machine learning by measuring the concentration of carbon dioxide gas rising from the surface of a carbonated beverage.

2.3 Adjustment of Carbonated Beverage Stimuli

Studies have been conducted to change the perceived stimuli when drinking carbonated beverages. Kanayama et al. have shown that the stimulation of carbonated beverages can be controlled using electro-gustatory sensation [10]. Ranasinghe et al. claimed the sense of taste can be controlled by external stimuli such as electric current and heat to the tongue [11]. However, these methods require electrodes to contact the human body when drinking carbonated beverages.

As a method for adjusting the stimuli of carbonated beverages without electrical stimulation, Mielby et al. found that the subjects felt more carbonation when the cup's weight was heavier [20]. This method can increase and decrease the perceived stimuli when drinking carbonated beverages, but it is difficult to adjust the intensity of a particular stimulus in real-time according to the user's requirements. This study applied ultrasonic to a cup with a carbonated beverage to change the carbonation level, thereby adjusting the carbonated beverage's stimuli to the user's requirements.

3   System Design

We developed a system allowing real-time stimuli adjustment of carbonated beverages according to the user's requirements.

3.1   System Requirement

We assumed that users would straightly drink the carbonated beverages after adjusting the carbonated beverage stimuli with our system. Therefore, the system must have a mechanism to measure and adjust the carbonated beverage stimuli in a hygienic method. In the following, we gave the requirements for developing the system.

1. **No contact between beverage and gas volume measurement device**
   Avoiding contact between the beverage and the stimulus measurement device is necessary to realize hygienic stimulus measurement. Therefore, in the proposed system, we placed the CO_2 sensor for stimulus measurement above the top of the cup.
2. **Estimation of stimulation intensity of carbonated beverages**
   The proposed system measures the carbonation level using a CO_2 sensor and applied machine learning to the measured data to estimate the carbonated beverage stimulus.

3. **Adjustment of stimulation intensity of carbonated beverages**
   If the stimulation intensity of carbonated beverages can be freely adjusted, it will be possible to provide carbonated beverages that meet users' needs. The proposed system adopts ultrasonic waves to quickly remove the diffused carbon dioxide from carbonated beverages. It reduces the stimuli of the carbonated beverage by applying ultrasonic waves to the cup containing the beverage.

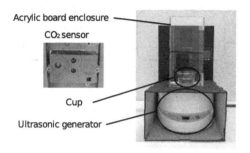

Acrylic board enclosure

CO₂ sensor

Cup

Ultrasonic generator

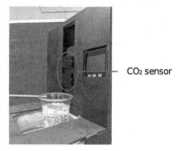

CO₂ sensor

Fig. 1. Overview of system

Fig. 2. Location of cup and CO_2 sensor

Based on the above requirements, we propose a system estimating the stimuli in carbonated beverages hygienically without contact between the stimuli measurement device and the beverage and adjusting the stimuli in carbonated beverages using ultrasonic.

3.2 Proposed System

The proposed system implemented to meet the requirements described in Sect. 3.1 is shown in Fig. 1, the positional relationship between the cup and the CO_2 sensor in the system is shown in Fig. 2, and the system configuration of the proposed system is shown in Fig. 3. The CO_2 sensor (Seeed Studio Co., Ltd. Grove-CO₂&Temperature&Humidity Sensor) was placed above a cup of carbonated beverage to measure the concentration of carbon dioxide rising from the cup to the surface of the carbonated beverage. The CO_2 sensor can be moved vertically to adjust its position according to the size of the cup. The data acquired by the CO_2 sensor was transmitted to a PC every 2 s via a microcontroller (M5Stack Co., Ltd. M5Stack Gray). An ultrasonic wave generator (Sanwa Supply Co., Ltd. 200-CD037) was placed at the bottom of the cup to reduce the carbonated beverage's stimuli by applying ultrasonic wave to the cup for a specified number of seconds. The frequency of the ultrasonic wave generator was 42 kHz.

The flow of using the proposed system is shown in Fig. 4. A cup filled with a carbonated beverage is placed below the CO_2 sensor to measure the concentration of carbon dioxide rising from the surface of the carbonated beverage. The measured carbonation level data and the liquid temperature of the carbonated beverage measured with an infrared thermometer (Ohm Electric Co., Ltd TN006) are used to calculate features for machine learning, and these features are used to estimate the carbonated beverage stimuli. In machine learning, 50 sets of data on carbonation level and liquid temperature and their GV values were collected and used to create an estimation model. In this paper, gas volume

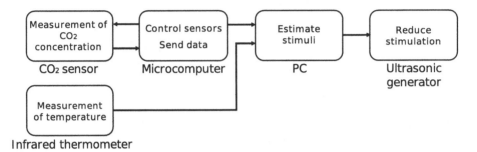

Fig. 3. System configuration diagram

(GV), which represents the amount of carbon dioxide gas per liter of beverage [L], indicates carbonated beverage stimuli. The GV was calculated from the mass of the carbonated beverage measured using an electronic scale (BOMATA Co., Ltd. 2604C).

If the estimated stimuli are stronger than the desired stimulus, the user inputs the desired value to the PC. Then the system calculates the time to apply ultrasonic waves to the cup to achieve the desired stimuli and applies ultrasonic waves in that time. This reduces the carbonated beverage's stimuli to a desired level for users before the beverage is consumed.

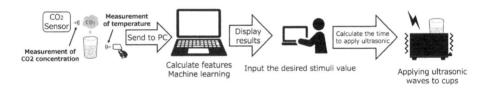

Fig. 4. Flow of using the proposed system

4   Evaluation Experiment

This section conducted the following four experiments to evaluate the accuracy of a CO2 sensor-based carbonated beverage stimuli estimation function and an ultrasonic-based carbonated beverage stimuli reduction function.

- Investigation of the relationship between GV and the stimuli that people perceive when drinking carbonated beverages
- Estimation of GV of carbonated beverages by machine learning and its evaluation
- Effect of volume and cup size of carbonated beverage on estimation accuracy
- Evaluation of ultrasonic-based methods for reducing carbonated beverage stimuli

Table 1. Maximum and minimum difference of GV when feeling and no feeling the difference of stimuli

Subjects	Perceived (min)	Unperceived (max)
A	0.41	0.51
B	0.27	0.20
C	0.78	0.78
D	0.51	0.47
average	0.49	0.49

The GV of the carbonated beverage as an index of stimuli was calculated using the mass m[g] of carbon dioxide contained in the beverage and the volume L[L] of the carbonated beverage, as follows.

$$GV = \frac{m}{1.977 \times L} \tag{1}$$

In this experiment, to obtain ground truth for machine learning, ultrasonic waves were applied to the carbonated water for a sufficient duration using an ultrasonic generator to determine the GV. The masses before and after were measured, and the difference was used as the mass m of the carbon dioxide contained in the beverage. The carbonated beverage is carbonated water produced by a soda maker (Sodastream Co., Ltd. Source v3).

4.1 Experiment 1: Relationship Between GV and Stimuli that People Perceive

Experimental Methods. To quantitatively evaluate how much difference users subjectively perceive between carbonated beverages when the difference in GV of the two beverages is far apart, we made subjects drink two kinds of carbonated water with different GVs produced by a soda maker and asked them whether or not they felt any difference in stimuli. We measured the difference in GV for each trial and investigated how much of a difference in GV could be perceived as a difference in the stimulation of carbonated water. Four male subjects were in their 20 s, and the number of trials was 10 times per subject.

Results and Discussion. Table 1 show the minimum difference in GV that felt a different carbonated level and the maximum difference in GV that did not feel a difference. The mean of the minimum difference in GV when the four subjects felt the difference in stimuli and the mean maximum difference in GV when they did not feel the difference in stimuli were both 0.49. These results suggest that when people drink carbonated water, they feel a difference in stimuli when the difference in GV is greater than 0.49. Therefore, the GV estimation error must be less than this value. In the following experiment, the threshold for evaluating whether the GV was correctly estimated or reduced was set at 0.49.

Table 2. GV Estimation Error

k	Linear	RandomForest	k-NN	SVM	KStar
5	0.49	0.50	0.44	0.49	0.41
6	0.41	0.44	0.40	0.45	0.39
7	0.42	0.39	0.39	0.42	0.31
8	0.42	0.36	0.38	0.44	0.33
9	0.43	0.35	0.37	0.43	0.30
10	0.43	0.36	0.37	0.42	0.34

4.2   Experiment 2: GV Estimation Accuracy

Experimental Methods. The accuracy of the proposed system's estimation of carbonated beverage stimuli was evaluated. The proposed system performs machine learning using the carbonation level measured by the CO_2 sensor to estimate the carbonated beverage stimuli. Immediately after carbonated water is poured into a cup, the carbon dioxide concentration rising from the surface of the carbonated water increases, and after a certain period of time, the carbon dioxide concentration tends to decrease and the fluctuation settles down. Therefore, carbon dioxide gas concentration data CO_2 sensors were used to collect the data; the sampling interval of the CO_2 sensors was 2 s. The number of sampling k was experimentally varied from 5 to 10 times (about 10 s to 20 s) for the same measured data, and the estimation accuracy at each number of sampling was evaluated. Five features, the maximum, minimum, average, and difference between the maximum and minimum carbon dioxide concentrations, were calculated for each of the data in the range at each number of sampling, and at the same time, the water temperature at the beginning of the measurement was measured, and these data were used for machine learning. A total of 50 measurements were made with different GV of carbonated water, and 10-fold cross-validations (regressions) were performed on representative learners using the calculated features to evaluate the estimation accuracy for each number of samplings. Mean absolute error (MAE) was used to evaluate accuracy. The measured values used as the correct data were those obtained from equation (1). We used the machine learning software Weka [21].

Results and Discussion. The estimation results are shown in Table 2. The minimum value of the MAE for all the algorithms and the data was 0.30 for KStar with k=9. This result is below 0.49, the threshold at which people perceive a difference in carbonated water stimuli, and falls within the acceptable estimation error range. Therefore, it is possible to estimate carbonated water's GV using the CO_2 sensor. Since KStar showed the smallest error throughout the estimation, KStar was the algorithm in the subsequent estimation system.

Table 3. GV estimation results for different volumes

volume	Measured value	Estimated value
100 ml	2.88	2.21
	1.97	2.27
200 ml	2.48	2.26
	2.48	2.31
300 ml	2.02	2.35
	2.29	2.39

Table 4. GV estimation results for two types of cups

The size of a cup	Measured value	Estimated value
	2.28	2.11
Big	2.11	1.97
	1.80	1.26
	1.59	2.05
	2.29	2.46
Small	2.16	2.07
	1.75	1.16
	1.62	2.26

4.3 Experiment 3: Effect of Amount of Beverage Volume and Cup Size

Experimental Methods. We investigated whether the proposed estimation fiction can estimate GV with high accuracy the carbonated water volume and the cup size for the carbonated water are changed. We used a single cup for volume estimation and three different volumes of carbonated water (100, 200, and 300 mL) to estimate the GV of each volume. The number of trials was two times for each. On the other hand, when investigating the effect of containers, we used two types of cups, a large and a small cup, poured 150 ml of carbonated water into each cup, estimated the GV, and compared the estimated results. The number of trials was four, and the GV of the carbonated water was approximately 2.00. The training data used for estimation are the 50 measurements in Sect. 4.2.

Results and Discussion. The results of GV estimation, when the volume of carbonated water was varied from 100, 200, and 300 mL, are shown in Table 3. There was no significant difference between the measured and estimated GV. MAE was 0.30, which is almost the same MAE estimated by KStar as described in Sect. 4.1. The MAE was below the threshold value of 0.49 obtained in Sect. 4.1, suggesting that the volume of carbonated water does not affect the estimation system and could estimate GV accurately.

The results of the GV estimation for two different cup sizes are shown in Table 4. MAE was 0.37 for the small cups and 0.33 for the large cups. The MAEs for large and small cups are below the thresholds determined in Sect. 4.1. Although the error is larger than when the volume is varied, the accuracy of the estimation is maintained, and the difference in container size is considered acceptable. In conclusion, the carbonated water volume and the container size do not affect the GV estimation system proposed here, and the system can estimate GV with high accuracy.

4.4   Experiment4: Carbonated Level Reduction Using Ultrasonic

Experimental Methods. We estimated the GV of carbonated water using the proposed estimation system and investigated whether the GV can be reduced to user's desired GV from the estimated GV with high accuracy by applying ultrasonic waves to the cup containing carbonated water. First, we measured the change in the GV of carbonated water when ultrasonic waves were applied to it using an ultrasonic generator and calculated an approximate equation that expresses the relationship between the time of ultrasonic wave application and the GV of the carbonated water. Cups were large, and the volumes were 100 mL, 200 mL, and 300 mL with measurement frequencies of 3, 5, and 7 s, respectively, for a total of nine measurements, one for each volume. In measuring the change in GV over time, the measurement was terminated when there was no change in GV for three consecutive measurements. Next, we set the target values of the amount of GV to be reduced from the estimated GV to 0.50, 1.00, and 1.50, and the duration of ultrasonic wave application was determined using an approximation formula. Ultrasonic waves were applied to the cups for that time, and the accuracy of reducing carbonate stimuli was evaluated. The number of trials was 27 times, three trials for each volume (100, 200, and 300 mL) at each target reduction GV value.

Results and Discussion. The time variation of GV when the ultrasonic wave was applied to carbonated water is shown in Fig. 5. There was no significant difference in the time variation for each volume. Therefore, when all the graphs were superimposed so that the GVs were almost the same, ignoring the time axis, the graph shown in solid red using the square marker in Fig. 5, which passes through the approximate center of all the graphs, was used as a base, and in addition, considering that it corresponds to a wide range of GVs, an approximate formula was created by referring to the graph shown in solid yellow using the triangle marker with the highest GV at 0 s. Figure 6 shows the time variation of the GV combining red and yellow solid lines in Fig. 5. The inverse function of the graph shown in Fig. 6 was taken to derive an approximate equation, the result of which is shown in Fig. 7. The dotted line in Fig. 7 is the approximate curve, which was derived by a logarithmic approximation. The derived approximate curve can be expressed as in equation (2), where T represents the time of ultrasonic wave application. This paper uses this equation to calculate the relationship between the time of ultrasonic wave application and GV.

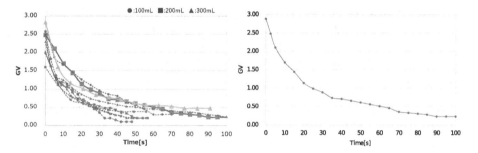

Fig. 5. Relationship between ultrasonic application time and GV

Fig. 6. Graph used to calculate the time to apply ultrasonic

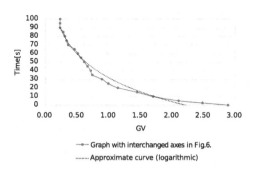

Fig. 7. Approximate curve for calculating the time to apply ultrasonic wave

$$T = -39.75ln(GV) + 31.41 \tag{2}$$

Assuming the GV at the time of estimation is GV_s and the target GV desired by the user is GV_g, the ultrasonic wave application time T required to reduce the GV_s to the GV_g can be derived as in Eq. (3) using Eq. (2).

$$
\begin{aligned}
T &= (-39.75ln(GV_g) + 31.41) - (-39.75ln(GV_s) + 31.41) \\
&= -39.75(ln(GV_g) - ln(GV_s)) \\
&= -39.75ln\frac{GV_g}{GV_s}
\end{aligned}
\tag{3}
$$

Using Eq. (3), we investigated the accuracy of the GV reduction by ultrasonic waves for three types of carbonated water with volumes of 100, 200, and 300 mL and with target reduction GV values of 0.50, 1.00, and 1.50, respectively. First, we present the results for each target reduction GV value. When the target reduction GV values were set to 0.50, 1.00, and 1.50, the average GV reduction by ultrasonic wave was 0.71, 0.99, and 1.15, respectively. The box-and-whisker plots of the error between the target reduction GV value and the reduction GV value for each target reduction GV value are shown in Fig. 8. The threshold value of GV at which people perceive a difference in the carbonated water's stimuli, which was calculated in Sect. 4.1, is indicated by the dotted line in Fig. 8. When the target reduction GV value was set at 0.50, the MAE was 0.23, much lower than the threshold value. When the target reduction GV value was set to 1.00, the MAE was 0.23, significantly below the threshold value. When the target GV reduction value was set to 1.50, the MAE was 0.35, below the threshold value, but the error was larger than when the target GV reduction value was set to 0.50 or 1.00. Figure 8 shows that the error and error range was small when the target GV reduction value was set to 0.50 and 1.00, but the error range was larger when the target GV reduction value was set to 1.50 compared to when the target GV reduction value was set to 0.50 and 1.00. However, there are cases where the adjustment can be made with a small error, and it is considered that the error can be reduced by improving the accuracy.

Next, we show the results focusing on each volume. When the volume of carbonated water was 100 mL, the MAE was 0.23; at 200 mL, the MAE was 0.34; and at 300 mL, the MAE was 0.25. Figure 9 shows a box-and-whisker plot of each volume's target reduction GV value and the reduction GV value. The GV thresholds at which people perceive a difference in carbonated water stimuli are indicated by the dotted lines in Fig. 9. The figure shows that the error in 200 mL is generally larger, and the adjustment accuracy is lower. 300 mL also has a larger error range, but the overall average error is smaller, suggesting that the accuracy is higher than that of 200 mL. The error range was the smallest at 100 mL, and the error itself was small, suggesting that the adjustment could be made with the highest accuracy. In conclusion, it is possible to reduce the GV of carbonated beverages by ultrasonic waves using an ultrasonic wave generator regardless of the target reduced GV or volume, and it is possible to provide carbonated beverages with the stimuli desired by the user.

5   Discussion

5.1   Thresholds and Error Issues

In Sect. 4.1, we determined the threshold at which an individual perceives a difference in stimulation when drinking two different carbonated beverages. Although all four subjects showed a preference for carbonated beverages, Table 1 shows that the minimum value for perceiving a difference in stimulation was 0.24 for subject B and the maximum value was 0.78 for subject C. From the above, it should be noted that the threshold value of 0.49 may not be universally accepted by all users, as the perception of stimulation when consuming carbonated beverages varies greatly from person to person.

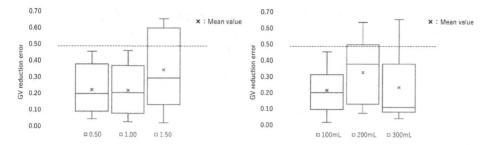

Fig. 8. Error in GV reduction by ultrasonic for each target GV

Fig. 9. Error in GV reduction by ultrasonic for each volume

Table 5. Combined error from estimation and adjustment

	Estimation error	Adjustment error	Combined error
MAE	0.30	0.27	0.57

On the other hand, the error in the proposed estimation system and the reduction using ultrasonic waves were evaluated separately in this experiment. In the use of the proposed system, the error in the estimation and the error in the reduction should be considered together. The combined errors are shown in Table 5. The error in the estimation system was 0.30 when estimating with KStar at k = 9 the number of sampling, and the error in the reduction using ultrasonic waves was 0.27. Thus, these combined errors resulted in an MAE of 0.57. When the estimation and reduction errors were compared to the thresholds, the combined error was above the thresholds. Considering that the errors here are absolute values and that both downward and upward swings appeared in the estimation error, and that the reduction error tended to be downward for smaller target reduced GV and upward for larger target reduced GV, it is not necessarily considered that the errors are as large as the MAE value in the combined error.

5.2 Approximation Formulas and Adjustment Issues

The approximate formula for reducing the GV of carbonated beverages obtained in Sect. 4.4 is a simplified formula obtained in this experiment by using the graph passing through the center of the total and the data with the highest measured GV among the nine-time variation data measured. The formula was used to reduce the GV of carbonated beverages. The values were close to the target when the target reduced GV was 0.50 and 1.00, the volume was 100 mL and 300 mL, and when the target reduced GV was 1.50, the volume was 200 mL, the GV was reduced to the target, although the accuracy was slightly lower. However, since the approximation formula is simple, the larger the amount of carbon dioxide to be reduced, the larger the error and the accuracy may have become low. Also, when the target GV reduction amount is 1.50, the accuracy may have been affected because carbon dioxide is almost completely removed from the carbonated beverage as it approaches the target GV reduction amount, depending on the original amount of carbon dioxide contained in the carbonated beverage. Therefore, it is necessary to increase the number of data to calculate a more accurate approximation formula and to set the reduction according to the GV of the carbonated beverage. The ultrasonic wave application time derive for stimulus reduction was specified only within an integer range because the ultrasonic waves were applied manually. In addition, the frequency of the ultrasonic waves was constant. Therefore, the accuracy of the reduction might be improved by improving these points because enabling a more detailed reduction.

5.3 Future Work

In this study, we estimated the stimuli of carbonated beverages using an indirect method and reduced the stimuli through the application of ultrasonic waves. However, consumers who enjoy carbonated beverages may request an increase in the level of stimulation. As a result, it becomes essential to enhance the system and incorporate a mechanism that can amplify the stimuli of carbonated beverages, such as enabling the addition of carbon dioxide. Moreover, while the experiment solely utilized carbonated water as the carbonated beverage, it is imperative to validate whether the proposed estimation function and ultrasonic adjustment function are effective for various types of carbonated beverages.

6   Conclusion

In this study, we proposed a non-contact system that can estimate the intensity of carbonated beverage stimulation and adjust the stimulation according to user's preferences. In this paper, we developed a stimulus estimation function using a CO2 sensor and machine learning and a stimulus reduction function using ultrasonic waves. To investigate the accuracy of the proposed system, we conducted four kinds of experiments. The results showed that the stimulus estimation function and the ultrasonic stimuli reduction function could accurately estimate and adjust carbonated beverage stimuli. In the future, we aim to improve the accuracy of the stimulus estimation further and develop a function that not only reduces the stimuli of carbonated beverages but also increases it.

Acknowledgements. This work was supported by JST CREST Grant Number JPMJCR18A3, Japan.

References

1. Storey, M.L., Forshee, R.A., Anderson, P.A.: Beverage consumption in the US population. J. Am. Diet. Assoc. **106**(12), 1992–2000 (2006)
2. Wakisaka, S., Nagai, H., Mura, E., Matsumoto, T., Moritani, T., Nagai, N.: The effects of carbonated water upon gastric and cardiac activities and fullness in healthy young women. J. Nutr. Sci. Vitaminol. **58**(5), 333–338 (2012)

3. Suzuki, M., Mura, E., Taniguchi, A., Moritani, T., Nagai, N.: Oral carbonation attenuates feeling of hunger and gastric myoelectrical activity in young women. J. Nutr. Sci. Vitaminol. **63**(3), 186–192 (2017)
4. Miura, Y., Morita, Y., Koizumi, H., Shingai, T.: Effects of taste solutions, carbonation, and cold stimulus on the power frequency content of swallowing submental surface electromyography. Chem. Senses **34**(3), 325–331 (2009)
5. Saiki, A., et al.: Effects of thickened carbonated cola in older patients with dysphagiay. Chem. Senses **34**(4), 325–331 (2022)
6. Wendrick, N.A., Sims, C.A., MacIntosh, A.J.: The effect of carbonation level on the acceptability and purchase intent of muscadine and fruit wines. MDPI Beverages **7**(3), 66–74 (2021)
7. Komai, M., Bryant, B.P.: Acetazolamide specifically inhibits lingual trigeminal nerve responses to carbon dioxide. Brain Res. **612**(2), 122–129 (1993)
8. Chandrashekar, J., et al.: The taste of carbonation. Science **326**(5951), 443–445 (2009)
9. Speers, R.A., MacIntosh, A.J.: Carbon dioxide solubility in beer. J. Am. Soc. Brew. Chem. **71**(4), 242–247 (2013)
10. Kanayama, J., Nomura, I., Mochizuki, N., Koike, T., Nakamura, S.: Basic evaluation of carbonate stimulus amplification and taste change using AC electric stimulation. In: 2021 IEEE/SICE International Symposium on System Integration. SII, pp. 819–820. IEEE, Iwaki, Fukushima, Japan (2021)
11. Ranasinghe, N., Nakatsu, R., Nii, H., Gopalakrishnakone, P.: Tongue mounted interface for digitally actuating the sense of taste. In: ISWC'12 Proceedings of the 2012 16th Annual International Symposium on Wearable Computers, ISWC 2012, pp. 80–87, IEEE, Newcastle, UK (2012)
12. Simons, C.T., Dessirier, J.M., Carstens, M.I., Mahony, M.O', Carstens, E.: Neurobiological and psychophysical mechanisms underlying the oral sensation produced by carbonated water. J. Neurosci. **19**(18), 8134–8144 (1999)
13. Liu, G.H., et al.: Determination of concentration of free carbon dioxide in artificial seawater by difference balance system/Henry's law. MDPI Sustain. **15**(6), 5096–5109 (2023)
14. Whitehill, J., Serpell, Z., Lin, Y.C., Foster, A., Movellan, J.R.: The faces of engagement: automatic recognition of student engagement from facial expressions. IEEE Trans. Affect. Comput. **5**(1), 86–98 (2014)
15. Banerjee, A., Srinivasan, K.: WiNE: monitoring microwave oven leakage to estimate food nutrients and calorie. In: Proceedings of the ACM on Interactive Mobile, Wearable and Ubiquitous Technologies, pp. 1–24, Assosiation for Computing Machinary, New York, USA (2022)
16. Viejo, C.G., Fuentes, S., Torrico, D., Howell, K., Dunshea, F.R.: Assessment of beer quality based on foamability and chemical composition using computer vision algorithms, near infrared spectroscopy and machine learning algorithms. J. Sci. Food Agric. **98**(2), 618–627 (2018)
17. Galdo, B., Rivero, D., Fernandez-Blanco, E.: Estimation of the alcoholic degree in beers through near infrared spectrometry using machine learning. In: Proceedings of the 2nd XoveTIC Conference, XoveTIC 2019, pp. 48–50, MDPI, A Coruña, Spain (2019)
18. Gunaratne, T.M., Viejo, C.G., Gunaratne, N.M., Torrico, D.D., Dunshea, F.R., Fuentes, S.: Chocolate quality assessment based on chemical fingerprinting using near infra-red and machine learning modeling. MDPI Foods **8**(10), 425–436 (2019)

19. Liu, H., Li, Q., Yan, B., Zhang, L., Gu, Y.: Bionic electronic nose based on MOS sensors array and machine learning algorithms used for wine properties detection. MDPI Sensors **19**(1), 45–55 (2022)
20. Mielby, L.A., et al.: See, feel, taste: the influence of receptacle colour and weight on the evaluation of flavoured carbonated beverages. MDPI Foods **7**(8), 119–132 (2018)
21. Waikato University: Weka 3. https://www.cs.waikato.ac.nz/ml/weka/. Accessed 20 July 2023

A Knee Injury Prevention System by Continuous Knee Angle Recognition Using Stretch Sensors

Ayumi Ohnishi⬤, Kota Kirinoe, Tsutomu Terada⁽✉⁾⬤,
and Masahiko Tsukamoto⬤

Kobe University, Hyogo, Japan
{ohnishi,tsutomu}@eedept.kobe-u.ac.jp, info@ubi.eedept.kobe-u.ac.jp,
tuka@kobe-u.ac.jp

Abstract. The knee is the most common site for running injuries. Fatigue causes changes in the knee angle at landing, which increases the impact acceleration at landing and leads to injury. To prevent such injuries, this paper proposes a wearable system that acquires knee bends and estimates the knee angle in real-time during running using a supporter-shaped device equipped with a stretchable sensor. The result of the running experiment outdoors on flat and sloping roads shows that the proposed system can present the double-knee action, which is an indicator of the knee bending in running. For knee angle recognition based on treadmill running data, the average MAE was 5.8° in ranged from approximately 4 to 8° individuals, when using training data of the same subject's other trial. For recognition of the knee angle during running under fatigued condition, the result shows that the proposed system can recognize the knee angle with MAE approximately 5.0, when using training data of the user's own non-fatigued data.

Keywords: Wearable computing · Knee angle · Double knee action · Running

1 Introduction

Running is popular among all generations as an exercise that can be performed on a daily basis, however, many people are injured while running. The most frequently injured part of the body during running is the knee, which accounts for 42.1% of all injuries [18].

Knee injuries are caused by an increase in impact acceleration at the time of landing. This occurs when the running form is not suited to various environments, such as hills, or when the knee lands in a more deeply bent position than normal due to fatigue from prolonged running. Mizrahi et al. reported that fatigue from prolonged running causes the knee angle to bend from 4 to 10° larger on landing, and the impact acceleration on landing is increased by about 50% [10].

The appropriateness of shock absorption is generally measured by whether the angle of the joint at the time of landing is suitable [10], and whether a

P. Delir Haghighi et al. (Eds.): MoMM 2023, LNCS 14417, pp. 93–103, 2023.
https://doi.org/10.1007/978-3-031-48348-6_8

movement known as double knee action is performed [21]. Double knee action, as shown in Fig. 1, is a movement where the knee bends twice in one cycle of periodic movement in running, where the foot contacts the ground, pushes off the ground and contacts the ground again. If this movement is inadequate, the knee cannot absorb the impact of landing well, which can lead to injury.

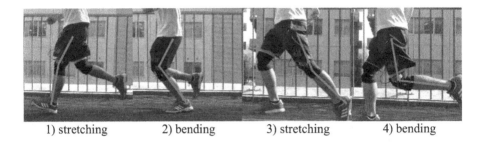

| 1) stretching | 2) bending | 3) stretching | 4) bending |

Fig. 1. Knee bending and stretching in double knee action.

Traditionally, running form analysis and training have been primarily conducted on a treadmill under the supervision of professional trainers. Joint angles and the presence or absence of double knee action are then analyzed from recorded video images [17]. However, it is not designed for actual running situations and is unsuitable for citizen runners to constantly check and correct their forms. Therefore, there is a need for a system that can constantly measure the knee condition.

In this study, we proposed and implemented a supporter-type device equipped with an elastic stretch sensor to acquire the state of knee flexion and estimate the knee angle in real time during running. The proposed system alerts the user to changes in knee motion due to prolonged running, allowing the user to stop running before injury occurs. The users also learn running strokes that reduce the impact on their knees during running, allowing them to enjoy running safely and injury-free without the need to be constantly monitored by a professional trainer. The contributions of this research are as follows.

- We proposed a supporter-type system equipped with a stretch sensor that can constantly monitor knee flexion and knee angle during running in an outdoor environment.
- We confirmed that the proposed system can acquire double knee action during running in outdoor environments.
- We evaluated that the proposed system can recognize the knee angle during running with an error margin of approximately 4 to 8°.

The remainder of this paper is structured as follows: Sect. 2 introduces related research, Sect. 3 describes the proposed system, and Sect. 4 presents the evaluation. The limitation are discussed in Sect. 5, and the paper is concluded in Sect. 6.

2   Related Research

2.1   Running Analysis Using Wearable Devices

Many studies and products exist that analyze the running condition of users using wearable devices. Devices such as the medilogic Foot Pressure Measurement System [8] and those developed by Huang et al. [6] and our previous work [14], utilize pressure sensors to analyze gait and running. Hassan et al. [5] propose a system to identify and correct different running styles (forefoot strike and rear foot strike) through data from sensor units placed in shoe insoles. However, these studies do not target acquiring knee movement, a crucial parameter for impact absorption.

Several researches have utilized sensors to identify running styles and provide feedback to runners. Stearne et al. [16] employ 3D motion capture, and McGrath et al. [7] utilize gyro sensors. Nylander et al. [11] developed 'RunRight,' an app providing real-time auditory feedback on running pace based on data from a body harness device.

Schütte et al. investigated the effects of fatigue on symmetry and stability during running using accelerometer attached to a runner [15]. Beéck et al. proposed a method to estimate RPE (Rating of Perceived Exertion), a subjective evaluation index of fatigue, using machine learning based on the values of acceleration sensors attached to the arms, wrists, and shins of runners [1].

Although wearable devices are proposed to analyze running contexts in outdoor environments, to the best of the authors' knowledge, knee bending state has not been measured. In this study, a knee supporter-type wearable device, which is easy to attach and detach, is used to measure the knee bending state.

2.2   Measurement of Joint Flexion

Various studies and products exist to measure joint flexion states. However, they are not designed for use in outdoor running.

Microsoft's Kinect [9] can detect user posture and gestures via infrared. Xsens' MVN Link [20] uses a motion capture suit equipped with IMU sensors, transmitting joint coordinates to a PC wirelessly. Sykes measured estimating joint angles during running from video [17]. Gioberto used stretch sensors sewn into flexible pants [3]. Wood et al. proposed a method of estimating the angle of knee flexion and extension in a standing position for home rehabilitation [19]. The device is instrumented with sixteen piezo resistive sensors mounted on the knee. As a result, subject-specific models average root mean square errors(RMSE) of 7.6 and 1.8° for flexion/extension and internal/external rotation, respectively. Device-specific models average RMSE of 12.6 and 3.5° for flexion/extension and internal/external rotation, respectively. These methods have limitations to use for various outdoor environments targeted in this study.

Some research measures joint flexion states in outdoor environments using wearable devices. Haladjian et al. proposed a system to record knee movement during patient rehabilitation with a sensor-equipped bandage [4]. O'Donovana et al. utilized sensors attached to the shin and instep or above and below the kneecap to measure knee angles in real-time [2,12,13]. However, these methods require expertise for proper placement and may constrain running motion due to wiring.

This study proposes a system targeting recreational runners, considering long-term outdoor use. We aim to measure knee flexion states with a method considering easy attachment and removal, using stretch sensors installed on a knee supporter.

3   Proposed System

3.1   Device Design

To prevent knee injuries during running, it is important to be able to check double knee action and know the angle of the knee to prevent excessive sinking [10]. Since the device is intended for use during running in an outdoor environment, it is necessary to consider a design that does not detract from the appearance of the device when worn, and wearability that does not restrict the running motion. In addition, measurement errors caused by attaching and detaching must also be reduced.

In this study, we focused on a knee supporter that is comfortable for runners to wear and implemented a device using a stretch sensor. The proposed device acquires the knee bending state during running from the value of a stretch sensor attached to the supporter and estimates the knee angle based on the obtained sensor value. In addition, calibration is performed during the bending exercise performed as a warm-up exercise to reduce errors due to changes in fitting or body shape during a series of running activities.

3.2   System Configuration

The configuration of the proposed system is shown in Fig. 2. A stretch sensor (C-STRETCH, Bando Chemical Industries) is attached to the patella of a sports knee supporter (ZAMST EK-1, NIPPON SIGMAX) so that the sensor responds to knee bending and stretching movements. In the proposed system, data obtained from a stretch sensor attached to a supporter is wirelessly transmitted to a mobile terminal. The mobile terminal processes the data and displays the flexion waveform during running in real-time. Moreover, the knee angle is estimated from the acquired sensor values by machine learning. Based on these two indicators of shock absorption, the knee bending state that is called double knee action and knee angle, the system provides feedback to the user on changes in running form and fatigue due to over-running.

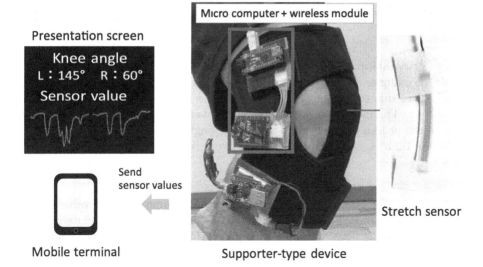

Fig. 2. Proposed system.

Calibration Procedure. The obtained sensor values depend on the size of the individual's legs and wearing. To prevent measurement errors due to fitting, the training data are normalized in advance using the maximum and minimum values for each trial. Data acquired in real-time are normalized based on the maximum and minimum values at the time of calibration. During calibration, the knee bending and stretching movements are performed three times and the sensor values are recorded.

Presentation Method of Double Knee Action. The user should be able to check if his/her running form is appropriate while running. In the proposed device, the stretch sensor is attached to the patella of the supporter, so when the knee is flexed, the sensor stretches, and the output sensor value increases. This property is used to measure the double knee action, which indicates the knee bending state during running. Stretch sensor values during running are graphed in real-time, allowing the user to check his or her running form at any time.

Knee Angle Recognition Method. For knee angle recognition, we use k-NN, a machine learning algorithm. Twelve features were used: the instantaneous sensor values, the sensor values of the last nine samples, and the mean and variance of the last nine samples. Training data were collected by running on a treadmill. Three colored stickers were placed on knee joints during the run, and a video recording was also conducted at the same time. The actual knee angle was calculated from the coordinates of three points obtained by tracking the colored stickers in the captured video using image processing. The parameter k

of the K-NN algorithm was set to $k = 9$, which was the most accurate in our preliminary measurements.

Injury Prevention Feedback. The application continuously estimates and records knee angles during running. It detects excessive running by recognizing sinking knees due to fatigue [10], prompting the user to improve their running form or rest. The method involves taking the average knee angle A_{ave} from the initial ten steps as a reference, and if the knee angle at landing $A_{landing}$ becomes $4°$ or more than A_{ave}, it is determined as excessive running.

$$A_{landing} - A_{ave} > 4 \tag{1}$$

The knee angle at landing is estimated from the minimum sensor value of the last 100 samples since the average running time per step is approximately 1 s. If excessive running is detected, a message prompting the user to rest is displayed on the device.

4   Evaluation

4.1   Double Knee Action During Running Outdoor

The stretch sensor values of the proposed system were investigated to confirm the double knee action when running in an outdoor environment, such as on a flat road, an uphill, and a downhill. Subjects ran on a flat road, uphill, and downhill while wearing the proposed device, and the sensor data were acquired. The measurement frequency was 100 Hz. The subjects were three males with an average age of 22.6 ± 0.6 years, an average height of 172.5 ± 4 cm, and an average BMI of 22 ± 1.2. The acquired stretch sensor values were compared with the video images captured during running. We confirmed that the waveforms showed knee bending twice per step cycle, which is a characteristic of double-knee action.

Figure 3 shows graphs of the stretch sensor values for one step in each of Subject A's runs in an outdoor environment. In the figure, steps 1 to 4 represent the characteristic movements of one step cycle during running in Fig. 1: 1) extension at landing, 2) flexion for shock absorption, 3) extension at kicking off, and 4) flexion during the motion of bringing the foot forward. Thus, for all subjects, double knee action could be confirmed in all three outdoor environments from the waveforms of the proposed system.

4.2   Knee Angle Recognition

Normal Condition (not Fatigued). We evaluated the accuracy of knee angle recognition based on the stretch sensor values acquired by the proposed system. The subjects were 10 males, including 3 subjects in Sect. 4.1, with an average age of 22.5 ± 0.8 years, an average height of 171.8 ± 4.7 cm, and an average BMI of 20 ± 1.5. They ran on a treadmill at three different speeds (6 km/h, 8 km/h, and

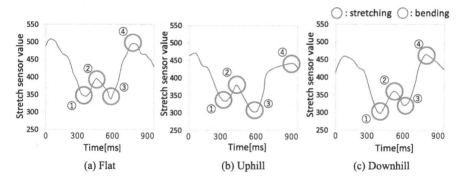

Fig. 3. Observed waveform of double knee action.

Table 1. Average accuracy of knee angle recognition under normal conditions.

Cross-validation Patterns	R	MAE	RMSE
Intra-individual and intra-trial	0.99	2.7	3.5
Intra-individual and inter-trial	0.93	5.8	7.7
Inter-individual	0.91	8.3	10.3
Intra-individual and inter-speed	0.92	6.4	8.5

10 km/h) for 30 s each while wearing the proposed device. Trials were performed three times each. The device was attached and detached between trials, and a few minutes of rest was taken between trials to prevent the effects of fatigue.

The recognition accuracy for each of the cross-validation methods under normal conditions is shown in Table 1. Cross-validation under conditions of intra-individual and intra-trial, which means we divided a trial to train and test data, showed that the average of MAE was 2.7°. Compared to this, the MAE under the condition of intra-individual and inter-trial, which means the same subject's data from a different trial were used as training data, was 5.8° and its error of each subject in MAE was approximately 4 to 8°. Therefore, it is considered that the recognition accuracy was slightly decreased due to differences in the way of attaching and detaching the device.

The average of MAE under the condition of inter-individual, which means when the sample data of others were used as training data, was 8.3°. The result was less accurate than the MAE of intra-individual cross-validation.

Furthermore, the MAE was 6.4° under the condition of intra-individual and inter-speed, which means the same subject at different speeds was used as training data. The recognition accuracy was improved when the training data contained data with speeds that were closer to the test data.

Since changes in running form due to prolonged running are represented by changes in the knee angle at landing, it is important to be able to acquire the knee angle at landing. Figure 4 shows that the waveform was estimated with high accuracies and small errors during one step of the running cycle, including

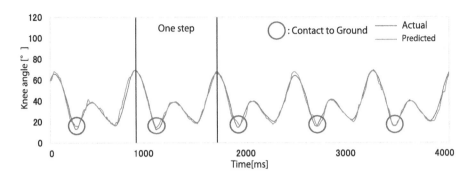

Fig. 4. A waveform of knee angle recognition result (intra-individual and inter-trial).

the landing phase. Such waveforms were observed in about approximately 80% of the subjects' total results and could be estimated with high accuracy.

The evaluation experiments showed that the knee angle could be estimated with an average MAE of 5.8, even on different trials, if the system learned the user's own data. This is not sufficient for capturing changes of 4 to 10° [10], however, the knee angle during running is recognized with some high degree of accuracy. Four participants had the recognition accuracy of approximately 4 to 5°, which is considered to be sufficient for practical use in capturing large changes.

The knee angle recognition error in the evaluation is considered to be caused by the attachment/detachment of the proposed device and noise in the sensor values. In the future, we will design devices and calibration methods to reduce noise even further. Experiments suggest that collecting training data on similar speeds contributes to improving the recognition accuracy. Since the difference in running motions may have affected the error, the recognition accuracy may be improved by collecting more data from participants with similar running behaviors to those with large errors.

Fatigued Condition. We evaluated whether the proposed system could be used to recognize the knee angle when running under fatigue conditions. The participants were three of the participants in Sect. 4.2.1. They were given 5 km run to make them fatigued. Immediately after 5 km running, they performed one trial of running on a treadmill for approximately 30 s at a speed of 8 km/h while wearing the proposed device. One set of the measurement was performed for each person.

The results of the experiment are summarized in Table 2. Cross-subject validation using data from one trial per person during fatigue showed that the average MAE was 8.8°. Using the same subject's training data under normal, non-fatigued conditions, the MAE of the knee angle during fatigue was 5.0° (Intra-individual from normal). These results indicate that the proposed system can be estimated the knee angle to some extent without acquiring data during fatigue by training the person's data under normal conditions.

Table 2. Average accuracy of knee angle recognition under fatigued conditions.

Cross-validation Patterns	R	MAE	RMSE
Inter-individual under fatigue	0.89	8.8	10.9
Intra-individual from normal	0.96	5.0	6.3
Inter-individual under normal	0.94	6.5	8.1

5   Limitation

Regarding subject bias, the prototype device implemented in this study uses a commercially available supporter, which limits the body size of those who can wear the device. Specifically, we targeted participants with a thigh circumference of 40 to 44 cm at 10 cm above the kneecap. Moreover, the age and gender of the participants were only males in their 20 s. Therefore, the accuracy of knee angle recognition for people with different physical characteristics may differ even if the appropriate size supporter device is made.

Participants who exercise daily were recruited for the evaluation of the fatigue experiment. Therefore, a person who does not normally exercise may have a large change in form, which may affect the accuracy of knee angle recognition.

The result in fatigued condition indicates that the knee angle can be estimated to some extent without acquiring data during fatigue by training the person's data under normal conditions. However, we did not evaluate knee angle recognition rate when running in various outdoor locations, which is a limitation of this study.

6   Conclusion

This paper proposes a wearable system that acquires knee bending state and estimates the knee angle in real-time during running using a supporter-shaped device equipped with a stretchable sensor. In the proposed system, data obtained from a stretch sensor attached to a supporter is wirelessly transmitted to a mobile terminal. The mobile terminal processes the data and displays the flexion waveform during running in real-time. Moreover, the knee angle is recognized from the acquired sensor values by machine learning. Based on these two indicators of shock absorption, the knee bending state that is called double knee action and knee angle, the system provides feedback to the user on changes in running form and fatigue due to over-running.

The result of the running experiment outdoors on flat and sloping roads shows that the proposed system can present the double-knee action, which is an indicator of knee bending in running. For knee angle recognition based on treadmill running data, the average MAE was 5.8° in ranged from approximately 4 to 8° in individuals, when using training data of the same subject's other trial. For recognition of the knee angle during running under fatigued conditions, the result shows that the proposed system can recognize the knee angle with an average MAE of approximately 5.0 when using training data of the user's own non-fatigued data.

The proposed device that can constantly measure the knee condition at various locations. We believe it will have a wide range of applications, not only for daily running but also for monitoring people undergoing rehabilitation in their daily life.

Acknowledgments. This research was supported in part by JST CREST Grant Number JPMJCR18A3.

References

1. Beéck, T.O.D., Meert, W., Schütte, K.H., Vanwanseele, B., Davis, J.: Fatigue prediction in outdoor runners via machine learning and sensor fusion. In: Proceedings of the 24th ACM SIGKDD International Conference on Knowledge Discovery and Data Mining, pp. 606–615 (July 2018)
2. Burns, A., et al.: Shimmer – a wireless sensor platform for noninvasive biomedical research. IEEE Sensors J. **10**, 1527–1534 (Sep 2010)
3. Gioberto, G.: Garment-integrated wearable sensing for knee joint monitoring. In: Proceedings of the 2014 ACM International Symposium on Wearable Computers (ISWC 2014), pp. 113–118 (Sep 2014)
4. Haladjian, J., et al.: Kneehapp: A bandage for rehabilitation of knee injuries. In: Proceedings of the 2014 ACM International Symposium on Wearable Computers (ISWC 2015), pp. 181–184 (Sep 2015)
5. Hassan, M., Daiber, F., Wiehr, F., Kosmalla, F., Krüger, A.: Footstriker: an ems-based foot strike assistant for running. Proc. ACM Interact., Mobile, Wearable Ubiquitous Technol. (IMWUT) **1**(2), 1–18 (2017)
6. Huang, P.Y., Lin, C.F., Kuo, L.C., Liao, J.C.: Foot pressure and center of pressure in athletes with ankle instability during lateral shuffling and running gait. Scand. J. Med. Sci. Sports **21**, 461–467 (2011)
7. McGrath, D., Greene, B.R., O'Donovan, K.J., Caulfield, B.: Gyroscope-based assessment of temporal gait parameters during treadmill walking and running. In: Proceedings of the International Sports Engineering Assosiation 2012, pp. 207–213 (2012)
8. medilogic: medilogic foot pressure measurement system (2018). https://medilogic.com/en/medilogic-wlan-insole/
9. Microsoft: Azure kinect dk (2019). https://azure.microsoft.com/en-us/products/kinect-dk/
10. Mizrahi, J., Verbitsky, O., Isakov, E., Daily, D.: Effect of fatigue on leg kinematics and impact acceleration in long distance running. Hum. Mov. Sci. **19**, 139–151 (2000)
11. Nylander, S., Jacobsson, M., Tholander, J.: Runright – real-time visual and audio feedback on running. In: Proceedings of the 2014 CHI Conference Extended Abstracts on Human Factors in Computing Systems (CHI 2014), pp. 583–586 (2014)
12. O'Donovan, K., Ayer, S.: Real-time joint angle measurement using the shimmer wireless sensor platform. In: Proceedings of the First ACM Workshop on Mobile Systems, Applications, and Services for Healthcare, pp. 1–2 (Nov 2011)

13. O'Donovana, K.J., Kamnikb, R., O'Keeffea, D.T., Lyonsa, G.M.: An inertial and magnetic sensor based technique for joint angle measurement. J. Biomech. **40**(12), 2604–2611 (2007)
14. for Review: our paper., B
15. Schütte, K.H., Seeden, S., Venter, R., Vanwanseele, B.: Fatigue-related asymmetry and instability during a 3200m time-trial performance in healthy runners. In: Proceedings of the 34rd International Conference on Biomechanics in Sports, pp. 933–936 (Nov 2016)
16. Stearne, S.M., Alderson, J.A., Green, B.A., Donnelly, C.A., Rubenson, J.: Joint kinetics in rearfoot versus forefoot running: implications of switching technique. Med. Sci. Sports Exerc. **46**, 1578–1587 (2014)
17. Sykes, K.: Technique and observation of angular gait patterns in running. British J. Sports Med. **9**(4), 181–186 (1975)
18. Taunton, J.E., Ryan, M.B., Clement, D.B., McKenzie, D.C., Lloyd-Smith, D.R., Zumbo, B.D.: A retrospective case-control analysis of 2002 running injuries. Br. J. Sports Med. **36**, 95–101 (2002)
19. Wood, D.S., et al.: Accurate prediction of knee angles during open-chain rehabilitation exercises using a wearable array of nanocomposite stretch sensors. Sensors **22**(7), 2499 (2022)
20. Xsens: Mvn link (2019). https://www.xsens.com/
21. Yamamoto, H.: The change in knee angle during the gait by applying elastic tape to the skin. J. Phys. Ther. Sci. **26**(7), 1075–1077 (2014)

Ubiquitous Mobile Application for Conducting Occupational Therapy in Children with ADHD

Jonnathan Berrezueta-Guzman[1]([✉]) [iD], Melissa Montalvo[2] [iD],
and Stephan Krusche[1] [iD]

[1] Technical University of Munich, Munich, Germany
{s.berrezueta,krusche}@tum.de
[2] Universidad Politécnica Salesiana, Cuenca, Ecuador
mmontalvo1@est.ups.edu.ec

Abstract. Attention Deficit Hyperactivity Disorder (ADHD) is a prevalent neurodevelopmental disorder that affects a significant number of children worldwide. It represents learning challenges, profoundly impacting the child's attention and behavior. Occupational therapies face these challenges by involving the child in mirroring activities of daily life.

This article presents the creation and assessment of a mobile application that assists therapists in remotely observing children's behavior during occupational therapy at home. This mobile application belongs to a smart-home environment designed to conduct occupational therapies for children with ADHD. It uses Firebase to acquire and manipulate data from this environment. Therapists can obtain clear details about the children's behavior, better than in a conventional clinical setting. The 16-week experiment reveals that therapists find the application useful for decision-making in therapeutic matters and lets parents be more involved in the therapy. This leads to new ideas on how to use the app.

Keywords: Ubiquitous occupational therapy · Mobile application development · Cloud computing · Remote monitoring · Behavior tracking · Therapeutic Decision-Making

1 Introduction

Attention Deficit Hyperactivity Disorder (ADHD), recognized as the most common Neurodevelopmental Disorder (NDD), poses significant challenges to children worldwide. It is typified by a triad of characteristic symptoms: inattention, hyperactivity, and impulsivity. Despite extensive research in the field, the origin of ADHD remains enigmatic, with the precise underlying mechanisms yet to be fully clarified [1].

The clinical manifestations of ADHD frequently endure into adulthood and often exhibit comorbidity with other disorders, such as Autism Spectrum Disorder (ASD) or Anxiety Disorder. The presence of ADHD can have a detrimental impact on an individual's daily functioning, academic accomplishments,

P. Delir Haghighi et al. (Eds.): MoMM 2023, LNCS 14417, pp. 104–119, 2023.
https://doi.org/10.1007/978-3-031-48348-6_9

and productivity in the workplace [2]. Empirical studies indicate a potential correlation between ADHD in childhood and subsequent success in adulthood, underscoring the necessity for early detection and efficacious treatment strategies [3]. Therapeutic interventions span from pharmacological remedies to behavioral approaches like occupational therapy [4–6]. Therefore, ensuring accessibility to these treatment options is primary for enhancing the quality of life for children with ADHD and their families.

The main goal of occupational therapy is to help children become more independent in their daily tasks. This includes things they do at home and school, especially homework [7]. Nevertheless, many children with ADHD find doing homework on their own very hard. Because it takes a lot of effort and there's no immediate reward, they often get frustrated and give up. This can hurt their school performance over time [8].

This paper introduces an Android mobile application as part of a smart-home environment intended to monitor children with ADHD during in-home occupational therapies. The application delivers meaningful information to therapists and parents using cloud-centric data processing by Firebase.

The organization of this paper is articulated as follows: Sect. 2 reviews related literature and projects, highlighting what makes our study different and unique compared to others. Section 3 gives a brief look at the smart-home system from earlier research. This helps readers understand why we made this mobile application. Section 4 delineates the research methodology employed in this study, and gives details about the application's features, its role in the smart-home system, and how data was handled. In Sect. 5, we describe the main parts of our experiments and the test methods we used. This section also explains how the app might help children with ADHD, their parents, and therapists. Section 6 wraps up the paper by summarizing the main findings and suggesting future research directions in this area.

2   Related Work

In the healthcare field, Pozo-Guzman et al. introduced an IoT system within a cyber-physical setup to monitor COVID-19 patients in hard-to-reach areas, allowing for timely medical check-ins [12]. This system uses the Firebase real-time database for two-way communication: 1. Doctors can see patient data (like heart rate and blood oxygen levels) from online devices on a web application. This application shows patient recovery trends with clear charts. 2. Through the same app, doctors can send important advice and medicine details to the patient or their family. This technology helped reduce hospital crowding by keeping patient numbers manageable. Patients could recover at home, while healthcare workers closely monitored for any problems.

In ADHD diagnostics, Chandrasena et al. created a mobile application that incorporates a questionnaire and gaming activities designed to identify and diagnose symptoms indicative of ADHD, including hyperactivity, impulsivity, inattention, and organizational disorders. Firebase serves as the central server facilitating information processing within the application. While the system's precision may not currently meet optimal standards, the authors believe using machine learning can make it better. This would improve diagnosis accuracy [13].

In the area of ADHD treatment, Doan et al. described CoolCraig, a mobile app to help children with ADHD and their caregivers manage behaviors and emotions. The app works on two devices: a smartwatch for children and a smartphone for caregivers. The authors illustrate a usage scenario delineating how CoolCraig supports children and their caregivers using goals, rewards, and tracking emotions and behavior. A key part of the application is its notifications, reminding children to note their feelings and actions. Results show that using the app regularly has helped children behave better in different settings [14].

Relatedly, Dolon-Poza et al. created a machine learning system using Firebase to see how well occupational therapy works on a child with ADHD over time. This system takes data from a smart home setup to check behavior. It also predicts how a child might progress with their treatment with an accuracy above 80 %. This helps therapists adjust the therapy to better fit the child's needs [15].

Out of the mentioned studies, [12] is most similar to our work, but it centers on clinical settings. Meanwhile, [13,14] mainly create apps for ADHD diagnosis. On the other hand, [15] does not make an app, instead, it uses an algorithm in Firebase to predict how well occupational therapies might work.

Consequently, the application presented in this study encompasses distinct functionalities tailored to enhance occupational therapies for children diagnosed with ADHD, thereby complementing the previous work [15,16]. A comprehensive exposition of these functionalities can be found in the methodology and experiments sections of this paper.

3 Background

This mobile application acts as the primary interface in delivering occupational therapy to children with ADHD within a smart-home setting. It streamlines the monitoring process for therapists and parents, allowing them to oversee the therapeutic progress of their charges. The application not only grants access to data sourced from the smart-home environment and processed via Firebase but also enables customization of the smart-home settings to ensure ideal conditions for therapy sessions [16].

In previous research, we designed a smart-home setting characterized by a sensor network specifically placed in the children's study space at home for real-time behavioral tracking. This network incorporates various sensors-including pressure, motion, and distance-fitted into the child's desk and chair. These sensors detect behaviors like distraction, fidgeting, or leaving the workspace [17].

Additionally, we introduced a robotic assistant to this sensor network. Equipped with a camera, the robot uses shape recognition algorithms to identify other signs of distraction. Such behaviors might involve the child stopping their writing tasks or misusing their study materials, actions therapists often refer to as 'playing on the table' [18].

The robotic assistant performs two main functions: it acts as a bridge between the child and therapist and serves as a tool for behavior change. Using pre-recorded voice commands, it directs the child to adjust their actions during homework, offering useful feedback and encouragement similar to a therapist's guidance [19]. Moreover, the robot has interactive features via its built-in touch screen. This interface shows various menu options, allowing the child to convey needs like needing a bathroom break, asking for a pause, and seeking help, among others.

Figure 1 depicts the arrangement of the smart environment, highlighting the position and function of key components like the smart chair and smart desk, essential for evaluating the child's behavior. The integration of the robotic assistant in this setup is also showcased. Additionally, the figure visually represents how the mobile application connects and interacts with the smart-home environment. This application is crucial for real-time communication, data handling, and carrying out commands within this smart framework.

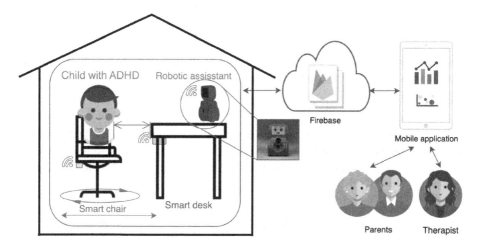

Fig. 1. Schematic of the SmartHome environment designed for pervasive occupational therapy for children with ADHD. This depiction shows the placement of various sensor devices and the robotic assistant within the house. These tools capture detailed information about the workspace, which is then relayed to Firebase for processing. The processed data can subsequently be accessed and visualized by therapists and parents via the mobile application developed in the course of this research.

4   Methodology

The application we developed incorporates four main features, as shown in Fig. 2. First, it supports real-time tracking of behavior and relevant therapy data. Second, it provides therapists with vital data from different therapy sessions. Third, it allows for remote customization of the smart environment and robotic assistant based on the child's unique requirements. Finally, it includes an authentication feature, ensuring only specific users, like parents and therapists, can access it.

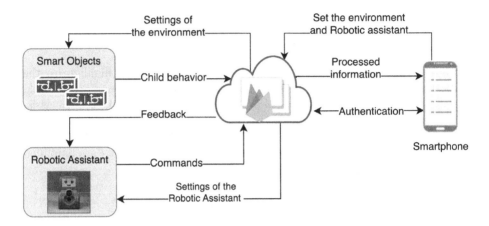

Fig. 2. Illustration of the interaction mechanism among the smart objects, the robotic assistant, and the mobile application, facilitated via Firebase. This diagram underscores the communication flow and data exchange among these entities in the context of the SmartHome environment.

We utilized Firebase[1] for the development of the smart home environment and the application presented in this paper. Here, we briefly discuss how Firebase facilitates the establishment of the smart environment and, in turn, the mobile application described in this article.

Feature 1. Remote Monitoring: The 'smart chair' and 'smart desk' are equipped with WiFi-enabled sensor devices, and a Raspberry Pi-based robotic assistant gathers acceleration, positional, and visual data during therapeutic sessions. After an initial pre-processing phase, significant distraction events are sent to Firebase. Moreover, children can engage with the robotic assistant to log task updates, request breaks, or seek help, and these interactions are recorded as events. Real-time synchronization with Firebase ensures that all events are thoroughly logged by the session's conclusion.

To tap into the real-time database, one must first establish a DatabaseReference instance, enabling data reading or writing. Data references can then have listeners attached to them, allowing for real-time data change tracking. Figure 3 depicts how data from Firebase's real-time database is mirrored in the mobile

---

[1] A platform owned by Google designed to streamline web and mobile application development. It offers various services such as real-time data storage, processing, user authentication, and push notifications. Moreover, it is compatible with many programming languages and integrates smoothly with Google tools [9–11].

application, facilitating child behavior monitoring. While Firebase's real-time database organizes the data alphabetically, the app offers flexibility in data presentation, allowing for custom ordering.

Feature 2. Information Processing in Firebase: Data stored in Firebase's real-time database is transformed into valuable therapeutic insights through protocols set by therapists for each child diagnosed with ADHD. These protocols are actioned by the Firebase cloud functions [18].

To deploy Cloud Functions, specific functions are written and triggered by events, such as updates in the real-time database. As demonstrated in Fig. 3 (Right), one distraction is labeled as "good". This suggests that a single distraction during the duration of the homework might not be detrimental. Cloud functions determine other such labels.

The valuable insights derived from the cloud functions are updated in the real-time database. Therapists then view these within the mobile application through graphical displays. These graphs chart the behavioral trends of each child during therapy sessions, for different tasks, or over specified durations.

Various behavioral patterns manifested by children diagnosed with ADHD can be identified and tracked. These include:

– **Hyperactivity.** This is discerned when the events recorded by the smart chair during task execution show unusual movements such as spinning, sudden bouncing, or acceleration in any direction. Therapists perceive these movements as indications of distraction stemming from playfulness.
– **Impulsivity.** This behavior is detected when events captured by both the smart chair and smart desk during the task indicate that the child often and for extended periods, leaves the workspace.
– **Wandering.** Even in the absence of hyperactive or impulsive events, if the image recognition by the robotic assistant determines that the child isn't actively participating in his/her task, it is termed wandering. Therapists label this state of disengagement as "the child is wandering".

The child's interaction with the robotic assistant, made possible through its touch-sensitive interface, generates crucial data. After each session, this data is sent to and analyzed by cloud services on the server side.

The generated data offers insights into three primary dimensions:

1. **Distraction Metrics:** Events categorized as distractions are numerically evaluated, accompanied by the duration from the initial distraction point until the child refocuses. A post-session analysis is carried out to assess the percentage of the session time wherein the child was distracted.
2. **Pause Metrics:** Situations in which the child signals the robotic assistant to pause are recorded, including the duration of each pause. These metrics are then contextualized as a fraction of the total session time, serving as a reference for comparison.

Fig. 3. (Left) Depiction of real-time data acquisition as represented within the Firebase real-time database, demonstrating the process of sensor reading collection. (Right) Visualization of the processed information within the mobile application, structured for easy comprehension and practical use by therapists and parents.

3. **Assistance Request Metrics:** When a child encounters obstacles that prevent task continuation, they can initiate an assistance request. This action triggers a specific cloud function, which, in turn, sends real-time push notifications to the parents via the designated application, ensuring they are updated about their child's needs. Moreover, the child can reach out to their therapists if necessary. Based on this request, the therapist can plan a follow-up session, providing interim feedback through the mobile app. This feedback is subsequently conveyed to the child through the robotic assistant.

In Fig. 4 (center), we illustrate the analytical findings of a homework session held on November 22, 2022. This compilation amalgamates data sourced from the integrated sensors of the smart environment as well as the interactive components of the robotic assistant.

Feature 3. Environment and Robotic Assistant Configuration: Distraction criteria vary, reflecting the unique attributes of each child. Hence, an initial calibration of the environment becomes imperative. The mobile application caters to personalized child profile adjustments, facilitating the meticulous configuration of both the smart devices and the robotic assistant. Such customizations can be carried out seamlessly through the application interface, without necessitating changes to the inherent code of the smart objects. Figure 4 (right) delineates how therapists can modulate sensitivity levels using predefined categories: highly sensitive, sensitive, normally sensitive, less sensitive, and non-sensitive, represented as intuitive sliding scales. This obviates the need for entering specific acceleration or distance metrics. A parallel approach is employed to tweak the response delay of the robotic assistant's feedback mechanism.

Feature 4. Authentication and Security: Firebase's security framework ensures that access to the application and individual child data is limited to authenticated users: specifically, therapists and the pertinent parents. The registration process mandates a two-step verification process executed through email. The extent of access granted to each user is inherently governed by their association with the child. Parents are granted access exclusively to their child's data. Conversely, therapists have the prerogative to both access and modify the data for all children under their professional supervision. For enhanced user convenience, the option to register via existing Google accounts is also incorporated. In facilitating these authentication dynamics, our application leverages Firebase Authentication APIs to effectively manage user registrations, log-ins, and user data management. The visual representation of the user account creation interface can be perused in Fig. 4 (left).

Through our endeavors, we have ascertained that Firebase furnishes an all-encompassing array of four salient features, all of which are seamlessly navigable through its intuitive console interface. These four distinct features were seamlessly embedded within the Android application by leveraging Firebase's Android-specific libraries. The assimilation procedure encompasses the integration of dependencies pertinent to Firebase libraries within the 'build.gradle' file, the subsequent initialization of Firebase within the application's milieu, and the definitive execution of the inherent capabilities of each respective service within the application's foundational code.

By harnessing Firebase's robust capabilities, we succeeded in crafting a versatile, highly scalable Android application that amalgamates an array of intricate functionalities. These include but are not limited to user authentication protocols, adept real-time data orchestration, cloud-centric functions, expansive data repository management, and dynamic user interactive modules. This application underwent rigorous evaluation through three distinct experimental methodologies, conclusively demonstrating its efficacy as an instrumental tool in facilitating occupational therapy for children diagnosed with ADHD.

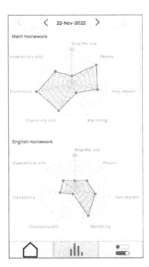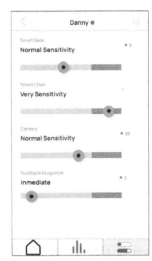

Fig. 4. (Left) The graphical user interface exhibited assists in the registration process for new accounts via the mobile application. (Center) The interface displayed here presents a detailed analysis of data gathered during a specific math and English homework session. This particular session illustrates the varying impacts of different homework assignments on a child, leading therapists to infer that math tasks necessitate a significant degree of exertion from the child. (Right) This interface enables the tuning of sensitivity parameters associated with the smart objects, in addition to the adjustment of feedback response latency in the robotic assistant.

5   Experiment and Results

The mobile application's effectiveness, when integrated with the smart environment, underwent rigorous validation across three distinct experiments over a 16-week duration. These experiments involved the collaboration of six seasoned therapists who meticulously selected a sample group of 32 children aged between 4 to 8 years, each exhibiting potential ADHD diagnostic indicators. Notably, to mitigate any experimental biases, the selected cohort exclusively comprised children without any comorbidities related to other disorders such as ASD (Autism Spectrum Disorder) or ODD (Oppositional Defiant Disorder). Before the onset of these experiments, informed consent was duly acquired from the parents, thereby ensuring the voluntary participation of their children in the study.

Table 1. Categorization of children into age-specific groups. Tasks have been allotted to each group by their cognitive developmental stage. For each group, two therapists are designated to observe and document the children's behavior, the first one with the mobile application and the second one without it.

Group	Age	Children	Task	Session time	Therapists	Period
1	4	2	Drawing	40 min	2	Week 1-2
2	5	2	Drawing	40 min	2	Week 1-2
3	6	4	Language homework	1 h	4	Week 3-4
4	7	5	Math and English homework	1 h	2	Week 5-6
5	8	3	Math and English homework	1 h	2	Week 5-6

5.1   The Experiments

During each experimental session, two groups were closely observed as they carried out their respective tasks. While one therapist utilized the application to monitor real-time results, the other conducted traditional monitoring, making manual notes on their observations. Post-session, the application's results were presented by the first therapist, and the second therapist shared their notes.

As depicted in Table 1, the initial two weeks saw both therapists overseeing activities involving 4 and 5-year-old children, who were assigned drawing tasks. Drawing, though seemingly simple, demands sustained attention-a quality often challenging for ADHD-diagnosed children. The therapist's roles alternated between weeks. In the initial week, Therapist 1 employed the application, leaving Therapist 2 with traditional monitoring. In the subsequent week, they switched roles.

Key observed behaviors included acts of impulsivity, instances of distraction, signs of hyperactivity, wandering, calls for assistance, pauses, and instances where tasks were abandoned. Yet, there remains potential for therapists to identify additional parameters to further refine the model's accuracy.

Notably, the therapists refrained from directly intervening or providing feedback to the children. The robotic assistant was solely responsible for this. While the first therapist's primary duty was passive observation, the second therapist meticulously documented interactions for post-session review.

5.2   Results from the Initial Experiment (Weeks 1 and 2)

During the initial experimental phase, we evaluated both the application's effectiveness in setting up the environment and establishing children's profiles and the accuracy of the smart objects compared to therapist observations.

From Fig. 5, it's clear that therapists not using the application had a reduced ability to record distraction events in the first week. In a role reversal in the second week, therapists who had previously used the application were less accurate than their counterparts. Their feedback suggested that having used the application, they found manual note-taking during standard monitoring to be redundant.

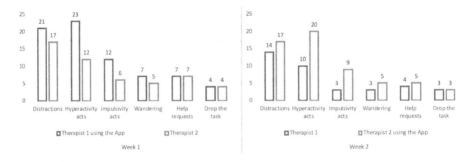

Fig. 5. Comparative analysis of the accuracy in identifying distraction parameters during sessions, between therapists employing the application and those not using it. The results depicted within the application are deemed to be the most accurate, as inferred from prior clinical validations of the smart-home environment [19].

At the end of each therapy session week, therapists' conclusions and reports varied noticeably. However, those utilizing the application consistently provided a more detailed and holistic overview of the children's progress in occupational therapy.

Finally, the therapists did not provide any feedback on enhancements for the application or the smart environment.

5.3   Results from the Second Experiment (Weeks 3 and 4)

During weeks 3 and 4, an identical experimental approach was applied to a sample of four 6-year-old children focusing on language tasks. Each child read three uniform short texts and discussed their interpretations post-reading with individual therapists to avoid fatigue; four therapists in total participated. Half of these therapists used the application for monitoring during the reading, while the others relied on traditional note-taking methods.

The experiment aimed to discern correlations between children's distraction metrics, as determined by both the app and manual therapist reports, and their comprehension of the readings. Responses to the text were graded on a scale from 1 to 5, with 1 indicating a poor response and 5 indicating a perfect understanding. While therapists were encouraged to remain objective in evaluations, a standardized rubric was provided to ensure consistent assessment across the board.

We cannot suggest that the children's performance is affected by the monitoring technique (with or without the use of the mobile application). However, it can be observed that therapists who used the application were more capable of drawing correlations between the children's performance during evaluations and the application's generated report.

Analyzing Fig. 6, it's evident that children monitored without the application displayed fewer distractions, implying better performance. However, Table 2 shows that the average grades across all children are relatively consistent. This

Table 2. Compilation of the average grades secured during the therapy sessions in the second experiment (weeks 3 and 4).

Child	Grade Text 1	Grade Text 2	Grade Text 3	Average grade
1	2.5	3.2	3.1	2,9
2	3.5	2.8	3.0	3,1
3	2,9	4.1	2.9	3,3
4	3.0	2.3	3.1	2,8

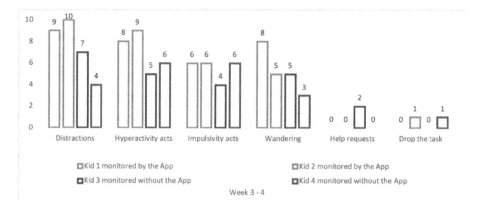

Fig. 6. Comparative analysis of the accuracy in detecting distraction parameters during sessions, contrasting between therapists employing the application and those abstaining from its use. The results presented within the application are regarded as the most accurate, backed by prior clinical validations of the smart-home environment [19].

suggests that therapists using the application could more effectively convey and support their observations about performance in each reading session's final evaluations. In contrast, therapists relying on traditional monitoring methods had limited data to validate these findings.

5.4   Results of the Final Experiment (Weeks 5 and 6)

The third and concluding experiment focused on the remote monitoring of eight children, all aged between 7 and 8 years, as they undertook their math and English homework assignments. Additionally, this trial involved the active participation of the children's parents, summing up to eight involved parents in total.

Our primary aim with this experiment was to gauge the application's clarity and understandability to parents, particularly those unacquainted with the nuances of occupational therapy. Following every therapy session, parents were presented with a questionnaire to assess their ability to comprehend and interpret the data and insights shared by the application.

The ensuing results were promising. Parents demonstrated a comprehensive understanding of their children's behavior. They were notably adept at recognizing instances when their children were becoming distracted during tasks. Of particular interest to the parents was the data about the time their children took to finish their homework and the weekly count of distractions they faced. This newfound knowledge inspired parents to be more proactive in aiding their children with their tasks and engaging in conversations to pinpoint potential domestic sources of distraction.

This trial served to reaffirm the outcomes of the first two experiments, where therapists employed the mobile application. The app proved instrumental in offering a detailed insight into the children's behavior, paving the way for a more refined and tailored approach to subsequent occupational therapies.

5.5   Findings

In our study, after careful experiments and analysis, we identified several key findings. These insights showed the effectiveness of the application and its impact on therapists and parents, highlighting the potential of technology to enhance ADHD therapies.

> **Finding 1:** The app enables effective remote tracking, showing a child's behavior during tasks. This simplifies therapy planning and improves timely decisions, including ADHD medication adjustments.

From a usability standpoint, our research brought to light a significant discovery. This observation not only underscored the importance of user experience but also highlighted the effectiveness and ease with which therapists and parents interacted with the application.

> **Finding 2:** Users found the app easy to use without facing any errors or issues. Parents have become more involved in their child's therapy and therapists could set up and personalize the smart-home environment, even without technical expertise.

The findings prove that the app is a transformative tool for managing ADHD challenges during occupational therapies at home. Its capacity for effective remote monitoring provides real-time insights into a child's behavior, streamlining therapy planning and enabling prompt therapeutic decisions, including medication adjustments. Its user-friendly interface ensures that parents engage more deeply in their child's therapy, and therapists, irrespective of their technical acumen, can seamlessly configure the smart-home environment. This cohesive integration of technology, parents, and professionals suggests a promising future for ADHD management.

6   Conclusions

The developed mobile application contributes as a critical tool enabling the ubiquitous execution of occupational therapies. It delivers real-time data capabilities, granting therapists and parents the necessary means to observe a child's behavior during tasks, and critically evaluate their progress promptly.

To enable comprehensive data interpretation, the application incorporates advanced visualization features that generate structured and categorized graphs and tables. These sophisticated tools provide a high-resolution view of the therapeutic journey for each child, tracing their progress over a designated time frame and allowing for a detailed longitudinal analysis.

This systematically collated information is stored within individual child profiles. Utilizing this accumulated data, therapists are better equipped to make informed decisions about the therapy's course, thereby promoting dynamic adjustments based on a child's demonstrated progress and immediate needs.

The application also offers robust customization capabilities for therapists, enabling them to calibrate the smart-home environment and robotic assistant according to specific requirements. This includes the capacity to fine-tune the sensitivity of smart objects, such as the chair and desk, to detect events like distraction or abandonment of the workstation. Additionally, therapists can define how the robotic assistant processes the actions captured through its camera, allowing for greater discernment between distraction, brief pauses, or the emergence of novel behavioral patterns.

Following experimental trials, the application has received favorable responses from both therapists and parents, who view it as an invaluable resource in therapeutic analysis. Its ability to simplify the acquisition and interpretation of data, tailor insights to individual child profiles, and present outcomes derived from therapy sessions, underscore its utility.

Regarding scalability, the application exhibits potential for adaptation across varied therapy scenarios, transcending the constraints of a home environment. Therefore, the utilization of Firebase as a robust and scalable platform for the application seems highly appropriate. Future work should focus on broadening the application's functionality to cater to a wider range of therapeutic needs, including the treatment of conditions like ASD and Anxiety Disorder.

References

1. Voeller, K.K.: Attention-deficit hyperactivity disorder (ADHD). J. Child Neurol. **19**(10), 798–814 (2004)
2. Banaschewski, T., Zuddas, A., Asherson, P., Buitelaar, J.: ADHD and Hyperkinetic Disorder. Oxford Psychiatry Library (2015)
3. Muris, P.: Relation of attention control and school performance in normal children. Percept. Mot. Skills **102**(1), 78–80 (2006)

4. World Health Organization: International Classification of Functioning, Disability, and Health: Children & Youth Version: ICF-CY. World Health Organization (2007)
5. Purper-Ouakil, D., Ramoz, N., Lepagnol-Bestel, A.-M., Gorwood, P., Simonneau, M.: Neurobiology of attention deficit/hyperactivity disorder. Pediatr. Res. **69**(8), 69–76 (2011)
6. Gabaldón-Pérez, A., Dolón-Poza, M., Eckert, M., Máximo-Bocanegra, N., Martín-Ruiz, M., Pau De La Cruz, I.: Serious game for the screening of central auditory processing disorder in school-age children: development and validation study. JMIR Serious Games **11**, e40284 (2023). https://doi.org/10.2196/40284
7. American Psychiatric Association: Diagnostic and statistical manual of mental disorders: DSM-5. American Psychiatric Association, Washington, DC (2013)
8. Ramdass, D., Zimmerman, B.J.: Developing self-regulation skills: the important role of homework. J. Adv. Acad. **22**(2), 194–218 (2011)
9. Google: Firebase: A Platform for Building Mobile and Web Applications. https://firebase.google.com/ (Accessed January 2023)
10. Sarkar, S., Gayen, S., Bilgaiyan, S.: Android based home security systems using internet of things (IoT) and Firebase. In: 2018 International Conference on Inventive Research in Computing Applications (ICIRCA), pp. 102–105. IEEE (2018)
11. Li, W.-J., Yen, C., Lin, Y.-S., Tung, S.-C., Huang, S.: JustIoT Internet of Things based on the firebase real-time database. In: 2018 IEEE International Conference on Smart Manufacturing, Industrial and Logistics Engineering (SMILE), pp. 43–47 (2018)
12. Pozo-Guzman, L., Berrezueta-Guzman, J.: IoT as an alternative way to improve the telemedicine methods against COVID-19 in vulnerable zones. In: Proceedings of Conference on Information and Communication Technology, Ecuador, pp. 64–76 (2020)
13. Chandrasena, A., Weerasinghe, G.D., Dilshan, K.T., Sadun, G.P., Samarakoon, U., Ratnayake, P.: IHI:-a mobile application for ADHD analysis and detection. In: 2022 7th International Conference on Information Technology Research (ICITR), pp. 1–6. IEEE (2022)
14. Doan, M., et al.: CoolCraig: a smart watch/phone application supporting co-regulation of children with ADHD. In: Extended Abstracts of the 2020 CHI Conference on Human Factors in Computing Systems, pp. 1–7 (2020)
15. Dolón-Poza, M., Berrezueta-Guzman, J., Martín-Ruiz, M.-L.: Creation of an intelligent system to support the therapy process in children with ADHD. In: Rodriguez Morales, G., Fonseca C., E.R., Salgado, J.P., Pérez-Gosende, P., Orellana Cordero, M., Berrezueta, S. (eds.) TICEC 2020. CCIS, vol. 1307, pp. 36–50. Springer, Cham (2020). https://doi.org/10.1007/978-3-030-62833-8_4
16. Berrezueta-Guzman, J., Pau, I., Martin-Ruiz, M.-L., Maximo-Bocanegra, N.: Smart-home environment to support homework activities for children. IEEE Access **8**, 160251–160267 (2020)
17. López-Pérez, L., Berrezueta-Guzman, J., Martín-Ruiz, M.-L.: Development of a home accompaniment system providing homework assistance for children with ADHD. In: Rodriguez Morales, G., Fonseca C., E.R., Salgado, J.P., Pérez-Gosende, P., Orellana Cordero, M., Berrezueta, S. (eds.) TICEC 2020. CCIS, vol. 1307, pp. 22–35. Springer, Cham (2020). https://doi.org/10.1007/978-3-030-62833-8_3

18. Berrezueta-Guzman, J., Krusche, S., Serpa-Andrade, L., Martín-Ruiz, M.-L.: Artificial vision algorithm for behavior recognition in children with ADHD in a smart home environment. In: Proceedings of SAI Intelligent Systems Conference, pp. 661–671. Springer (2023). https://doi.org/10.1007/978-3-031-16072-1_47
19. Berrezueta-Guzman, J., Pau, I., Martin-Ruiz, M.-L., Maximo-Bocanegra, N.: Assessment of a robotic assistant for supporting homework activities of children with ADHD. IEEE Access **9**, 93450–93465 (2021)
20. Moroney, L., Moroney, L.: Cloud functions for firebase. In: The Definitive Guide to Firebase: Build Android Apps on Google's Mobile Platform, pp. 139–161 (2017)

Wearable Device Supporting Light/Dark Adaptation

Hiroki Sato, Ayumi Ohnishi(iD), Tsutomu Terada(✉)(iD),
and Masahiko Tsukamoto(iD)

Kobe University, Hyogo, Japan
hiroki-sato@stu.kobe-u.ac.jp, {ohnishi,tsutomu}@eedept.kobe-u.ac.jp,
tuka@kobe-u.ac.jp

Abstract. Human eyes maintain visual function by adapting to changes in brightness. There are two types of adaptation to changes in brightness. Light and dark adaptations occur when the surroundings become bright and dark, respectively. Human eyes cannot adapt immediately when brightness changes rapidly. Therefore, a decline in visual function and accidents can occur when entering and exiting places, such as tunnels and buildings. In this study, we proposed a wearable device that supports light/dark adaptation when brightness changes rapidly. The proposed device controls the brightness of the field of vision using LEDs and light-shielding films. Evaluation results showed that the recovery time of visual function was significantly faster with the support of light/dark adaptation using our system than without any support.

Keywords: Light adaptation · Dark adaptation · Wearable computing

1 Introduction

Human eyes can maintain the visual function by adapting to changes in ambient brightness. There are two types of adaptation to changes in brightness. Light adaptation occurs as the surroundings become brighter, while dark adaptation occurs as the surroundings become darker. Human eyes cannot immediately adapt to rapid changes in brightness [1]. Therefore, visual function declines, and accidents may occur when brightness changes rapidly in real-life situations. For example, when driving in and out of tunnels, there is a risk of accidents because of rapid changes in brightness that make it challenging to observe the surroundings clearly. In this study, we propose a wearable device that supports light/dark adaptation. The device controls the brightness of the field of vision only when the brightness changes rapidly. Figure 1 shows a prototype of the proposed device. The proposed device has two functions to support light adaptation. One is to accustom the eyes to brightness by illuminating them with LED light just before the ambient light becomes bright. The other is to moderate rapid changes in brightness by using light-shielding films immediately after the ambient light becomes bright. To support dark adaptation, the proposed device has a function to accustom the eyes to darkness by using light-shielding

P. Delir Haghighi et al. (Eds.): MoMM 2023, LNCS 14417, pp. 120–125, 2023.
https://doi.org/10.1007/978-3-031-48348-6_10

LED light illuminates eyes.   Light-shielding films covers eyes.

Fig. 1. Prototype Device Attached.

films just before the ambient light becomes dark. In the experiment, we assessed whether the three functions of the prototype could reduce visual acuity loss when brightness changes rapidly in the experimental environment.

2 Related Work

Humans can see objects under various brightness conditions by light/dark adaptation. However, eyes cannot immediately adapt to rapid changes in brightness. This can result in a decline in visual function, such as visual acuity and color discrimination ability [3,4]. When the ambient brightness changes rapidly, there is a risk of accidents because visual function declines until the eye adapts. For example, there is a risk of crashing owing to the decline in visual function caused by rapid changes in ambient brightness when driving in and out of tunnels. Pervez et al. found that there is a high risk of accidents at tunnel entrances and exits [5]. In addition, even while walking, there is a risk of stumbling and crashing by rapid changes in ambient brightness when entering or exiting a building. To prevent such risks, we propose a device that suppresses the decline in visual function by accustoming eyes to changes in brightness in advance, and enabling eyes to quickly adapt to rapid changes in brightness.

Some studies supported visual function by using head-mounted displays (HMDs) to adapt to changes in ambient brightness. Hiroi et al. developed a device called AdaptiVisor that supports adaptation [2]. It reduces the rapid changes in the display brightness by darkening excessively bright areas and brightening excessively dark areas in the field of vision. Thus, seeing through the display narrows the field of vision and reduces visual information. To avoid such limitations, the proposed device enables the user to directly observe the surroundings, except when the brightness changes rapidly. Wicue proposed eShades, which are instant-dimming sunglasses that automatically adjust the light transmittance of the lenses in response to the ambient brightness [6]. eShades constantly control the brightness of the field of vision and cannot help the eye to adapt. It is difficult to observe the surrounding objects and scenery in their true colors. In addition, it is difficult to observe the surroundings in dark places because there is an upper limit to the light transmittance of the lenses. Support for visual function should be such that users can see the surrounding colors correctly. The proposed device swiftly controls the brightness of the field of vision only when the brightness changes rapidly, and supports light/dark adaptation to suppress the decline in visual function. It enables the user to see the true colors of surrounding objects and scenery, except when the brightness changes rapidly.

Fig. 2. Device Configuration.

3   Proposed Device

We propose a wearable device that supports light/dark adaptation when the ambient brightness changes rapidly between the inside and outside of rooms, buildings, tunnels, etc. Figure 2 shows a prototype of the proposed device. The prototype predicts the changes in brightness and supports light/dark adaptation. In adaptation support, the prototype controls the brightness of the field of vision with a microcontroller that controls a tape-like LED attached to the top of the glasses and motors at both ends of the glasses that quickly move two pieces of light-shielding films up and down. The motors independently raise and lower the light-shielding films to change the number of pieces covering the eyes. To support light adaptation, a film with a visible light transmittance of 71 % was installed on the outside, and a film with a visible light transmittance of 50 % was installed on the inside. To support dark adaptation, both films with a visible light transmittance of 50 % were installed. In addition, a distance sensor and an illuminance sensor, attached to both ends of the glasses, predict rapid changes in ambient brightness when transitioning from one place to another through a door.

The prototype has two functions to support light adaptation, one to support dark adaptation, and the other to predict rapid changes in brightness. In the light adaptation support using LEDs, the device illuminates eyes with LED light to enable them to adapt to the brightness of the surroundings before the surroundings become bright. Therefore, the user can quickly adapt to the rapid changes in brightness and reduce the deterioration of the visual function. In the light adaptation support using two light-shielding films, the device lowers two light-shielding films immediately after the ambient light becomes bright to reduce the amount of light entering the eyes, and then raises light-shielding films individually to slow the change in brightness. Therefore, the user can quickly adapt to the rapid changes in brightness and reduce the deterioration of the visual function. In the dark adaptation support, the device covers the eyes with two light-shielding films to enable the eyes to adjust to the darkness before the surroundings become dark. Therefore, the user can quickly adapt to the rapid changes in brightness and reduce the deterioration of the visual function. As

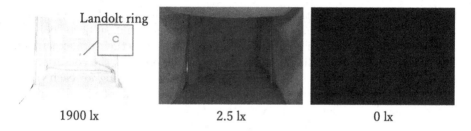

Landolt ring

1900 lx   2.5 lx   0 lx

Fig. 3. Experimental environment for each illuminance level.

illustrated above, our adaptation-supporting methods need to predict the timing of a drastic change in ambient brightness beforehand. The prediction function in our method predicts the timing using wearable sensors; a distance sensor detects the user's approach to the door, and an illuminance sensor predicts the brightness behind the door by measuring ambient illuminance.

4   Experiment

In this experiment, we evaluated whether the functions of the prototype to support light/dark adaptation would suppress visual acuity loss when brightness changes rapidly indoors. We used visual acuity as an evaluation index, in line with previous studies [7]. We evaluated each function of the prototype by measuring the time between a rapid change in brightness and recovery from visual acuity loss. The measured time is referred to as the recovery time of visual acuity. We used a Landolt ring to measure visual acuity. Figure 3 shows the experimental environment for each illuminance level. The illuminance was 1900 lx, 2.5 lx, and 0 lx. The subjects began measuring time with a stopwatch when they switched the illuminance. Subsequently, the subjects stopped measuring time immediately after they saw the direction of the Landolt ring. We recruited 12 subjects (11 male and one female) aged 20s for the experiment. Before the experiment, we measured the subjects' visual acuity in both eyes using a Landolt ring at 1900 lx and 2.5 lx illumination. In the experiment, we used the smallest size of the Landolt ring in which the subjects could determine its direction. We set the time for light adaptation support using LEDs and dark adaptation support using a light-shielding film to 3 s, considering that the prototype could predict the brightness 3 s at most before changes occurred. In addition, we set the time for dark adaptation support to 5 s, considering that dark adaptation takes longer time than light adaptation. After the experiment, we asked if the subjects had any concerns about light/dark adaptation.

Evaluation for Light Adaptation The subjects waited for 5 min in a dark area with an illumination of 0 lx, and then switched to an ambient illumination of 1900 lx. We performed one of the three conditions: no support (referred to as L_N), light adaptation support using LEDs (referred to as L_L), and light adaptation support using light-shielding films (referred to as L_F) at the timing of the brightness switch. One trial was performed up to this point. Furthermore, we performed the experiment in other conditions. After each trial, subjects looked at the outside scenery for 1 min and then moved their eyes to their pre-experiment state of adaptation. In addition, we randomized the order of the conditions for each subject. We also changed the direction of the Landolt ring for each trial.

Figure 4(a) shows a graph of the average recovery time of visual acuity in L_L for all subjects when the recovery time in L_N is set to 1. A t-test on L_N and L_L showed that L_L had a significantly shorter recovery time of visual acuity than L_N ($t(11) = 4.67$, $p < 0.05$). Thus, light adaptation support using LEDs suppressed visual acuity loss. In addition, according to some subjects, the LED lights made it difficult to observe the upper part of the field of vision. Figure 4(b) shows a graph of the average recovery time of visual acuity in L_F for all subjects when the recovery time in L_N is set to 1. A t-test on L_N and L_F showed that L_L had a significantly shorter recovery time of visual acuity than L_N ($t(11) = 2.28$, $p < 0.05$). Thus, light adaptation support using light-shielding films suppressed visual acuity loss.

Evaluation for Dark Adaptation The subjects waited for 1 min in a light area with an illumination of 1900 lx, and then switched to an ambient illumination of 2.5 lx. We performed one of the three conditions: no support (referred to as D_N), 3 s of dark adaptation support using light-shielding films (referred to as D_{F3}), or 5 s of dark adaptation support using light-shielding films (referred to as D_{F5}) at the timing of the brightness switch. One trial was performed up to this point. Moreover, we performed the experiment in other conditions. After each trial, subjects looked at the outside scenery for 1 min and then moved their eyes to their pre-experiment state of adaptation. In addition, we randomized the order of the conditions for each subject. We also changed the direction of the Landolt ring for each trial.

Figure 4(c) shows a graph of the average recovery time of visual acuity in D_{F3} and D_{F5} for all subjects when the recovery time in D_N is set to 1. We performed a one-factor within-participant analysis of variance, using the recovery time of visual acuity of each subject in the three conditions of D_N, D_{F3}, and D_{F5} as samples. The results showed that D_{F3} and D_{F5} had significantly shorter recovery times of visual acuity than D_N ($F(2,22) = 21.29$, $p < 0.05$). Thus, the 3 s and 5 s of dark adaptation support using light-shielding films suppressed visual acuity loss.

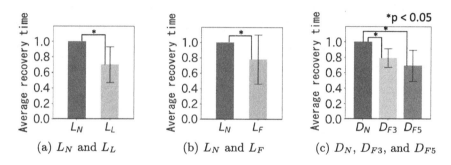

Fig. 4. The average recovery time of visual acuity.

5 Conclusion

We proposed a wearable device that supported light/dark adaptation to suppress the decline of visual function during rapid changes in brightness. The prototype supports the user's light/dark adaptation by using LEDs and light-shielding films to control the brightness of the field of vision. Furthermore, it predicts the timing of rapid brightness changes in situations, such as entering or leaving a door. In the experiment, we confirmed that the prototype could suppress visual acuity loss when the ambient brightness changed rapidly in the experimental environment. In the future, we will evaluate whether the prototype can support light/dark adaptation in an outdoor environment. In addition, we will improve the device to ensure that it can predict the timing of rapid changes in brightness by analyzing the brightness of the scenery toward the direction of the user.

Acknowledgement. This work was supported by JST CREST Grant Number JPMJCR18A3, Japan.

References

1. Dowling, J.E.: The Retina: An Approachable Part of the Brain, Harvard University Press (1987)
2. Hiroi, Y., Itoh, Y., Hamasaki, T., Sugimoto, M.: AdaptiVisor: assisting eye adaptation via occlusive optical see-through head-mounted displays. In: Proceedings of the 8th Augmented Human International Conference (AH 2017), no. 9, pp. 1–9 (2017)
3. Stevens, J.C., Stevens, S.S.: Brightness function: effects of adaptation. J. Opt. Soc. Am. **53**(3), 375–385 (1963)
4. Hunt, R.W.G.: Light and dark adaptation and the perception of color. J. Opt. Soc. Am. **42**(3), 190–199 (1952)
5. Pervez, A., Huang, H., Lee, J., Han, C., Wang, J., Zhang, X.: Crash analysis of expressway long tunnels using a seven-zone analytic approach. J. Transp. Saf. Secur. **13**(1), 108–122 (2019)
6. Wicue: Electronic Smart Sunglasses - Smart Eyewear - Products. https://www.wicue.com/info/109.html. Accessed 28 Apr 2023
7. Brown, J.L., Graham, C.H., Leibowitz, H., Ranken, H.B.: Luminance thresholds for the resolution of visual detail during dark adaptation. J. Opt. Soc. Am. **43**(3), 197–202 (1953)

Image and Video Processing

Face to Face with Efficiency: Real-Time Face Recognition Pipelines on Embedded Devices

Philipp Hofer[1]([✉]), Michael Roland[1], Philipp Schwarz[2], and René Mayrhofer[1]

[1] Johannes Kepler University Linz, Institute of Networks and Security, Linz, Austria
{philipp.hofer,roland,rm}@ins.jku.at
[2] Johannes Kepler University Linz, LIT Secure and Correct Systems Lab,
Linz, Austria
philipp.schwarz@jku.at

Abstract. While real-time face recognition has become increasingly popular, its use in decentralized systems and on embedded hardware presents numerous challenges. One challenge is the trade-off between accuracy and inference-time on constrained hardware resources. While achieving higher accuracy is desirable, it comes at the cost of longer inference-time. We first conduct a comparative study on the effect of using different face recognition distance functions and introduce a novel inference-time/accuracy plot to facilitate the comparison of different face recognition models. Every application must strike a balance between inference-time and accuracy, depending on its focus. To achieve optimal performance across the spectrum, we propose a combination of multiple models with distinct characteristics. This allows the system to address the weaknesses of individual models and to optimize performance based on the specific needs of the application.

We demonstrate the practicality of our proposed approach by utilizing two face detection models positioned at either end of the inference-time/accuracy spectrum to develop a multimodel face recognition pipeline. By integrating these models on an embedded device, we are able to achieve superior overall accuracy, reliability, and speed; improving the trade-off between inference-time and accuracy by striking an optimal balance between the performance of the two models, with the more accurate model being utilized when necessary and the faster model being employed for generating fast proposals. The proposed pipeline can be used as a guideline for developing real-time face recognition systems on embedded devices.

This work has been carried out within the scope of Digidow, the Christian Doppler Laboratory for Private Digital Authentication in the Physical World and has partially been supported by the LIT Secure and Correct Systems Lab. We gratefully acknowledge financial support by the Austrian Federal Ministry of Labour and Economy, the National Foundation for Research, Technology and Development, the Christian Doppler Research Association, 3 Banken IT GmbH, ekey biometric systems GmbH, Kepler Universitätsklinikum GmbH, NXP Semiconductors Austria GmbH & Co KG, Österreichische Staatsdruckerei GmbH, and the State of Upper Austria.

P. Delir Haghighi et al. (Eds.): MoMM 2023, LNCS 14417, pp. 129–143, 2023.
https://doi.org/10.1007/978-3-031-48348-6_11

Keywords: Face recognition pipeline · efficiency · embedded devices · face detection · inference-time/accuracy

1 Introduction

Biometric authentication in physical environments is becoming more and more widespread. For the past decade, each Chinese person has been given a score that changes depending on how the person's decisions are in line with the government [15]. In India, each person is assigned a 12-digit number, which is continuously supplemented with biometric characteristics and is required for many parts of life, such as banking, traveling, and even being admitted to schools [20]. In the Russian metro, there is a face recognition payment system [17]. The EU plans an entry/exit system, where fingerprints and facial images of travelers from third-countries will be collected [6]. These applications paint a scary picture for a privacy conscious user; biometrics from millions, in some cases billions, of users are stored in a single logical location. All requests for information must go through that point, creating a single point of failure that can be exploited by attackers or misused by operators:

1. A central place with potentially billions of personal data is an excellent target for technical, legal, and organizational attacks. Unfortunately, even with the highest security precautions, data breaches happen again and again, even (or especially) with the largest providers[1].
2. People must trust their providers. Users have to rely on the operator's integrity to ensure that their biometric data is only used for its intended purpose, without being shared or exploited for other purposes. Users have limited control over their data once it is collected.

To mitigate the risks associated with centralized biometric data storage, a decentralized approach is considered the gold standard [16]. By distributing biometric data across multiple instances, each instance becomes less attractive to potential attackers. However, decentralization also introduces additional complexity to the system, as Wolpert's no free lunch theorem suggests [22]: the gain in security comes at the cost of a more complex system.

One of the complexities associated with decentralized systems is the data economy perspective, whereby several smaller organizations operate sensors to reduce the amount of data available to any single entity [19]. As a result, decentralized systems aim to support as many sensors as possible by minimizing hardware requirements.

To address these challenges, this paper proposes an efficient face pipeline architecture capable of running on embedded systems. We tested its real-world behavior by mounting three cameras in front of our office doors and running the proposed pipeline. Furthermore, we evaluated if new systems and biometric architectures should provide additional metrics, to be able to make a

---

[1] A list with recent large-scale data breaches is visualized at https://informationisbeautiful.net/visualizations/worlds-biggest-data-breaches-hacks/.

more informed decision while deciding between components for face recognition pipelines.

Overall, this research underscores the importance of prioritizing security in biometric data management while considering the trade-offs between security and complexity in designing decentralized systems.

2   Background

Authenticating a person using biometrics requires two main steps: face detection, followed by face recognition. First, the system must accurately detect and locate the face within the image or video frame. Once the face is detected, the system can then extract the relevant facial features necessary for recognition. Recognition involves comparing these features to a database of known faces to determine the identity of the individual. Therefore, accurate detection and recognition are essential for effective and reliable biometric authentication.

The Labeled Faces in the Wild (LFW) dataset [18] is a widely-used benchmark dataset in the field of computer vision to assess the performance of recognition models. This dataset has become an important standard in the field and is commonly used for performance comparisons between different models and comprises over 13,000 images of faces with variations in pose, lighting, and facial expressions. As there are multiple images of the same person, the dataset is suitable for evaluating face recognition models. We utilized the dataset for evaluating the performance of both face recognition and face detection models. To evaluate face recognition models, LFW provides a test dataset that contains 3,000 true positive and 3,000 true negative matches.

Specifically, we used a metric in which a predicted bounding box is considered successful if it has an overlap of more than 50 % with the ground truth bounding box. This metric was chosen as it is a commonly used standard for evaluating the performance of face detection models on the LFW dataset, e.g. by Yang et al. [23]. By employing this metric, we were able to quantitatively measure and compare the accuracy of different face detection models.

2.1   Face Detection

Face detection is a computer vision task that identifies the presence and location of human faces in digital images and video frames. With the increasing demand for facial recognition technology, a wide variety of face detection models have been developed. Each model has certain advantages over their competitors. Some focus on finding tiny faces [12], occluded faces [11], or using multiple camera angles [7].

In order to quantify the quality of networks and being able to compare different models, they are evaluated on publicly available datasets. There is a focus on accuracy: Wider Face [23] shows precision-recall curve, LFW [18] shows the ROC-curve and the corresponding area under curve, VGGFace2 [2] shows false(-positive)-acceptance-rates and rank-accuracies, UMD Faces [1] shows the normalized mean error.

In this section, we will provide a brief overview of four popular choices of face detection networks.

Retinaface is based on a single-shot detector framework and uses a fully convolutional neural network (FCN) to detect faces in images. The architecture of Retinaface consists of three main components: a backbone network, a multiscale feature pyramid network, and three task-specific heads.

The backbone network is responsible for feature extraction and is typically a pre-trained ResNet or MobileNet. The feature pyramid network then takes the feature maps generated by the backbone network and produces a set of multiscale feature maps. Finally, the task-specific heads, which consist of a classification head, a regression head, and a landmark head, are applied to each of the feature maps to predict the presence of a face, its bounding box, and its facial landmarks.

ULFGFD is specifically designed to be lightweight and suitable for deployment on edge computing devices. The small size, just over 1 MB, stands out in particular. The network is based on a single-shot detector (SSD) architecture and consists of a backbone network and a prediction network. The backbone network is a lightweight MobileNetV2 architecture that is used to extract features from input images. The prediction network consists of a set of convolutional layers that are used to predict the bounding boxes and confidence scores of faces in the input images.

ULFGFD also uses a feature pyramid network (FPN) to detect faces at different scales. The FPN consists of a set of convolutional layers that are used to generate feature maps at different resolutions. These feature maps are then used to predict the bounding boxes and confidence scores of faces at different scales.

YuNet is a deep neural network architecture designed for efficient face detection and recognition in real-world scenarios [8].

YuNet is composed of three main components: a lightweight backbone network, a feature pyramid network (FPN), and a detection head. The backbone network is based on MobileNetV2, a popular architecture known for its efficiency and low computational cost.

The detection head of YuNet is responsible for predicting the locations of faces in the input image. It consists of a set of convolutional layers followed by two parallel branches. One branch performs classification to determine whether a given region of the image contains a face or not, while the other branch performs regression to predict the bounding box coordinates of the face.

Haarcascade is a widely used computer vision algorithm for face detection, having been introduced by Viola and Jones as early as 2001 [21]. Despite being around for over two decades, Haarcascade remains a popular choice for face detection in various applications due to its simplicity, efficiency, and effectiveness.

The Haarcascade algorithm works by using a series of classifiers to detect faces within an image. Each classifier is composed of a set of weak learners, which are typically decision trees that evaluate simple features such as edges and corners. These features are calculated on a sliding window that moves across the image, with the goal of detecting faces at different scales and orientations.

One limitation of Haarcascade is that it can be sensitive to changes in lighting conditions and occlusion, which can result in false positives or missed detections.

2.2 Face Recognition

Face recognition is the process of identifying an individual based on their distinctive facial features. In recent years, the accuracy, reliability, and efficiency of this process have increased significantly due to advancements in deep learning algorithms and the availability of large datasets.

The majority of state-of-the-art (SOTA) algorithms requires a pre-processed RGB image as input, which is then used to create a high-dimensional vector that represents the individual's facial features. To ensure that the images are properly pre-processed, it is necessary to use landmarks from the individual's face. Typically, these landmarks consist of the eye, nose, and mouth points, which are used to ensure that the image is properly aligned and scaled.

For our pipeline, we tested a single instance of a state-of-the-art face recognition model. This decision was based on two factors: the model's negligible inference-time compared to face detection and its near-perfect accuracy. Therefore, our primary focus was not on selecting the best-performing face recognition model, but on optimizing the pipeline's overall efficiency.

Arcface. Arcface [4] is a SOTA face recognition method that uses a neural network-based approach to extract discriminative features from faces. The technical details of Arcface include a modified ResNet architecture with a large embedding size, a novel angular softmax loss function, and specific optimization techniques. The ResNet architecture consists of several convolutional layers, which extract features from the input face image. The embedding size of Arcface is a 512 dimensional floating point array.

Arcface is trained using a custom loss function (*Arcface loss*), based on cosine similarity between features because it enforces more inter-class discrepancy. Different distance functions are used for comparing two embeddings in practice. Typically, the L2 loss function is used as distance measurement. However, in certain applications different distance functions are preferable. For example, a zero knowledge proof might need an inner product for efficient calculation, therefore cosine distance might be the preferred function.

3   State-of-the-Art Face Recognition Pipeline

The typical SOTA setup for image-based face recognition consists of the following components:

Camera → Detection → Recognition → Comparison

The inference time is heavily influenced by the size of the retrieved camera image. For this paper, we assume that the camera produces 4K images. For the default pipeline, we use Retinaface [3] as face detection model because it has SOTA accuracy on many datasets and returns face landmarks which are needed for face recognition. Similarly, Arcface [4] is used because it gives SOTA accuracy.

Two embeddings are compared using a distance function. There has been no study on the impact of using different distance functions during inference. Therefore, we evaluated the impact of three popular distance metrics used with Arcface, namely absolute, L2, and cosine distance. We calculated the embeddings of the 6,000 test image-pairs from the LFW dataset and followed their protocol to verify the accuracy of Arcface using different distance metrics. Our findings reveal that the choice of distance metric does not have a significant effect on the analysis outcome. The precision-recall plot presented in Fig. 1 indicates only minor differences, which are only visible if we zoom in on the plot. The inference time is not affected significantly as well, our benchmark indicates roughly 1 μs computation time for all three variants (L2: $1.0939\,\mu s \pm 3.9\,ns$, Cos-Dist: $1.1549\,\mu s \pm 20.9\,ns$, absolute: $1.0956\,\mu s \pm 8.6\,ns$).

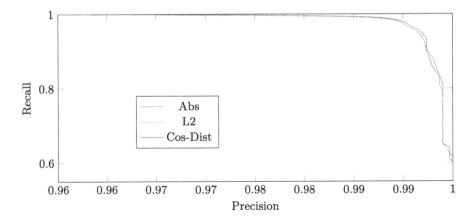

Fig. 1. Different distance functions for Arcface. Notice the magnified scale; plotting the whole spectrum (0-1) would yield no discernible distinction. The green line is not visible, as using L2 and COS distance functions yields an identical precision-recall curve. The Area Under Curve (AUC) is not significantly different either: $AUC_{L2} = 0.99884653$, $AUC_{ABS} = 0.9988512$, $AUC_{COS} = 0.99884653$. (Color figure online)

Due to popular use, the L2 norm is used for the rest of this paper. This gives us the following architecture for our default pipeline:

Camera → Detection → Recognition → Comparison
4k images   Retinaface   Arcface   L2 Norm

3.1   Performance

In order to establish a baseline for the performance, we implemented the pipeline in Rust using Tensorflow Lite (Retinaface and ULFGFD) and OpenCV (YuNet and Haarcascade). Due to popularity, all benchmarks are executed on a Jetson Nano[2], with an NVIDIA Maxwell GPU and a Quad-core ARM Cortex-A57 MPCore CPU.

There are two distinct performance metrics:

1. With respect to **time**: We established benchmarks using Criterion [10]. To ensure statistical significance and reliability, each component underwent 100 iterations, and the reported time is based on the median of these runs. The variance is less than 4.8% of the value for all components. It is noteworthy that the times reported are calculated per image, with Retinaface requiring a total of 91 s for inference.

$$\underbrace{\text{Camera (4k)}}_{0.02\,s} \rightarrow \underbrace{\text{Retinaface}}_{91\,s} \rightarrow \underbrace{\text{Arcface}}_{0.071\,s} \rightarrow \underbrace{\text{Comparison}}_{0.000028\,s}$$

Retrieving the 4k image from the camera is possible at that frequency, because hardware acceleration and MJPG compression are used.

2. With respect to **accuracy**: We use the 6,000 face comparisons proposed by LFW [18] and run the face recognition pipeline on it. If multiple faces are found, the one closest to the center is used, as the LFW images are pre-processed in that way. Retinaface manages to find all faces. As LFW primarily features single-person portraits, this accuracy was expected. Arcface uses the best threshold on that dataset to decide if the two faces are from the same person.

$$\text{Camera (4k)} \rightarrow \underbrace{\text{Retinaface}}_{100\%} \rightarrow \underbrace{\text{Arcface}}_{99.3\%} \rightarrow \text{Comparison}$$

3.2   Improvements

Time-performance (1.5 min per 4K image) is arguably too slow for real-time performance. Most time (99.9%) is spent on Retinaface. There are two options to reduce the inference time:

1. Reduce the input dimension, which yields the following time-performance:
   - 4k (3840×2160px): 91.24 s
   - Full HD (1920×1080px): 11.52 s
   - HD (1280×720px): 5.13 s
   - SD (640×480px): 1.72 s

---

[2] https://www.nvidia.com/en-us/autonomous-machines/embedded-systems/jetson-nano/.

How is accuracy-performance affected if input dimension is reduced? The theoretical lower-limit is detecting people of size 16 px × 16 px, as this is the smallest anchor used by Retinaface. We tested if such small faces are detected in practice. Starting with LFW's image size of 250 px × 250 px, we run our face recognition pipeline over all (test) images to determine the detected face size. Subsequently, the images were scaled down by 50 pixels, and the experiment was repeated until the image size was 50 × 50 px. The resulting face sizes were recorded. Figure 2 illustrates the widths and heights in pixels for detected faces. It is apparent that the smallest anchors are not only used for sub-features (for use in higher levels of the FPN [13]), but also to directly detect faces. Interestingly, the smallest detected face has a dimension of 10 px × 14 px. This is smaller than the smallest anchor (16 px × 16 px) and possible because the network refines its predicted bounding box in later stages.

Despite the successful detection of faces, there is no guarantee that the image has enough information for face recognition to recognize a person. Therefore, we created another experiment by performing the same shrinking of the images as before. An embedding of the scaled down version of the image is (L2) compared to the embedding of the full image. The results are plotted in Fig. 3.

As anticipated, our analysis reveals a distinct threshold at approximately 40 × 30 pixels, beyond which facial recognition accuracy is substantially diminished.

Even though an image of SD quality still has an inference time of 1.7 s, it skips 99.69% of potential input data (25,600 vs 8,294,400 pixel).

We can calculate the real-world impact of this dimension reduction. For this calculation, we need a few hardware assumptions.

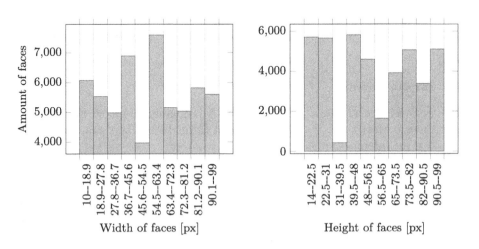

Fig. 2. The sizes of detected faces using Retinaface. Sizes larger than 99 pixels are not displayed as our focus was on identifying the smallest detectable faces.

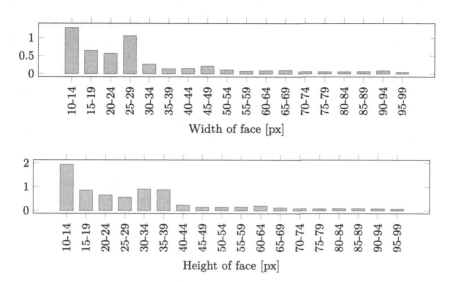

Fig. 3. L2 distance to reference embedding (full size face) using different face sizes (smaller is better).

- **Face dimensions** Being able to detect an object depends on its size. Since we want to detect a face, we have to assume the dimensions. The US Department of Defense measured the width (bitragion breadth) and height (menton-crinion length) of the face to be between 12–15 cm and 15–21 cm, respectively [5]. We want to find the lower limit of face recognition pipelines possibilities. Therefore, we use the upper end of the face dimension scale:

$$\text{face}_{\text{width}} = 0.15 \text{ m}, \text{face}_{\text{height}} = 0.21 \text{ m}$$

- **Camera** For the camera, we assume typical 70 mm focal length with a full frame 35 mm sensor:

$$\text{camera}_{\text{focallength}} = 0.07 \text{ m}$$

$$\text{camera}_{\text{imagewidth}} = 35 \text{ mm}, \text{camera}_{\text{imageheight}} = 24 \text{ mm}$$

Figure 3 demonstrates that facial recognition can reliably commence at sizes as small as 40×30 pixels.

$$\text{object}_{\text{width}} = 30 \text{ px}, \text{object}_{\text{height}} = 40 \text{ px}$$

We can now calculate the maximum distance in millimeters of a person with respect to the camera, such that the face is still recognizable:

$$\text{distance} = \frac{\text{camera}_{\text{focallength}} \times \text{pixel}_{\text{width/height}} \times \text{face}_{\text{width/height}}}{\text{object}_{\text{width/height}} \times \text{camera}_{\text{imagewidth/imageheight}}}$$

If we use pixel$_{width/height}$ of 640 and 480 respectively, we can detect faces up to 6.4 m. With a pixel$_{width/height}$ of 3840 and 2880 this distance increases to 38.4 m.

2. Use a different, more lightweight model. Due to the use of a large backbone network (ResNet [9]) and its computationally heavy use of feature pyramid networks [13], the inference time of Retinaface is slow. There are lighter networks with fewer parameters, such as ULFGFD. One major deficiency of fast face detection algorithms is their tendency to produce false positives. Retinaface, on the other hand, has been shown to have a very low false positive rate, making it a more reliable option for these types of applications.

As face recognition expects a pre-processed image and this pre-processing depends on the location of landmarks, it is not possible to calculate face recognition accuracy with ULFGFD.

4   Inference-Time/Accuracy Tradeoff

The accuracy of face detection models has been extensively studied and reported in modern research (as demonstrated by the reported metrics described in Sect. 2.1). However, an often overlooked aspect in the evaluation of these models is their inference time. This information is important, as a slow inference time can lead to delays and long queues, compromising the effectiveness of the system (cf. Sect. 3.1). Inference time can also impact the scalability and cost-effectiveness of a face detection system, as a slow model may require more powerful hardware or computing resources to achieve the desired performance. Furthermore, inference time is especially important when considering the deployment of face detection models on embedded hardware. These devices often have limited computing resources and require models that can perform in real-time. Therefore, evaluating face detection models based on their inference time is essential for ensuring that they can be deployed effectively on embedded hardware and meet the performance requirements of real-world applications. Despite its critical importance in real-world deployment scenarios, none of the existing datasets currently available comprehensively address this aspect of performance evaluation. As a result, there is a significant gap in our understanding of the practical implications of face detection model performance in real-world settings.

This paper evaluates SOTA face detection models with respect to these metrics. We assessed the performance and accuracy of four face detection models, Retinaface [3], ULFGFD [14], YuNet [8], and Haarcascade [21]. In this paper, Fig. 4 illustrates the space of performance-accuracy for current models. It is important to note that only the networks situated at the border of the performance-accuracy spectrum are relevant, and their selection depends on the specific application requirements. Different applications may require different points on the performance-accuracy spectrum, and our study provides insights into the trade-offs involved in selecting an appropriate face detection model for a given application. Our results, depicted in Fig. 4, clearly show that Haarcascade has a detection failure rate of over 50%, even for the relatively simple portrait-like datasets such as the LFW dataset. Retinaface achieves high accuracy but requires high inference time, while ULFGFD has lower accuracy but a faster inference time.

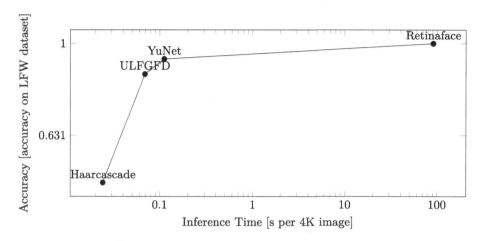

Fig. 4. The figure illustrates the trade-off between inference-time and accuracy for various face detection networks. The x-axis represents the inference time, while the y-axis represents the accuracy of the networks. The solid line in the figure represents the Pareto frontier, which is the optimal trade-off between accuracy and inference time.

5   Fast and Accurate Face Recognition Pipeline

In order to optimize face detection for both speed and accuracy, we propose an approach that combines two algorithms with distinct characteristics in the inference/time spectrum to harvest the strengths of each. A fast algorithm is used as a proposal generator to quickly create possible face detections. We prioritize minimizing false negatives in the proposal generator, as false positives can be verified by the subsequent algorithm. While our analysis shows Haarcascade to be the fastest method, it misses more than half of the faces even in the easy LFW dataset. Therefore, we use ULFGFD as our algorithm for generating proposals. These proposals are then confirmed and augmented with face landmarks by a more accurate algorithm, Retinaface. This yields the following pipeline:

Camera (4k) → ULFGFD → Retinaface → Arcface → Comparison

As discussed in Sect. 3, face recognition requires face dimensions of at least 30 px × 40 px. To achieve higher accuracy, we recommend using face images with dimensions of 50 px × 65 px or larger. Our experimental results indicate that performance degrades when face images are smaller than this threshold.

As the pipeline should take bounding box errors of ULFGFD into account, we performed a systematic search on a grid of possible dimensions and performed additional benchmarks on Retinaface with respect to inference time:

- 150 px × 150 px: 0.169 s
- 125 px × 125 px: 0.093 s
- 100 px × 100 px: 0.052 s
- 75 px × 75 px: 0.038 s
- 50 px × 50 px: 0.018 s

Subsequently, we constructed the complete pipeline and evaluated the accuracy of each individual component as follows:

$$\text{Camera (4k)} \rightarrow \underbrace{\text{ULFGFD}_{th=0.05}}_{96.45\%} \rightarrow \begin{matrix} \underbrace{\text{Retinaface}_{50\times50}}_{73.2\%} & \underbrace{\text{Arcface}}_{92.3\%} \\ \underbrace{\text{Retinaface}_{75\times75}}_{86.1\%} & \underbrace{\text{Arcface}}_{95.3\%} \\ \underbrace{\text{Retinaface}_{100\times100}}_{98.3\%} & \underbrace{\text{Arcface}}_{97.3\%} \\ \underbrace{\text{Retinaface}_{125\times125}}_{98.9\%} & \underbrace{\text{Arcface}}_{97.7\%} \\ \underbrace{\text{Retinaface}_{150\times150}}_{99.7\%} & \underbrace{\text{Arcface}}_{98.3\%} \end{matrix} \rightarrow \text{Comparison}$$

A size of 100 px × 100 px for the Retinaface input seems to be a good tradeoff between time and accuracy performance. With this, the full pipeline runs on $\sim$ 4.7 FPS on a Jetson Nano and achieves an overall accuracy of 92.3% (0.9645 ∗ 0.983 ∗ 0.973) on the LFW dataset.

Next, we can calculate both the inference time and accuracy of the full pipeline with these three combinations of networks and compare it to existing algorithms. Figure 5 clearly demonstrates that by integrating multiple different networks, the trade-off border in the inference-time/accuracy spectrum is increased and a better balance between these two metrics is achieved. This indicates the effectiveness of our approach in improving face detection performance.

Notably, the selection of suboptimal parameters, as observed in Fast50 and Fast75, can lead to an unexpected outcome where the desired effect is inverted. Specifically, this may result in a decrease in accuracy despite a slower inference time. Therefore, it is crucial to carefully select appropriate parameters by utilizing techniques such as analyzing the inference-time/accuracy plot to ensure the desired performance outcome is achieved.

6 Future Work

To improve the efficiency of face detection systems, future work can analyze the impact on inference time and accuracy if positional information of previously detected faces are utilized to narrow down the search area in subsequent readings,

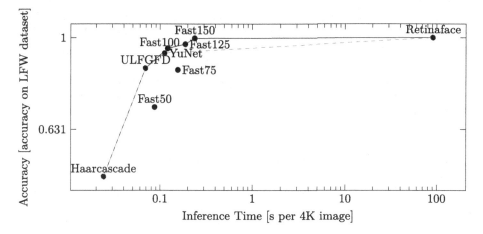

Fig. 5. This plot adds our proposed models to the initial plot of Fig. 4, which is represented by the dashed line. Our proposed Fast100, Fast 125, and Fast150 networks increase the Pareto front in the *inference-time/accuracy* spectrum, as visualized in the solid line. Fast50 and Fast75 do not increase the border, as they are slower and have less accuracy than ULFGFD.

instead of scanning the entire image each time. This strategy can significantly reduce the computational cost and time required for the detection process.

Furthermore, to enhance the system's resilience and prevent it from being deceived by fake representations, such as videos or photos, a liveness detection mechanism can be incorporated. This mechanism can distinguish between the presence of an actual person in front of the camera and a non-living representation, such as a still image or a pre-recorded video. By incorporating such a mechanism, our system can be more reliable and effective in real-world scenarios where security and authenticity are crucial factors.

7   Conclusion

In recent years, real-time face recognition has become increasingly popular, particularly for applications in decentralized systems and on embedded hardware. However, this popularity has come with several challenges, including the trade-off between accuracy and inference-time on constrained hardware resources. Achieving higher accuracy is desirable, but it often comes at the cost of longer inference-time, which is particularly problematic for embedded devices with limited processing power.

To address this challenge, we conducted a comparative study to investigate the effect of using different face recognition distance functions. Future datasets and models should include inference time as a metric for performance evaluation. This will allow researchers to better understand the trade-offs between accuracy and efficiency in real-world deployment scenarios, and enable the development of more effective and efficient face detection models that can be deployed in real-world applications. By including inference time as a metric, the practical relevance of face detection research is improved and models can be optimized for real-world deployment. We also introduced a novel inference-time/accuracy plot that enables the comparison of different face recognition models. Our analysis showed that different models have different strengths and weaknesses, and every application must strike a balance between inference-time and accuracy, depending on its focus.

To achieve optimal performance across the spectrum, we proposed a combination of multiple models with distinct characteristics. This approach allows the system to address the weaknesses of individual models and optimize performance based on the specific needs of the application. We demonstrated the practicality of our proposed approach by developing a multimodel face recognition pipeline. We utilized two face detection models positioned at either end of the inference-time/accuracy spectrum to achieve superior overall accuracy, reliability, and speed. Specifically, we employed the more accurate model when necessary and the faster model for generating fast proposals, thereby improving the trade-off between inference-time and accuracy.

Overall, our proposed pipeline can serve as a guideline for developing real-time face recognition systems on embedded devices. By striking an optimal balance between the performance of different models, we can improve the overall accuracy, reliability, and speed of such systems.

References

1. Bansal, A., Nanduri, A., Castillo, C.D., Ranjan, R., Chellappa, R.: UMDFaces: an annotated face dataset for training deep networks. In: IEEE International Joint Conference on Biometrics (IJCB), pp. 464–473. IEEE (2017). https://doi.org/10.1109/BTAS.2017.8272731
2. Cao, Q., Shen, L., Xie, W., Parkhi, O.M., Zisserman, A.: VGGFace2: a dataset for recognising faces across pose and age. In: 13th IEEE International Conference on Automatic Face & Gesture Recognition (FG 2018), pp. 67–74. IEEE (2018). https://doi.org/10.1109/FG.2018.00020
3. Deng, J., Guo, J., Ververas, E., Kotsia, I., Zafeiriou, S.: RetinaFace: single-shot multi-level face localisation in the wild. In: IEEE/CVF Conference on Computer Vision and Pattern Recognition (CVPR), pp. 5202–5211 (2020). https://doi.org/10.1109/CVPR42600.2020.00525
4. Deng, J., Guo, J., Xue, N., Zafeiriou, S.: ArcFace: additive angular margin loss for deep face recognition. In: IEEE/CVF Conference on Computer Vision and Pattern Recognition (CVPR), pp. 4685–4694 (2019). https://doi.org/10.1109/CVPR.2019.00482
5. Department of Defense: Human engineering design data digest (2000). https://apps.dtic.mil/sti/pdfs/ADA467401.pdf. Accessed 3 Apr 2023
6. Europa.eu: Entry/exit system (EES) (2023). https://home-affairs.ec.europa.eu/policies/schengen-borders-and-visa/smart-borders/entry-exit-system_en. Accessed 3 Apr 2023

7. Farfade, S.S., Saberian, M.J., Li, L.J.: Multi-view face detection using deep convolutional neural networks. In: Proceedings of the 5th ACM on International Conference on Multimedia Retrieval, pp. 643–650 (2015). https://doi.org/10.48550/arXiv.1502.02766
8. Feng, Y., Yu, S., Peng, H., Li, Y.R., Zhang, J.: Detect faces efficiently: a survey and evaluations. IEEE Trans. Biometrics Behav. Identity Sci. **4**(1), 1–18 (2022). https://doi.org/10.1109/TBIOM.2021.3120412
9. He, K., Zhang, X., Ren, S., Sun, J.: Deep residual learning for image recognition. In: Proceedings of the IEEE Conference on Computer Vision and Pattern Recognition, pp. 770–778 (2016). https://doi.org/10.1109/CVPR.2016.90
10. Heisler, B.: Criterion.rs: statistics-driven benchmarking library for rust (2014). https://github.com/bheisler/criterion.rs
11. Kumar, A., Kumar, M., Kaur, A.: Face detection in still images under occlusion and non-uniform illumination. Multimedia Tools Appl. **80**, 14565–14590 (2021). https://doi.org/10.1007/s11042-020-10457-9
12. Li, Z., Tang, X., Han, J., Liu, J., He, R.: PyramidBox++: high performance detector for finding tiny face. arXiv:1904.00386 (2019)
13. Lin, T.Y., Dollár, P., Girshick, R., He, K., Hariharan, B., Belongie, S.: Feature pyramid networks for object detection. In: IEEE Conference on Computer Vision and Pattern Recognition (CVPR), pp. 936–944 (2017). https://doi.org/10.1109/CVPR.2017.106
14. Linzaer: 1MB lightweight face detection model (2019). https://github.com/Linzaer/Ultra-Light-Fast-Generic-Face-Detector-1MB
15. Liu, C.: Multiple social credit systems in China. Econ. Soc. Eur. Electr. Newslett. **21**(1), 22–32 (2019)
16. Mayrhofer, R., Roland, M., Höller, T.: Poster: Towards an architecture for private digital authentication in the physical world. In: Network and Distributed System Security Symposium (NDSS Symposium 2020), Posters (2020)
17. mos.ru: The Face Pay system for fare payment was launched at all metro stations (2023). https://www.mos.ru/news/item/97579073/. Accessed 2 Feb 2023
18. Parkhi, O.M., Vedaldi, A., Zisserman, A.: Deep face recognition. In: Proceedings of the British Machine Vision Conference (BMVC), pp. 41.1–41.12. BMVA Press (2015). https://doi.org/10.5244/C.29.41
19. Roland, M., Höller, T., Mayrhofer, R.: Digitale Identitäten in der physischen Welt: Eine Abwägung von Privatsphäreschutz und Praktikabilität. HMD Praxis der Wirtschaftsinformatik **60**(2), 283–307 (2023). https://doi.org/10.1365/s40702-023-00949-1
20. uidai.gov.in: Unique Identification Authority of India (2023). https://uidai.gov.in/en/. Accessed 2 Feb 2023
21. Viola, P., Jones, M.: Rapid object detection using a boosted cascade of simple features. In: Proceedings of the 2001 IEEE Computer Society Conference on Computer Vision and Pattern Recognition. CVPR 2001, vol. 1, pp. I–I (2001). https://doi.org/10.1109/CVPR.2001.990517
22. Wolpert, D.H.: The lack of a priori distinctions between learning algorithms. Neural Comput. **8**(7), 1341–1390 (1996). https://doi.org/10.1162/neco.1996.8.7.1341
23. Yang, S., Luo, P., Loy, C.C., Tang, X.: WIDER FACE: a face detection benchmark. In: Proceedings of the IEEE Conference on Computer Vision and Pattern Recognition, pp. 5525–5533 (2016). https://doi.org/10.1109/CVPR.2016.596

Multi-camera Live Video Streaming over Wireless Network

Takashi Koyama[1] and Yusuke Gotoh[2(✉)]

[1] Graduate School of Natural Science and Technology, Okayama University, Okayama, Japan

[2] Faculty of Environmental, Life, Natural Science and Technology, Institute of Academic and Research, Okayama University, Okayama, Japan
`y-gotoh@okayama-u.ac.jp`

Abstract. Due to the development of wireless communication technology, more and more streamers are using cameras mounted on mobile devices for live streaming in a wireless LAN environment. Conventional live streaming systems, which employ multiple images captured by multiple cameras, require relay equipment for transmitting images to a computer for streaming and a network environment with sufficient bandwidth for live streaming. Therefore, the restrictions on using live streaming systems by streamers are severe. In this paper, we propose a multi-view live streaming system using multiple mobile devices in a wireless LAN environment. Our proposed system reduces the processing load on live streaming by using video streaming functions implemented on several mobile devices based on WebRTC. By sending and receiving data between mobile devices, the proposed system also reduces the bandwidth needed for delivering data. Furthermore, with a video switching function during live streaming, the system can dynamically change viewpoints. Performance evaluation results using the proposed system confirmed that the delay time between transmitting and delivering devices can be reduced compared to conventional systems that apply Motion-JPEG and RTMP.

Keywords: Live video streaming · multi-camera · wireless network

1 Introduction

With the proliferation of such mobile devices as smartphones and tablets as well as the development of wireless communication technology, Internet-based streaming services like Twitch [1] and YouTube Live [2] have become widespread. An increasing number of users employ applications for live streaming with video captured by cameras mounted on mobile devices. By using applications provided by live streaming services [3] and third-party developers [4,5], streamers can perform live streaming by mobile devices.

To deliver high-quality video that attracts many viewers during live streaming, streamers check multiple video shots in real time and switch to the video that offers the most appeal to their users. When a streamer captures multiple

P. Delir Haghighi et al. (Eds.): MoMM 2023, LNCS 14417, pp. 144–158, 2023.
https://doi.org/10.1007/978-3-031-48348-6_12

images in real time, a distribution system using a wired connection requires multiple cameras, relay equipment that transmits images to the streaming computer, and a network environment. In this case, streamers struggle to construct a live streaming environment because of the long time required to transport the equipment and the complicated connections among the different kinds of equipment. In addition, conventional live streaming systems using wireless connections require multiple mobile devices and both a computer and a network environment for live streaming. In this case, the amount of equipment required for distribution is smaller than for a wired connection, and the transportation burden is reduced. However, the delay time for video transmission is lengthened because the throughput is increased for communicating the video captured by the camera. In addition, the streamer needs expert knowledge for operating the video streaming server and constructing a communication environment. Therefore, streamers face many challenges to simply perform live streaming using multiple cameras.

In this paper, we propose a multi-view live streaming system in a wireless LAN environment. The proposed system provides both video distribution and video switching functions using multiple mobile devices. The following are the major contributions of our proposed multi-view live streaming system:

- We implement a video distribution server that can be operated on a web browser using Web Real-Time Communication (WebRTC), which transmits multiple video and audio streams.
- Streamers can live stream while switching between multiple video streams with less burden than with conventional systems.

The remainder of this paper is organized as follows. We explain live streaming with multiple cameras in Sect. 2. Related works are presented in Sect. 3, and our proposed method is described in Sect. 4. In Sects. 5 and 6, we design and implement our proposed system. We evaluate it in Sect. 7. Finally, we conclude in Sect. 8.

2   Live Streaming with Multiple Cameras

2.1   Live Streaming Technology Using Mobile Devices

The mobile vision mixer (MVM) [6] system performs live streaming outdoors while multiple mobile devices connected to a wireless LAN environment edit the streamed video. Videographers use mobile devices connected to a 3G network to capture video as they move around. Streamers live stream by selecting video from multiple videos taken by videographers.

Switcher Studio [7] is an application for the live streaming of video captured by an iOS device camera. By connecting up to nine iOS devices to a Wi-Fi network, a streamer can switch the video streaming offered to users during live streaming by multiple cameras both indoors and outdoors.

Streamers who have difficulty streaming video using multiple cameras and relay equipment can use these systems and applications for multi-camera live

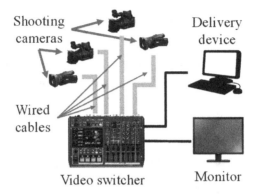

Fig. 1. Configuration of conventional live streaming system using a wired connection

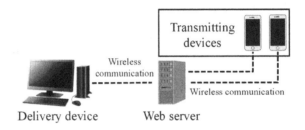

Fig. 2. Configuration of conventional live streaming system with wireless connection

streaming without specialized knowledge of such equipment. On the other hand, the related technologies do not consider the case where a mobile device that is used as a camera is changed to another device during live streaming, or where a device is added/removed from the network used for live streaming. Therefore, streamers need to create a streaming environment for a mobile device that is connected to the network before the live streaming starts, especially due to the complications of changing the mobile device's streaming environment during live streaming. For example, MVM [6] requires that multiple mobile devices be prepared in advance that can use the mobile network. Since the devices in Switcher Studio [7] are connected to the same Wi-Fi network, a Wi-Fi network must be prepared with sufficient bandwidth for the number of devices.

2.2   Conventional Live System Using Multiple Cameras

Figure 1 shows the configuration of a conventional live streaming system with a wired connection. In a multi-camera live streaming system, a streamer can streams by adjusting the amount and video quality of the multiple images captured by multiple video cameras and selects the images to be streamed. Examples of live streaming with multiple cameras with a wired connection include sports arenas, concert halls, and event places. Such venues have wide shooting areas and can capture multiple subjects from various perspectives. However, compared to a simple live streaming using one video camera, multi-camera live streaming with multiple viewpoints requires many delivery devices, a situation that also complicates the configuration of the delivery environment. Examples of distribution equipment include multiple video cameras, video monitors for checking the images from video cameras, a video switcher for integrating multiple captured images and determining the output image, a computer for live streaming, and various cables for connecting all of this equipment. If a network environment is unavailable at a sports or concert venue, one must be constructed that provides sufficient scale for live streaming. In addition, as the amount of distribution equipment grows, the workload required for transporting, installing, and connecting distribution equipment also increases. As the number of streamers increases, the streamers need to carry, install, and connect streaming equipment.

Figure 2 shows the configuration of a conventional live streaming system with a wireless connection. As an example of such a system with a wireless connection, we introduce Switcher Studio [7], which is popular for cooking and variety shows distributed by individual streamers, online conferences with relatively few shooting locations, and events where multiple subjects are simultaneously shot by multiple mobile devices. A live streaming system by a wireless connection requires less equipment than a wired connection, although streamers must prepare a video streaming server and construct a wireless network. The delay in video communication is also longer than in wired connections.

Conventional live streaming systems using multiple cameras require specialized knowledge and experience for exploiting such streaming equipment. This live streaming context also increases the burden on streamers. Therefore, streamers need a system that provides live streaming from multiple viewpoints using multiple cameras without increasing their burden.

3   Related Works

3.1   Video Delivery Technology Considering Network Environment

N-Screen technology [8,9] enables uninterrupted viewing of video data on multiple mobile devices, including smartphones, tablet PCs, and laptop computers. By downloading the same content, multiple users can simultaneously view it. However, when mobile devices share video data using N-Screen technology in a wireless LAN environment, all the devices connect to the same access point (AP) and share the channel bandwidth. In this case, the number of interruptions in video playback increases as the number of devices rises.

Kwon et al. [10] proposed a relaying method for scalable video streaming in a wireless LAN environment to address the increase of mobile devices. Their method reduces the load on mobile devices during video playback and lowers the interruptions during playback using video streaming over Wi-Fi Direct [11] networks and bandwidth control for downloading video data.

3.2   Multi-view Live Streaming

Research on multi-view live streaming using 360-degree cameras has also attracted much attention. Takada et al. [12] proposed a method for detecting the point of view (POV) of high interest to users in live streaming of a 360-degree camera on the internet. Their method collects and analyzes a user's POV data based on the assumption that the most intriguing images are displayed when the user faces a viewpoint other than the one directly opposite the camera in live streaming by a 360-degree camera.

Matsumoto et al. [13] proposed a distributed multi-view, internet live streaming system to reduce the processing load on devices when such effects as text and backgrounds are added to videos based on user preferences in multi-view live streaming. In this method, the delivery server classifies whether each effect in a video can be shared among users based on the elementary cellular automaton (ECA) rules. A streamer can reduce the processing load on the server by using the user's device for additional processing for effects that cannot be shared among users.

Kashif et al. [14] proposed a multi-view crowdsourcing streaming system (CMVCS) that collects and combines multiple videos on the cloud taken by numerous photographers at the same event for multi-view streaming. It automatically generates a multi-view live streaming video based on GPS information, shooting angles, and shooting times for each video.

3.3   WebRTC

WebRTC [15] is an open source project that has been attracting attention as a method that provides real-time video communication via APIs between web browsers and mobile applications.

Currently, the Internet Engineering Task Force (IETF) [16] and the World Wide Web Consortium (W3C) [17] are standardizing WebRTC. WebRTC supports such leading web browsers as Google Chrome and Mozilla Firefox and enables real-time communication of large amounts of data, including video and audio.

Maehara et al. [18] implemented a system that transmits multiple video and audio signals using WebRTC and compared its QoE with that of a system using MPEG-DASH in an environment with a heavy communication load. Their evaluations confirmed that a system using WebRTC has shorter communication latency and higher QoE than one using MPEG-DASH.

Tang et al. [19] proposed a video chat system using WebRTC and synchronized video and audio transmitted from multiple users by combining them in real time with the WebRTC protocol. They maintained video quality and audio with minimal delay.

SkyWay [20] provides SDK and API to facilitate the development of applications using WebRTC. By deploying SkyWay, streamers can use the signaling, STUN, TURN, and SFU servers, all of which are required to deploy WebRTC in their applications by the API. Since the SDK in SkyWay supports multiple platforms, users can reduce the development time of their applications.

By using WebRTC, the delay time in a delivery system for wireless communication can be reduced more than with conventional communication protocols. Streamers can construct a system without installing a dedicated application by communicating video through a browser that is standard on computers and mobile devices.

4 Proposed System

4.1 Outline

For a wireless LAN environment, we propose a multi-view live streaming system with multiple cameras. The proposed system exploits multiple mobile devices as transmitting devices and sends video to a distributor device in a wireless LAN environment by a streaming server that applies WebRTC, which transmits multiple video and audio streams. By using a mobile device as a camera for capturing video, streamers can reduce the required amount of equipment (for example, cables) compared to a wired multi-view live streaming system and also capture video outdoors or underwater that has very difficult operations with a wired connection. In addition, by using WebRTC for communication with a streaming server, our proposed system can use the standard browsers installed in mobile devices and computers. Therefore, the number of required applications can be reduced for implementing a delivery system.

In this study, we assume multi-view live streaming by an individual streamer who can display every multiple video sent from a transmitting device to a server on a web page. In addition, the streamer can switch the videos by selecting the viewpoints viewers want to watch on their screens in real time on a web page.

4.2 System Configuration

Our proposed system consists of four types of apparatuses: a transmission device, a web server, a signaling server and a STUN/TURN server, and a delivery device. The proposed system's configuration is shown in Fig. 3, and its details are described below.

- Sending device: connects to the web server by a browser and sends a room ID along with the device information. After completing the P2P connection with the delivery device, the transmission device sends the video to the delivery device by the web server.
- Web server: sends the device information and the room ID received from the transmission and delivery devices to the signaling server. After receiving the device information and the peer ID that is registered in the room ID from the signaling server, both the transmitting and delivery devices are connected through P2P communication. In P2P communication, the video from the transmitting device is sent to the delivery device by a web server. When

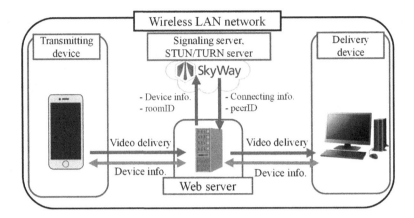

Fig. 3. Live streaming environment using proposed system

there are multiple transmitting devices, the streamer sends the video selected on the web server to the streaming device.

– Signaling and STUN/TURN servers: The former server receives information from the transmitting and delivery devices and generates a peer ID that corresponds to each device. Based on the room ID sent from each device, the signaling server sends the peer ID and the information on the connected device with the same room ID to the web server. Next the STUN server provides information about the IP addresses to each device in the communication between each device and the signaling server. If no P2P communication can be connected between the devices, they can communicate through the TURN server.

– Delivery device: connects to the web server by a browser and sends the device information and the room ID. After completing the P2P connection with the transmitting device, the streamer receives the selected video from the web server and transmits it to the live streaming service.

The viewers of the live streaming watch from the live streaming service by the internet on their own devices. In our proposed system, a streamer can stream another video during live streaming by adding a new transmitting device. In the device-to-device communication used in the proposed system, clients are connected to each other by P2P in a mesh-type communication.

4.3   Functions of Proposed System

Our proposed system provides two types of functions that reduce the burden on streamers in live streaming. They are explained in the following order.

Video Switching Function. During live streaming, the proposed system switches the video to be sent to the receiving device using multiple videos received by the streaming server from multiple sending devices. By using the video switching function, the streamer can live stream from multi-cameras on multiple mobile devices without any relay equipment that switch the videos.

Video Streaming Function. The delivery device sends by its camera the video captured and distributed by the transmitting device to the live streaming service. Viewers can watch live streaming video by connecting to such a service using the video streaming function.

5   Design

5.1   Software Configuration

Figure 4 shows the configuration of the modules in the proposed system. The four types of devices described in Sect. 4 are composed of multiple modules with independent functions. The modules required for each device are described below:

- Transmitting device:
    - Connection controller:
      a module that communicates from the transmitting device to the web server;
    - Camera manager:
      a module that controls the transmitting device's camera;
    - Video stream sender:
      a module that sends the video streaming data captured by the transmitting device's camera to the web server;
- Signaling and STUN/TURN servers:
    - Connection controller:
      a module that communicates from the signaling server to the web server;
- Web server:
    - Connection controller:
      a module that communicates from the web server to the transmitting device, the signaling server, and the delivery server;
    - Video switcher:
      a module that selects a video to be sent to the distribution device from among multiple videos received from the transmitting device;
    - Video stream receiver:
      a module that receives the video streaming data sent from a transmitting device;
    - Video stream sender:
      a module that sends the video streaming data selected by the video switcher;
    - Room manager:
      a module that manages the connection status of devices connected to the web server;

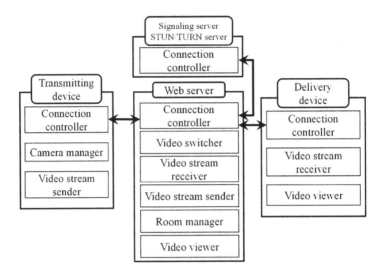

Fig. 4. Composition of modules in proposed system

  - Video viewer:
    a module for viewing the video received from the transmitting device;
 – Delivery device:
    - Connection controller:
      a module that communicates from the delivery device to the web server;
    - Video stream receiver:
      a module that receives video streaming data sent from the web server;
    - Video viewer:
      a module for viewing the video received from the web server.

5.2 Video Switching Function

Next we describe the process flow of the video switching function. The video switcher that changes the videos runs on a web server, which displays all the received videos on the device screen using the video viewer and selects one type using the video switcher.

5.3 Video Streaming Function

Here we describe the process flow of the video streaming function. The transmitting device sends the video captured by the camera to the web server using a video stream sender. The web server, which receives the video stream from the transmitting device using a video stream receiver, combines one or more types of videos selected by the video switcher from the multiple videos received by the video stream receiver and sends them to the delivery device. The delivery device receives the video sent by the web server using the video stream receiver.

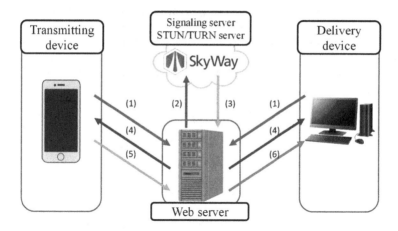

Fig. 5. Processing procedure of live streaming in proposed system

5.4 Processing Steps of Live Streaming in Proposed System

Figure 5 shows the live streaming procedure using the proposed system. Its details are described below:

(1) The transmitting and delivery devices connect to the web server by a browser and send the device information and the room ID.

(2) The web server sends both to the signaling server.

(3) The signaling server sends the ID of the peer with the same room ID and device information to the web server based on the device information and the room ID.

(4) The web server sends the peer ID and the device information of the connection destination to the transmitting and delivery devices for P2P communication between them.

(5) The transmitting device sends the video streaming data to the web server using P2P communication.

(6) The web server selects one of the multiple videos received from the transmitting device and sends it to the delivery device.

6 Implementation

We implemented the functions of the devices and the server in our proposed system. We used a mobile device with an Android OS as a transmitting device and a notebook computer as a delivery device. Table 1 shows the performance of the transmitting and distributing devices. The web server uses GitHub Pages, which is a function provided by GitHub [21]. The transmitting and delivery devices are connected in a wireless LAN environment by a router. The former sends the video images captured by the on-board camera to the delivery device, which transmits the video to YouTube Live [2] (a live streaming service) by

Table 1. Device performances

Device type	Transmitting device	Delivering device
Computer	HUAWEI MediaPad M5	Desktop PC
OS	Android 9.0	Windows 10 Pro
CPU	HUAWEI Kirin 960	AMD Ryzen 5 3600 6-Core Processor
Clock frequency	2.4 GHz	3.60 GHz
Memory	4.00 GB	32.00 GB
Wireless LAN standard	IEEE 802.11 a/b/g/n/ac	IEEE 802.11 a/b/g/n/ac

the internet. Clients can watch the video by connecting to YouTube Live from a browser on the web. The transmitting device uses the functions of acquiring camera images and transmitting them on a browser. In the web browser, we implemented image reception, transmission, display, switching, and device connection processes to the web server using HTML [22], JavaScript [23], and CSS [24]. The delivery device uses the functions of receiving and displaying video on the browser. By using Open Broadcaster Software (OBS) [25], which is open source, we implemented the video display and video distribution processes for a live streaming service.

7   Evaluation

7.1   Evaluation Environment

We evaluated the delay time between the transmitting and delivery devices in the video delivery by the proposed system and compared them with the conventional system. In the latter, we used two types of systems: one using Motion-JPEG as the communication protocol and another using RTMP.

In the conventional system using Motion-JPEG, the transmitting device functions as the server, and the streaming data of the camera images captured by the transmitting device are sent to the delivery device in Motion-JPEG. Next the conventional system using RTMP operates NGINX [26], which is a video distribution server, on a virtual environment constructed using VirtualBox [27] for the delivery device.

The transmitting device sends video to the server based on the RTMP protocol using LarixBroadcaster [28]. The VLC media player [29] receives the video sent by the transmitting device.

We constructed an evaluation environment (Fig. 6) using three transmitting devices and one delivery device. Table 2 shows the evaluation performance of the

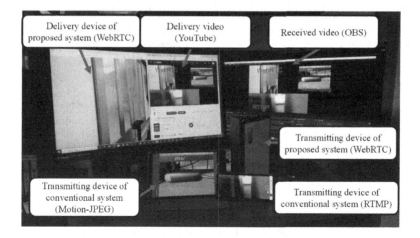

Fig. 6. Evaluation environment for latency

transmitting devices. Table 3 shows the format of the video content used by the transmitting devices.

7.2   Latency

Table 4 shows the latency that occurs in video streaming between the transmitting and delivery devices based on the elapsed time since the live streaming's start. We calculated the average of five measured latencies between the videos displayed on the transmitting device during shooting and on the delivery device sent from the transmitting device. No interruptions occurred in the live streaming using the proposed system during the measurements.

In WebRTC, the latency at 30 s after the start of live streaming is about 0.247 s; at 3,600 s, it is about 0.256 s Therefore, the latency did not increase significantly with processing time. Comparing WebRTC, which simultaneously communicates video and audio, and Motion-JPEG, which communicates only video, WebRTC's latency is about 0.1 s shorter than that of Motion-JPEG. Comparing WebRTC and RTMP, the former's latency is about 3.0 s shorter than the latter.

By using WebRTC for communication with a streaming server, our proposed system can use the standard browsers installed in mobile devices and computers. Therefore, the number of applications required by the proposed system can be reduced compared to conventional wireless systems without WebRTC.

7.3   Performance of Proposed System

When multiple streamers individually operate the transmitting and delivery devices, they need to consider the latency that occurs between them for the streaming and switching processes. Concerning the effect of latency in general

Table 2. Performance of transmitting devices

Communication protocol	WebRTC	Motion-JPEG	RTMP
Computer	HUAWEI MediaPad M5	HUAWEI MediaPad M5	Xperia 10 II
OS	Android 9.0	Android 9.0	Android 12.0
CPU	HUAWEI Kirin 960	HUAWEI Kirin 960	Snapdragon690 5G
Clock frequency	2.4 GHz	2.4 GHz	$2.0 + 1.7$ GHz
Memory	4.00 GB	4.00 GB	6.00 GB
Wireless LAN standard	IEEE 802.11	IEEE 802.11	IEEE 802.11

Table 3. Format of video contents

Communication protocol	WebRTC	Motion-JPEG	RTMP
Resolution	640×480 pixel	640×480 pixel	4032×1728 pixel
Frame rate	60 fps	30 fps	45 fps

teleconferencing, round-trip latency was about 0.50 s for delivery between speakers with high conversational speed and high speech frequency. In our proposed system's evaluation, the latency between the sending and delivery devices was about 0.25 s, and none occurred in the switching process. In addition, the proposed system with WebRTC, which simultaneously communicates video and audio, had latency more than 2 s shorter than the conventional system with RTMP. Therefore, in actual streaming, we confirmed that the proposed system allows multiple streamers to perform shooting and switching processes in cooperation between the transmitting and delivery devices.

8 Conclusion

We proposed a multi-view live streaming system using multiple mobile devices in a wireless LAN environment. In our proposed system, we designed and implemented two types of video streaming functions: a video switching function that

Table 4. Latency based on time elapsed from start of live streaming

Protocol	Elapsed time			
	60 s	600 s	1,800 s	3,600 s
WebRTC	0.247 s	0.235 s	0.245 s	0.256 s
Motion-JPEG	0.327 s	0.337 s	0.371 s	0.532 s
RTMP	3.347 s	3.328 s	3.373 s	3.374 s

changes video during live streaming and a video streaming function that distributes the video using mobile devices and delivers it by a streaming service. Our performance evaluation of the proposed system confirmed that the latency between the transmitting and delivery devices was as short as about 0.25 s.

In the future, we plan to implement a more usable interface and evaluate the proposed system with more transmitting devices.

Acknowledgment. This work was supported by JSPS KAKENHI Grant Numbers JP21H03429 and JP22H03587, a JSPS Bilateral Joint Research Project (JPJSBP120229932), and the JGC-S Scholarship Foundation.

References

1. Twitch Interactive Inc: Twitch. https://www.twitch.tv/ Accessed Aug 29 2023
2. YouTube: YouTube Live. https://www.youtube.com/live/ Accessed Aug 29 2023
3. Meta Platforms Inc: Instagram. https://www.instagram.com/ Accessed Aug 29 2023
4. Vault Micro Inc: CameraFi Live https://www.camerafi.com/camerafi-live/ Accessed Aug 29 2023
5. Google Play: Astra Streaming Studio. https://play.google.com/store/apps/details?id=miv.astudio&hl=en_US Accessed Aug 29 2023
6. Engstrom, A., Zoric, G., Juhlin, O., Toussi, R.: The mobile vision mixer: a mobile network based live video broadcasting system in your mobile phone. In: Proc. 11th International Conference on Mobile and Ubiquitous Multimedia (MUM'12), No.18 (2012). https://doi.org/10.1145/2406367.2406390
7. Switcher Inc: Switcher Studio. https://www.switcherstudio.com/ Accessed Aug 29 2023
8. Yoon, C., Um, T., Lee, H.: Classification of N-screen services and its standardization. In: Proceedings of the 14th International Conference on Advanced Communication Technology (ICACT), pp. 567–602 (2012)
9. Kim, J.W., Ullah, F., Lee, S.C., Jo, S.K., Lee, H.W., Ryu, W.: Dynamic addition and deletion of device in n-screen environment. In: Proceedings of the 4th International Conference on Ubiquitous and Future Networks (ICUFN), pp. 118–122 (2012)
10. Kwon, D., Je, H., Kim, H., Ju, H., An, D.: Scalable Video Streaming Relay for Smart Mobile Devices in Wireless Networks, *PLOS ONE*, Vol. 11, No. 12 (2016). https://doi.org/10.1371/journal.pone.0167403
11. Wi-Fi Alliance: Wi-Fi Direct. https://www.wi-fi.org/discover-wi-fi/wi-fi-direct Accessed Aug 29 2023
12. Takada, M., Nishioka, D., Saito, Y.: A detection method of viewers' interests based on pov for 360-degree internet live broadcasting in mobile environment. In: *Proceedingsofthe IEEE 8th Global Conference on Consumer Electronics (GCCE)*, pp. 367–370 (2019)
13. Matsumoto, S., Yoshihisa, T.: A distributed internet live broadcasting system for multi-viewpoint videos. Int. J. Inform. Soc. (*IJIS*). **11**(2), 117–124 (2019)
14. Bilal, K., Erbad, A., Hefeeda, M.: Crowdsourced multi-view live video streaming using cloud computing. IEEE Access **5**, 12635–12647 (2017)
15. WebRTC: Real-time communication for the web. https://webrtc.org/ Accessed Aug 29 2023

16. Internet Engineering Task Force (IETF). https://www.ietf.org/ Accessed Aug 29 2023
17. The World Wide Web Consortium (W3C). https://www.w3.org/ Accessed Aug 29 2023
18. Maehara, Y., Nunome, T.: WebRTC-Based multi-view video and audio transmission and its QoE. Int. Conf. Inform. Network. (ICOIN), pp. 181–186 (2019). https://doi.org/10.1109/ICOIN.2019.8718109
19. Tang, D., Zhang, L.: Audio and video mixing method to enhance WebRTC. IEEE Access **8**, 67228–67241 (2020). https://doi.org/10.1109/ACCESS.2020.2985412
20. SkyWay. https://skyway.ntt.com/en/ Accessed Aug 29 2023
21. GitHub. https://github.com/ Accessed Aug 29 2023
22. HTML: HyperText Markup Language: MDN Web Docs. https://developer.mozilla.org/en-US/docs/Web/HTML Accessed Aug 29 2023
23. JavaScript: MDN Web Docs. https://developer.mozilla.org/en-US/docs/Web/JavaScript/ Accessed Aug 29 2023
24. CSS: Cascading Style Sheets: MDN Web Docs. https://developer.mozilla.org/en-US/docs/Web/CSS Accessed Aug 29 2023
25. OBS Project: OBS studio. https://obsproject.com/ Accessed Aug 29 2023
26. NGINX. https://nginx.org/en/ Accessed Aug 29 2023
27. Oracle VM VirtualBox. https://www.virtualbox.org/ Accessed Aug 29 2023
28. Softvelum. https://softvelum.com/larix/ Accessed Aug 29 2023
29. VideoLAN. https://www.videolan.org/vlc/index.en_GB.html Accessed Aug 29 2023

Effects of Deep Generative AutoEncoder Based Image Compression on Face Attribute Recognition: A Comprehensive Study

Ahmed Baha Ben Jmaa[1(✉)] and Dorsaf Sebai[2,3]

[1] Efrei Research Lab, Paris Panthéon-Assas University, Paris, France
ahmedbaha.benjmaa@outlook.fr
[2] Images and Forms Research Group, CRISTAL Laboratory, ENSI,
University of Manouba, Manouba, Tunisia
[3] Department of Computer Science Engineering and Mathematics, INSAT,
University of Carthage, Tunis, Tunisia

Abstract. Face Attribute Recognition (FAR) is a computer vision task that has attracted a lot of attention for applications ranging from security and surveillance to healthcare. In real-world scenarios, setting up a FAR system requires an important step, which is image compression because of computational, storage, and transmission constraints. However, severe face image compression not adapted to FAR tasks can affect the accuracy of these latter. In this paper, we investigate the impact of image compression based on deep generative models on face attribute recognition performance. In particular, we present a case study on smile and gender detection by face attribute classification of compressed images. For this purpose, we use QRes-VAE (Quantized ResNet Variational AutoEncoder) for image compression, which is, to the best of our knowledge, the most powerful and efficient VAE model for lossy image compression. Unlike prior studies, we quantify the impact of using deep generative autoencoder for image compression on FAR performance. We also study the impact of varying compression rates on the FAR performance. Results obtained from experiments on the CelebA dataset highlight the potential trade-off between image compression by deep generative autoencoder and FAR performance.

Keywords: Face Attribute Recognition · Image Compression · Deep Generative Autoencoder · Quantized ResNet Variational AutoEncoder

1 Introduction

In recent years, Face Attribute Recognition (FAR), a computer vision task, has undergone a great evolution thanks to the rapid growth of information and communication technologies [11]. It has been introduced in several fields of application, including security and surveillance, health, education, and advertising.

P. Delir Haghighi et al. (Eds.): MoMM 2023, LNCS 14417, pp. 159–172, 2023.
https://doi.org/10.1007/978-3-031-48348-6_13

This evolution of FAR technologies has imposed constraints in real-world applications. In particular, efficient storage and transmission of face images without compromising recognition accuracy is highly recommended for a practical and efficient implementation of any FAR system.

To meet these constraints, image compression techniques are introduced in FAR systems as a solution in real-world use cases [2,3]. In fact, the purpose of image compression is to reduce the size of the image while maintaining its quality. In this context, the emergence of deep learning has strengthened these techniques [8,12,14,19], especially those that use generative models. Great revolutions are made by proposing new methods and improving existing methods. Especially, image compression methods that use generative models are becoming increasingly more demanding than conventional standards. These methods are the new trend as they achieve the required results. Recently, multiple approaches have been proposed to exploit autoencoder for image compression [19]. One of the most recent being Quantized ResNet Variational AutoEncoder (QRes-VAE) [6], a Deep Generative AutoEncoder (DGAE), which builds on previous work to build a powerful architecture capable of competing with the most popular architectures in image compression.

In real-world FAR systems, the dominant concern is the impact of image compression on FAR accuracy [3]. Therefore, our goal is to evaluate the effect of image compression based on a DGAE model on FAR performance. In particular, we are interested in the recognition of face attributes for smile and gender detection. By compressing and reconstructing face images using QRes-VAE, we use deep FAR algorithms based on Convolutional Neural Networks (CNNs) for the classification of these attributes.

So far, most existing works have mainly focused on the impact of conventional compression standards, such as JPEG and JPEG 2000, as well as discriminative deep learning models for image classification [1–3,13,15]. However, the compression artifacts generated by deep learning models differ from those produced by classical codecs [17], especially by generative models. That's why we focus on studying the impact of DGAE on FAR. Additionally, this is particularly relevant for computer vision applications since FAR is a crucial task for other applications like face recognition, and DGAEs have shown better results for image compression, especially the QRes-VAE model.

Our hypothesis is that the compression of face images by a DGAE model can lead to a loss or modification of face features, which then leads to distortions in the FAR system and erroneous interpretations. While we expected compression to negatively impact FAR performance in most cases [13], we did not have an accurate measure of this decrease. Indeed, the exact measure of this decrease cannot be established without carrying out an in-depth study. It was, therefore, essential to quantify this impact through our study, especially since DGAEs do not only compress and reconstruct images but are also able to generate new images. This characteristic of compression methods, different from other compression techniques that only focus on the compression task, can play a crucial role in the impact of DGAE-based compression on FAR, making our study novel.

Another peculiarity of our study is to master the trade-off between image compression rate and FAR accuracy for a FAR system that is both robust and efficient in real-world applications. In light of the above, we establish our research questions as follows:

- How does image compression using DGAE affect the FAR performance?
- How does the use of DGAE-based image compression during both the training and testing phases impact the performance and generalizability of FAR models?
- What are the trade-off between image compression rate and FAR accuracy?
- What are the limitations of using DGAE-based image compression for FAR in real-world scenarios?

Contributions. We summarize our contributions mainly in the following two points:

- Conducting the first study that evaluates the effects of image compression based on a DGAE model (QRes-VAE) on FAR performance, specifically for smile and gender detection, using the CelebA (CelebFaces Attributes) dataset [11], the most dedicated benchmark for FAR tasks, to ensure the applicability of our results in real-world use cases.
- Uncovering the trade-off between compression rates and FAR performance according to the use case and the constraints of the implemented application. Additionally, we highlight potential limitations and challenges that may arise in real-world scenarios.

Paper Organization. In the following, Sect. 2 presents QRes-VAE, explaining its working principle and evaluating its performance for image compression. Section 3 describes the evaluation methodology used for deep attribute recognition in compressed face images. In Sect. 4, we present the results and findings of this study. Finally, Sect. 5 concludes the paper and suggests future perspectives.

2 Quantized ResNet Variational AutoEncoder for Image Compression

Quantized ResNet Variational AutoEncoder (QRes-VAE) is a novel quantized hierarchical model based on VAEs, introduced by Duan et al. in [6], for lossy image compression. Duan et al. propose modifications to existing methods in this field, leading to better quality reconstructions at very low bit rates. They present a compression model similar to ResNet VAE [9] to better adapt such a model to this task in real-world use cases. They experimentally show that the visual quality of the reconstructions of their method is superior to previous lossy compression methods [6], thus reducing the gap between the reconstruction of input images and the generation of new images and providing better computational efficiency.

In this section, we briefly summarize the compression process of QRes-VAE. More details are provided in [5,6]. Section 2.1 is dedicated to the presentation of the working principle of this method. Section 2.2 will be devoted to experiments and evaluation of the method, in terms of image quality and compression efficiency.

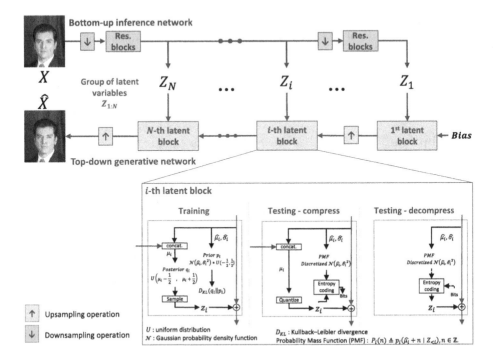

Fig. 1. Illustration of the QRes-VAE framework

2.1   Architecture and Working Principle

The architecture of QRes-VAE is organized, as shown in Fig. 1, into a bottom-up inference network and a top-down generative network, where each network is a hierarchy of modules. To further explain what is happening, we consider an image X as an example. This image will be passed to the bottom-up inference network, where it will be encoded to create a latent variable group $Z_{1:N} \triangleq \{Z_1, Z_2, ..., Z_N\}$, which will then be transmitted to the generative network from top to bottom. At the top-down generative network level, the model starts with a learnable constant feature that propagates through the network to generate the reconstruction of the input, X.

The bottom-up inference network is organized into several levels. Each level has a downsampling operation and a residual block. The downsampling operation is carried out by a patch embedding [4] and the residual block used is the ConvNeXt block [10], which empirically ensures better performance [6]. The output of each level of the hierarchy is a latent variable, Z_i, capturing features at different resolutions. The generative network, from top to bottom, is also organized as a hierarchy of levels, where each level includes an oversampling operation and a latent block. The oversampling operation is performed by sub-pixel convolution [16] interpreted as the inverse of the downsampling operation (patch embedding). As detailed in Fig. 1, the latent block behaves differently depending on the task performed: training, compression, or decompression.

During QRes-VAE training, the goal is to learn a group of latent variables from the input data, $Z_{1:N}$, providing a low-dimensional compressed representation that captures its underlying structure. This is achieved by minimizing the loss function, $\mathcal{L}_{QRes-VAE}$, presented in Eq. 1, where λ is a scalar hyperparameter and $d(\cdot)$ is a distortion metric.

$$\mathcal{L}_{QRes-VAE} = \mathbb{E}_{X,Z_{1:N}} \left[\sum_{i=1}^{N} \log \frac{1}{(Z_i \mid Z_{<i})} + \lambda \cdot d(X, \hat{X}) \right] \tag{1}$$

$\mathcal{L}_{QRes-VAE}$ can be formalized as a trade-off between rate and distortion using the Lagrangian method (rate-distortion Lagrangian) [19] which balances two important aspects: rate and distortion. Mathematically, this trade-off can be expressed as follows:

$$\mathcal{L}_{QRes-VAE} = R + \lambda \cdot D \tag{2}$$

where :

- R represents the rate, which in our case is the number of bits required to represent the input X in latent space.
- D represents the distortion, which in our case is MSE (Mean Squared Error), thus quantifying the difference between input X and output $\hat{X}$.
- λ represents the Lagrange multiplier, also called the rate-distortion parameter, a parameter that controls the trade-off between rate and distortion.

2.2   Compression Performances Evaluation

In this section, we will perform some experiments to answer the most important questions that arise when working with the QRes-VAE architecture. To do this, we will first objectively evaluate the performance of the compression process performed by QRes-VAE using different metrics on the CelebA dataset [11]. We chose to work with the CelebA dataset to ensure the applicability of our results to real-world use cases. Indeed, CelebA is a celebrities' human face dataset that contains 202,599 images (162,770 images for training set, 19,867 images for validation set and 19,962 images for test set). To attain a comprehensive perspective on performance, we used both an objective evaluation and a subjective evaluation. For the objective evaluation, we are interested in the PSNR (Peak Signal to Noise Ratio) and MS-SSIM (MultiScale Structural SIMilarity) metric values calculated for each bit rate with QRes-VAE. We first calculate the metric for each image and then the average over all images in the test set. The results are shown in Fig. 2.

The results were fascinating and convincing, showing that this approach allows for better reconstruction according to MS-SSIM, particularly at low bit rate, where the quality of the reconstruction degrades gracefully when the compression increases. The hierarchical latent approach seems reasonable and could be more robust, especially since it does not require computational complexity [5,6]. This architecture also effectively tackles the difficult problem of maintaining realism and high-level semantic content in the scenario of image compression at very low bit rate.

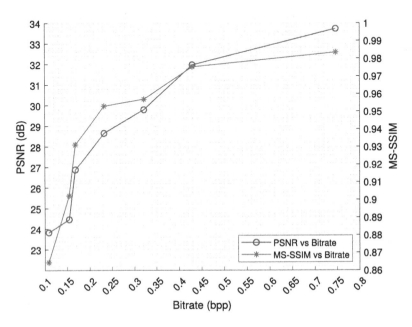

Fig. 2. Bitrate vs. PSNR and MS-SSIM curves for QRes-VAE-based compression and reconstruction of CelebA test set

We are currently conducting a subjective evaluation. The choice to have a subjective evaluation is based on the fact that the objective evaluation can be slightly different from human perception and human judgment. For this purpose, we used the visual evaluation methodology (see Table 1). Subsequently, the interpretation will be based on the results of the images we obtained. Overall, the architecture gave excellent results. However, our main concern will be the comparison between the results of the architecture at different compression rates. The compression rate translates into the lambda value. A higher lambda value means a higher bitrate and better reconstruction quality, while a smaller lambda value results in potentially lower bitrate and reconstruction quality. We can say that for $\lambda \geq 8$, the QRes-VAE architecture gives excellent results, where the human faces are visible and similar to the original faces, while for $\lambda < 8$, the QRes-VAE architecture gives results that are composed of lots of artifacts and noise. We can see that the subjective evaluation verifies the results found with the objective evaluation, where the architecture gives excellent results with CelebA.

Table 1. Reconstructed CelebA images with QRes-VAE at different levels of compression corresponding to λ

3 Deep Attribute Recognition of Compressed Face Images: Evaluation Methodology

Deep learning models have given impressive results in the FAR context [18]. However, the accuracy of these models may vary depending on the input image quality. In this section, we set up deep learning models for the recognition with precision of faces that were compressed by QRes-VAE in Sect. 2.

In the following, Sect. 3.1 presents the evaluation framework as well as the experimental setups used to assess the impact of compression based on DGAE on FAR. In Sect. 3.2, we explore real-world applications through the use cases of FAR studied in this paper.

3.1 Evaluation Framework

We present the working principle of the evaluation framework for attribute recognition of compressed face images in Fig. 3, where a face image is passed through the compression & reconstruction framework presented by QRes-VAE to produce a reconstructed face image. The reconstructed input is then introduced into a FAR system based on CNNs to learn deep face descriptors and map these descriptors via a classifier to the different classes of face recognition attributes according to the use case.

In order to determine the impact of lossy compression on FAR performance, we perform all our experiments with a compression rate corresponding to $\lambda = 1$, which allows severe compression of face images. There are three main Experimental Setups (ES) used in this paper:

- **ES 1:** Training and testing set are uncompressed.
- **ES 2:** Training set is uncompressed; testing set is compressed.
- **ES 3:** Training and testing set are compressed.

We use the CelebA dataset in all experimental setups.

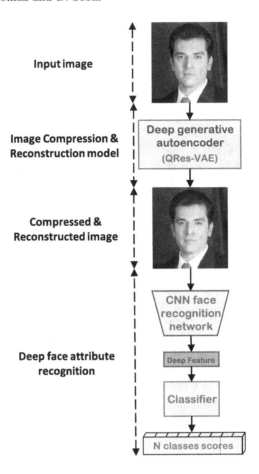

Fig. 3. Illustration of the evaluation framework

3.2   Face Attribute Recognition Use Cases

Face attribute recognition has a wide range of use cases. In this paper, we are interested in these two use cases: *Smile Detection for Emotion Recognition and User Engagement* and *Gender Detection for Security, Healthcare, and Advertising*.

Use Case 1 - Smile Detection for Emotion Recognition and User Engagement. Smile detection is a computer vision task that can identify whether or not a person is smiling from face images. It is commonly used in a variety of application areas, including:

 – Education: Smile detection can identify students' level of interest during online teaching sessions, which then allows teachers to adjust their teaching methods according to their students' needs for better student engagement.

– Healthcare: Specifically, in the case of psychological illnesses, smile detection can identify and monitor the psychological state of patients. This allows the doctor to properly diagnose the case and take the necessary measures accordingly for the patient's health.

In this section, we set up a deep learning model for smile detection. To do this, we implement the VGG-16 architecture [7,20] on the CelebA face dataset to train a smile classification model. This model allows us to classify a face image into one of two classes: "Smiling" and "Not Smiling".

Use Case 2 - Gender Detection for Security, Healthcare, and Advertising. Gender detection is the task of determining whether a person is male or female. It can be done from images, videos, or even text. Several use cases for gender detection arise in real life, including:

– Healthcare: Gender detection makes it possible to adapt medical treatment according to the gender of the patient.
– Security and surveillance: Gender detection helps ensure access to spaces restricted to a specific gender (such as restrooms or locker rooms). It also allows, in some cases, the prevention of crime and the identification of missing persons.
– Advertising: Gender detection makes it possible to adapt advertisements according to the gender of the target.

In this section, we set up a deep learning model for gender detection. We implement the ResNet-50 architecture [7,20] on the CelebA face dataset to train a gender classification model that classifies a face image into one of two classes: "Male" and "Female".

4   Results and Discussion

For the use cases studied in this paper, the face attribute recognition models used are classification models. In order to evaluate the performance of these models, we report in Table 2, following standard practice, these classification metrics: accuracy, precision, recall and F1-score, calculated on the test set for all experimental setups. Next, we evaluate these metrics for each class. All results are shown in Table 2.

Impact of Compression on Face Attribute Recognition. In this part, we analyze the results presented in Table 2 to show the effect of image compression on face attribute recognition performance. The results of the experimental setup ES1 serve as a reference to evaluate the recognition performance of uncompressed face images. The two models set up for smile and gender detection present reasonably high performances according to the four metrics (accuracy, precision,

Table 2. Accuracy, precision, recall and F1-score for face attribute recognition model. ✓: Compressed images, ✗: Uncompressed images

Experimental Setup (ES)		ES1	ES2	ES3
Train set		✗	✗	✓
Test set		✗	✓	✓
Smile classifier model				
Smiling	Precision	89,23%	80,37% (↓ 8,89%)	87,5% (↓ 1,73%)
	Recall	92,26%	95,85% (↑ 3,59%)	91,25% (↓ 1,01%)
	F1-score	90,72%	87,43% (↓ 3,29%)	89,34% (↓ 1,38%)
Not Smiling	Precision	92%	94,87% (↑ 2,87%)	90,87% (↓ 1,13%)
	Recall	88,88%	76,62% (↓ 12,26%)	86,98% (↓ 1,9%)
	F1-score	90,41%	84,77%(↓ 5,64%)	88,88%(↓ 1,53%)
ALL	Accuracy	90,57%	86,23% (↓ 4,34%)	89,11% (↓ 1,46%)
	Precision	90,61%	87,62% (↓ 2,99%)	89,19% (↓ 1,42%)
	Recall	90,57%	86,23% (↓ 4,34%)	89,11% (↓ 1,46%)
	F1-score	90,56%	86,10% (↓ 4,46%)	89,11% (↓ 1,45%)
Gender classifier model				
Male	Precision	98%	95,15% (↓ 2,85%)	97,24% (↓ 0,76%)
	Recall	98,38%	93,48% (↓ 4,9%)	96,36% (↓ 2,02%)
	F1-score	98,19%	94,31% (↓ 3,88%)	96,8% (↓ 1,39%)
Female	Precision	97,42%	89,94% (↓ 7,48%)	94,3% (↓ 3,12%)
	Recall	96,81%	92,43% (↓ 4,38%)	95,66% (↓ 1,15%)
	F1-score	97,11%	91,17%(↓ 5,94%)	94,97%(↓ 2,14%)
ALL	Accuracy	97,78%	93,08% (↓ 4,7%)	96,09% (↓ 1,69%)
	Precision	97,77%	93,13% (↓ 4,64%)	96,1% (↓ 1,67%)
	Recall	97,78%	93,08% (↓ 4,7%)	96,09% (↓ 1,69%)
	F1-score	97,77%	93,09% (↓ 4,68%)	96,09% (↓ 1,68%)

recall, and F1-score). Indeed, the accuracy of the smile classifier model and gender classifier model are respectively 90.57% and 97.78%.

With the introduction of compression, performance drops from the baseline. We are interested in this part in the analysis of the results under the experimental configuration ES2. The performances of the smile classification model and the gender classification model deteriorate respectively by 4.34% and 4.7% in terms of accuracy. This supports our hypothesis that generative model-based image compression has a negative effect on the model's ability to correctly detect smile (and gender). Although it was expected, our goal is to measure and quantify this effect, which can only be achieved through these experiments. The idea is to quantify the impact of compression using QRes-VAE on the performance of FAR.

So far, we have used the overall recognition performance for the evaluation. We now analyze performance behavior by class. According to F1-score, which combines precision and recall, the gender classifier model, for example, obtains lower results in both classes. The "Female" class remains a challenge because it is characterized by the lowest value according to the three metrics (precision, recall, and F1-score): a decrease of 7.48% in precision, 4.38% in recall, and 5.64% in F1-score.

This decrease is huge, especially in real-world use cases. This gives rise to significant ethical considerations as it can distort decisions and lead to inequitable treatment in the context of gender detection. In the field of healthcare, this reduced performance leads to inappropriate medical treatments and erroneous predictions of health outcomes. Medical decision-making is critical, and a wrong decision has very dangerous consequences. In the field of security, for example, in gender-based access control systems, detection errors could lead to unauthorized persons gaining access to secure areas.

Impact of Training Set Compression on Face Attribute Recognition. We are interested in this part in the evaluation of the performances of the two models under the two experimental configurations ES2 and ES3. When the model is trained on original uncompressed images, the accuracy as well as the other metrics, calculated on the test set of compressed images, decrease considerably compared to the reference obtained with the test set of uncompressed images. Meanwhile, when the model is trained on compressed images, the decrease is less significant. For example, for the smile classifier model, the accuracy decreases by 4.34% if the model is trained on uncompressed images and tested on compressed images, and when the model is trained and tested on compressed images, the accuracy decreases by 1.46%: an improvement of 2.88% when compression is introduced during training.

Each of these configurations replicates certain expected real-life scenarios. For example, the second configuration, where the training set is uncompressed and the test set is compressed, is feasible in the case where the training data is collected in its original uncompressed format and the model is trained before use. In use, especially in real time, data is compressed for efficient storage or transmission.

Compression Rate vs. Face Attribute Recognition Performance Trade-Off. We are interested in this part in the analysis of the impact of compression level on face attribute recognition performance. As mentioned in Sect. 2.2, the quality of the reconstructed images deteriorates considerably for $\lambda < 8$. For this, we limit ourselves to the effect of the resulting reduction in image quality for compression levels corresponding to $\lambda = \{1, 2, 4, 8\}$. Figure 4 shows substantial degradation in the accuracy of both models as the level of compression increases (i.e., λ decreases). The highest compression rate corresponding to $\lambda = 1$ leads to the most significant reduction in performance: a reduction of 4.34% in the accuracy of the smile classifier model and of 4.7% in the accuracy of the gender classifier model compared to the baseline achieved with uncompressed images. Thus, severe compression results in the most significant decrease in face attribute recognition performance. A moderate compression rate, corresponding to $\lambda = 8$ in our case, does not lead to a difference in accuracy: a reduction of 0.38% in the accuracy of the smile classifier model and of 0.73% in the accuracy of the gender classifier model compared to the baseline achieved with uncompressed images.

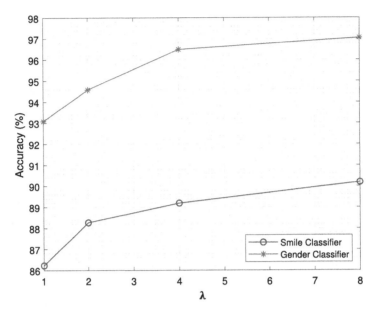

Fig. 4. Accuracy of face attribute recognition model for compressed face images at different compression levels corresponding to λ under experimental setup 2.

This allows us to underline the interest of making a compromise between compression rate and face attribute recognition accuracy, depending on the use case and the constraints of the implemented application. Several factors must be taken into account. The nature of the application is a crucial factor. In critical security or healthcare applications, such as access control systems or medical diagnostic aids, attention must be paid to system efficiency, which implies greater face attribute recognition accuracy. Therefore, low compression is preferable. However, in consumer applications focused on user experience, fast and efficient real-time processing is advantageous, which means a higher compression rate may be acceptable while maintaining satisfactory face attribute recognition performance. Another factor to consider is the hardware resources available. In the case of limited resources for storage, calculation, or transmission, higher compression allows efficient use of resources. However, if the resources are available, we can favor higher face attribute recognition accuracy, which allows for better system efficiency. If processing time and calculation speed play a critical factor in the application, for example, in real-time monitoring systems, it is necessary to compromise by slightly sacrificing accuracy to obtain faster results. The nature of the solution is also a factor to consider. If the solution is embedded, such as a face attribute recognition device integrated into an autonomous system, the resources are generally limited, which implies a high compression rate. If the solution is IoT (Internet of Things), i.e., the face attribute recognition system will be integrated into an IoT environment, network resource constraints (limited bandwidth, low-speed communication protocols, etc.) are taxed. Hence, the need in such cases for a high compression rate for better optimization of the use of network resources.

5 Conclusion

In this paper, we study the impact of image compression based on QRes-VAE, a deep generative autoencoder model, on face attribute recognition performance, in particular, smile and gender detection in real-world uses. We focus on the challenges and considerations involved in balancing compression rate and recognition performance. The results of the experiments performed on the CelebA dataset have highlighted the limitations of image compression based on QRes-VAE in face attribute recognition applications.

This allows us to consider other techniques and methods for a more efficient and robust end-to-end framework for attribute recognition of compressed face images. We propose as a prospective the use of attention mechanisms in the recognition network to help the model focus on relevant features and compensate for distortions due to compression. We also propose as prospects to add a module based on Generative Adversarial Networks (GAN) between the reconstruction network and the recognition network, which allows generating high-quality uncompressed versions of compressed images. A last perspective is to propose a new cost function for an end-to-end training of the whole framework sensitive to the FAR task.

References

1. Benbarrad, T., Salhaoui, M., Anas, H., Arioua, M.: Impact of standard image compression on the performance of image classification with deep learning. In: Ben Ahmed, M., Boudhir, A.A., Karaş, İR., Jain, V., Mellouli, S. (eds.) SCA 2021. LNNS, vol. 393, pp. 901–911. Springer, Cham (2022). https://doi.org/10.1007/978-3-030-94191-8_73

2. Bian, N., Liang, F., Fu, H., Lei, B.: A deep image compression framework for face recognition. In: 2019 2nd China Symposium on Cognitive Computing and Hybrid Intelligence (CCHI), pp. 99–104 (2019)

3. Delac, K., Grgic, S., Grgic, M.: Image compression in face recognition - a literature survey. In: Delac, K., Grgic, M., Bartlett, M.S. (eds.) Recent Advances in Face Recognition, Chap. 1. IntechOpen, Rijeka (2008)

4. Dosovitskiy, A., et al.: An image is worth 16x16 words: transformers for image recognition at scale. In: International Conference on Learning Representations, May 2021

5. Duan, Z., Lu, M., Ma, J., Huang, Y., Ma, Z., Zhu, F.: QARV: quantization-aware ResNet VAE for lossy image compression. ArXiv abs/2302.08899 (2023)

6. Duan, Z., Lu, M., Ma, Z., Zhu, F.: Lossy image compression with quantized hierarchical VAEs. In: 2023 IEEE/CVF Winter Conference on Applications of Computer Vision (WACV), pp. 198–207 (2023)

7. He, K., Zhang, X., Ren, S., Sun, J.: Deep residual learning for image recognition. In: 2016 IEEE Conference on Computer Vision and Pattern Recognition (CVPR), pp. 770–778 (2016)

8. Jamil, S., Piran, M.J., Rahman, M., Kwon, O.J.: Learning-driven lossy image compression: a comprehensive survey. Eng. Appl. Artif. Intell. **123**, 106361 (2023)

9. Kingma, D.P., Salimans, T., Jozefowicz, R., Chen, X., Sutskever, I., Welling, M.: Improved variational inference with inverse autoregressive flow. In: Advances in Neural Information Processing Systems, vol. 29, December 2016

10. Liu, Z., Mao, H., Wu, C.Y., Feichtenhofer, C., Darrell, T., Xie, S.: A convnet for the 2020s. In: 2022 IEEE/CVF Conference on Computer Vision and Pattern Recognition (CVPR), pp. 11966–11976 (2022)

11. Liu, Z., Luo, P., Wang, X., Tang, X.: Deep learning face attributes in the wild. In: Proceedings of International Conference on Computer Vision (ICCV), December 2015

12. Mishra, D., Singh, S.K., Singh, R.K.: Deep architectures for image compression: a critical review. Signal Process. **191**, 108346 (2021)

13. Ozah, N., Kolokolova, A.: Compression improves image classification accuracy. In: Meurs, M.-J., Rudzicz, F. (eds.) Canadian AI 2019. LNCS (LNAI), vol. 11489, pp. 525–530. Springer, Cham (2019). https://doi.org/10.1007/978-3-030-18305-9_55

14. Patel, M.I., Suthar, S., Thakar, J.: Survey on image compression using machine learning and deep learning. In: 2019 International Conference on Intelligent Computing and Control Systems (ICCS), pp. 1103–1105 (2019)

15. Sebai, D., Missaoui, N., Zouaghi, A.: Signal extraction for classification of noisy images compressed using autoencoders. In: International Conference in Central Europe on Computer Graphics, Visualization and Computer Vision (2021)

16. Shi, W., et al.: Real-time single image and video super-resolution using an efficient sub-pixel convolutional neural network. In: Proceedings of the IEEE Conference on Computer Vision and Pattern Recognition, pp. 1874–1883, June 2016

17. Valenzise, G., Purica, A.I., Hulusic, V., Cagnazzo, M.: Quality assessment of deep-learning-based image compression. In: 2018 IEEE 20th International Workshop on Multimedia Signal Processing (MMSP), pp. 1–6 (2018)

18. Wang, X., Peng, J., Zhang, S., Chen, B., Wang, Y., Guo, Y.H.: A survey of face recognition. ArXiv abs/2212.13038 (2022)

19. Yang, Y., Mandt, S., Theis, L.: An introduction to neural data compression. Found. Trends Comput. Graph. Vis. **15**(2), 113–200 (2023)

20. Zhang, K., Tan, L., Li, Z., Qiao, Y.: Gender and smile classification using deep convolutional neural networks. In: 2016 IEEE Conference on Computer Vision and Pattern Recognition Workshops (CVPRW), pp. 739–743 (2016)

Implementation of a Video Game Controlled by Pressing the Upper Arm Using PPG Sensor

Kazuki Yoshida[✉][ORCID], Goro Mizuno, Naoki Kurata, and Kazuya Murao[ORCID]

Ritsumeikan University, Kusatsu, Shiga, Japan
{kazuki.yoshida,goro.mizuno,naoki.kurata}@iis.ise.ritsumei.ac.jp,
murao@cs.ritsumei.ac.jp

Abstract. Many interaction methods between users and wearable devices have been proposed until now. In previous works, an interaction method to input commands by controlling the photoelectric pulse wave sensor value is proposed. In this paper, we propose a new interaction method using pulse wave control, a video game played using pulse wave control as a game input. The proposed method uses a pulse wave like a game controller. Two types of video games were implemented: a side-scrolling game and a quick-fire shooting game. A total of 18,360 logs were collected and evaluated. As a result, the idea of the proposed method was well appreciated; however, the operability of the game remained an issue.

Keywords: Wearable · Pulse wave · Interaction · Game · Controller

1 Introduction

Various wearable devices have been developed and are becoming widely available. Wearable devices can collect a wide range of information related to the device's motion and physiological information. As an example of using data collected by a wearable device, an interaction method between the user and the wearable device has been proposed [8,9]. However, these methods cause noise and vibration, and the environmental noise causes a loss of accuracy. To solve this problem, Akimoto et al. [1] proposed an interaction method that modifies the photoelectric pulse wave sensor value by pressing on the upper arm (hereafter referred to as pulse wave control) to input commands to the smartwatch.

In this study, we propose a video game that uses pulse wave control for game input. The proposed video game uses a pulse wave like a game console. The processing in this game is based on whether the pulse wave control is performed. A side-scrolling game and a quick-fire shooting game were implemented. Two games were played by the visitors at the exhibition hall.

The primary contributions of this study are as follows:

- We suggest the potential in interaction using pulse wave control by upper arm pressure for game input.
- A game using pulse wave control was implemented and exhibited for four months to conduct a large-scale evaluation experiment.

P. Delir Haghighi et al. (Eds.): MoMM 2023, LNCS 14417, pp. 173–178, 2023.
https://doi.org/10.1007/978-3-031-48348-6_14

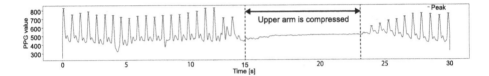

Fig. 1. The PPG values at fingertip during upper arm compression.

2   Related Works

Various methods exist for interactions with smart devices. Reyes et al. [8] proposed a method to control a smartwatch based on the sound generated by the user's breath movement. Yeo et al. [9] proposed a method to recognize finger poses and hand gestures by including a camera in a wrist-worn wearable device. Akimoto et al. [1] proposed an input interface to a wearable device that inputs commands by pressing on the upper arm. As described above, many interaction methods have been proposed. However, to our knowledge, there is no study on using pulse wave control interaction technology as a game controller.

On the other hand, many methods are proposed using pulse waves. Robert et al. [2] estimated the peak time of an ECG by calculating the time difference between pulse wave peaks. Liu et al. [6] proposed a method for estimating blood pressure using pulse wave data. Yoshida et al. [10] proposed a method for estimating the sensor wearing position based on the pulse wave arrival time difference. As described above, many methods exist for using pulse waves. However, to the best of our knowledge, no studies focus on modifying pulse waves or using the controlled pulse wave as the game controller. In addition, stopping blood flow is conducted during blood pressure measurement [3,4]; however, it does not control the pulse wave dynamically as in this study.

3   Proposed Method

This section describes the proposed method. In this study, the upper arm pressed is called a "pressed state," and the upper arm not pressed is called a "not-pressed state."

3.1   Pressed and Not-Pressed States Detection

This study targets a photoelectric pulse wave (PPG: Photoplethysmogram) sensor. The PPG sensor uses the property of hemoglobin in the blood to absorb light. Therefore, by pressing the upper arm and decreasing the blood volume, the sensor value becomes smaller at the end of the fingertips. Figure 1 shows that the pulse wave sensor value is so small when the upper arm is pressed. Based on this fact, the proposed method detects the pressed and not-pressed states. When a pulse wave peak is detected by the peak detection program [5], it is assumed to be in the not-pressed state. Hereafter, t is the time of the most recent peak

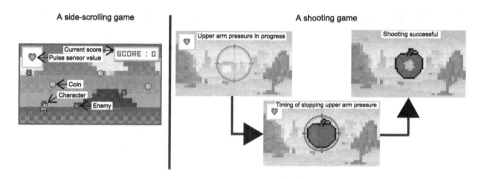

Fig. 2. The game-play screen of the implemented game. The left side is a side-scrolling game, and the right is a shooting game.

among the detected peaks. The pressed state is assumed when no new peaks are detected by the peak detection program more than $t + 1000$ ms later.

3.2   Video Games

In this study, we implemented two games: a side-scrolling game and a quick-fire shooting game (hereafter referred to as a "shooting game").

In the side-scrolling game, the player collects coins while avoiding enemies by moving the character on the screen using pulse wave control. The character moves upward in the pressed state and downward in the not-pressed state. Figure 2 on the left shows the game-play screen of a side-scrolling game. The score increases by 1,000 when the character touches a coin. The game is finished when the character hits an enemy. The coins and enemies flow constantly from right to left on the screen. When the game ends, the final and highest scores are displayed on the screen. A heart-shaped image is displayed in the upper left corner of the screen, whose image size changes according to the pulse wave sensor value. The player can check that the pulse wave is measured correctly through the heart-shaped image.

In shooting game, the player competes in the time from pressed state to not-pressed state. Figure 2 on the right shows the game-play screen of a shooting game. When the game starts, the player presses his or her upper arm to display a green target. After a random time in the $1 - 5$ s range from displaying a green target, the apple target appears as shown on the screen. When the apple target appears, the time measurement starts, and the player stops the upper arm pressure as quickly as possible. After the not-pressed state is detected, the time measurement stops, and the game ends. When the game is finished, the time of this play and the shortest time in the score are displayed on the screen.

Table 1. Results of the evaluation criteria calculated from the play logs.

Evaluation criteria	Evaluation result			
	Average	Median	Maximum	Minimum
(1) Play score [points]	1126	1000	38000	0
(2) Playtime [s]	38.902	29.740	510.244	15.944
(3) Coin get rate [%]	28.635	0.0	100.0	0.0
(4) Play score [s]	3.504	2.038	3418.12	0.204
(5) Playtime [s]	28.143	15.886	3587.25	1.333
(6) Time taken for the target [s]	12.064	5.601	3122.39	1.816
(7) Number of times target appeared [times]	1	1	21	1

4   Evaluation Experiment

This section describes an evaluation experiment using play logs and survey responses from players.

4.1   Experiment Environment

The implemented game was exhibited and played by visitors at The Lab. at Grand Front Osaka, Osaka, Japan. Posters describing how to play each game and control the pulse wave were placed near the exhibition. An evaluation was conducted on 18,360 logs (side-scrolling game: 8,410 logs, shooting game: 9,950 logs) collected from October 5, 2022 (15:00) to February 28, 2023 (20:00). An Arduino program [5] was used to detect pulse wave peaks. The pulse wave sensor made by pulsesensor.com [7] is used. The game was implemented in Python. The player can select the game by pressing up or down arrow keys. The pulse wave sensor was attached to a desk surface. The following evaluation criteria were used: (1) play score (side-scrolling game), (2) playtime (side-scrolling game), (3) a coin get rate (side-scrolling game), (4) play score (shooting game), (5) playtime (shooting game) (6) the time taken for the apple target to appear (shooting game), (7) the number of times the target appeared before the score is displayed (shooting game). In addition, some players were asked to the difficulty and operability of this game by the exhibition staff.

4.2   Results and Consideration

Table 1 shows the results of each evaluation criterion calculated from the play logs. First, we focus on the side-scrolling game. In (1) play score, the average score is 1,126 points; conversely, the maximum score is 38,000 points, indicating a big difference between players. In (2) playtime, there is a big difference between the average and maximum values. It is thought that it was difficult for beginners without knowledge to control the pulse wave by holding the blood vessels accurately. Therefore, it is necessary to modify the method of information display and the pressed state detection part to the pulse wave control more accurately.

Table 2. Opinions on game difficulty and operability.

· The response was sometimes not very good, but I did not feel difficulty

· I was good at stopping the pulse because I had done anatomy.

· It is difficult because it does not move as expected

· The idea is interesting but difficult to control.

· Having the mother hold the child's arm was better

· I played with my sleeves rolled up, as there was no response through my jacket.

In (3) a coin get rate, the average was 28.635%. The reason is thought to indicate that the lag in the pulse wave control was not used. The farther away the pulse wave is from the heart, the longer the sensor receives the pulse wave. A lag occurs before the sensor measures the change in blood volume passing through the upper arm. Therefore, it is thought that implementing a tutorial that allows the user to experience the lag between the upper arm pressure will improve the coin get rate.

Next, we focus on the shooting game. In (4) play score, the average is 3.5 s, while the maximum is 3418.12 s, showing a large difference. Also, focusing on the maximum values of (6) the time taken for the apple target to appear, it takes time for the target to appear. This is because the player could not perform the desired controls, and the game-play was left in the process of playing. It is necessary to improve the pulse wave control part so that it is not left. In (7) the number of times the target appeared, focusing on the average and median, many players could finish the game, as we had expected with one pulse wave control. However, focusing on the maximum value, the results showed that 21 times were tried. This is because the player's upper arm pressure position was incorrect, and insufficient pressure was given. It is necessary to show the pressure position more clearly.

Finally, we focus on the survey for this game. Table 2 shows the responses received about players' impressions of playing the game. In the survey results, many respondents commented that the idea was interesting; however, they were negative about the game's difficulty, saying that the pulse wave control was difficult. This game requires the player to press down on blood vessels accurately, so it is thought to be easier to operate by a person who knows the position of blood vessels. This result indicates that it is necessary to provide information to make it easier for players to find the position of blood vessels. On the other hand, some respondents indicated that it was more difficult for children to control the pulse wave with their grip strength, so it was more successful to have their parents do it. Another respondent rolled up their sleeves to play the game because the game did not respond when played through their jacket. In both cases, it is considered that pulse wave control could not be performed due to not enough pressure on the upper arm. The additional device that adds pressure, such as a cuff for blood pressure measurement, would allow more players to play the game.

5   Conclusion

In this study, we proposed a video game played with pulse wave control by upper arm pressure. A side-scrolling game and a quick-fire shooting game were implemented, and the games were exhibited and collected data from visitors' experiences. As a result, the proposed method idea was well appreciated; however, the operability of the game remained an issue.

In the future, the game will improve to make the game easier to play for beginners. In addition, we plan to design a method for estimating vascular age and pulse wave velocity by playing proposed game.

Acknowledgements. This research was funded by the Japan Science and Technology Agency, PRESTO grant number JPMJPR1937, Japan.

References

1. Akimoto, Y., et al.: Design and implementation of an input interface for wearable devices using pulse wave control by compressing the upper arm. In: Proceedings of the Augmented Humans International Conference 2021, pp. 280–282. Association for Computing Machinery, New York, NY, USA (2021). https://doi.org/10.1145/3458709.3458998
2. Dürichen, R., et al.: Prediction of electrocardiography features points using seismocardiography data: a machine learning approach. In: Proceedings of the 2018 ACM International Symposium on Wearable Computers, pp. 96–99. Association for Computing Machinery, New York, NY, USA (2018). https://doi.org/10.1145/3267242.3267283
3. Geddes, L., et al.: The efficient detection of korotkoff sounds. Med. Biol. Eng. **6**(6), 603–609 (1968). https://doi.org/10.1007/BF02474723
4. Geddes, L., et al.: Characterization of the oscillometric method for measuring indirect blood pressure. Ann. Biomed. Eng. **10**(6), 271–280 (1982). https://doi.org/10.1007/BF02367308
5. Gitman, Y., et al.: Pulsesensor_amped_arduino (2018). https://github.com/WorldFamousElectronics/PulseSensor_Amped_Arduino
6. Liu, Z.D., et al.: Cuffless blood pressure estimation using pressure pulse wave signals. Sensors **18**(12), 4227 (2018). https://doi.org/10.3390/s18124227
7. Murphy, J., et al.: pulsesensor.com (2018). https://pulsesensor.com/
8. Reyes, G., et al.: Whoosh: non-voice acoustics for low-cost, hands-free, and rapid input on smartwatches. In: Proceedings of the 2016 ACM International Symposium on Wearable Computers, pp. 120–127. Association for Computing Machinery, New York, NY, USA (2016). https://doi.org/10.1145/2971763.2971765
9. Yeo, H.S., et al.: Opisthenar: hand poses and finger tapping recognition by observing back of hand using embedded wrist camera. In: Proceedings of the 32nd Annual ACM Symposium on User Interface Software and Technology, pp. 963–971. UIST 2019, Association for Computing Machinery, New York, NY, USA (2019). https://doi.org/10.1145/3332165.3347867
10. Yoshida, K., et al.: Load position estimation method for wearable devices based on difference in pulse wave arrival time. Sensors **22**(3), 1090 (2022). https://doi.org/10.3390/s22031090

Immerscape: Supporting the Creation of Immersive Soundscapes by Users in Cultural Heritage Contexts

Carolina Ferreira, Sofia Cavaco, Armanda Rodrigues(✉),
and Nuno Correia

NOVA School of Science and Technology and NOVA LINCS, Universidade NOVA de Lisboa, Campus da Caparica, 2829-516 Quinta da Torre, Caparica, Portugal
{scavaco,a.rodrigues,nmc}@fct.unl.pt, crd.ferreira@campus.fct.unl.pt

Abstract. In this paper, we introduce Immerscape, an interactive tool for composing immersive soundscapes. Immerscape can be used to support the study and creation of historical soundscapes, enhancing the experience for visitors at culture and heritage sites. The tool allows non-technical users to compose immersive auditory scenes, by simply combining different sound recordings that simulate moving sound sources, as well as sound sources positioned in different locations in the scene. A preliminary evaluation of the tool's usability and acceptance has been conducted, involving domain users and other volunteers.

Keywords: Historical Soundscapes · Digital Heritage · Spatial Audio · Immersive Audio · Audio-visual Interaction · Immersive experiences · User Generated Content

1 Introduction

The use of soundscapes enriches the dissemination of the history of places and contributes to enhance the visitors experience in tourism contexts [1,9]. Listening to historical soundscapes of a place can help the visitor travel back in time when visiting a location, as soundscapes provide a unique way of experiencing auditory memories of a specific period in history. However, making historical soundscapes available to the general public may be a real challenge, due to the nonexistence of original audio captures of the past.

Researchers who study the interdisciplinary connections of historical soundscapes, use written testimonies to support the creation of structured descriptions of historical events (Fig. 1.a). They combine current audio clips to create simplified soundscapes that mimic the auditory event, as described in historical documentation. It is relevant, for these researchers, to acquire skills to understand immersive audio technology and use current recordings for generating simple simulated soundscapes.

Here we propose Immerscape, an interactive tool for composing immersive soundscapes which can be used to support the study of historical soundscapes.

P. Delir Haghighi et al. (Eds.): MoMM 2023, LNCS 14417, pp. 179–186, 2023.
https://doi.org/10.1007/978-3-031-48348-6_15

The tool, which uses audio recordings as a basis to compose immersive auditory scenes, can convert them into immersive 3D audio files. This process includes the composition and spatialisation of sound, using Head Related Transfer Functions (HRTFs) [11], to generate audio files that provide a sense of immersion in the scene, when using personal devices, such as headphones, to reproduce them. The user can add audio clips to the tridimensional environment (provided by the Unity game engine[1]), associate them to 3D generic representations, and define their locations and movement throughout the unravelling of the scene. A preliminary user study was conceived to evaluate Immerscape, with results showing that the tool includes the essential features to support the target users produce simplified immersive audio scenes.

Immerscape was developed in the context of the PASEV[2] project, which is set to contribute to the patrimonialization of the Portuguese city of Évora's soundscapes. Évora is located in the southern region of Alentejo and has been classified as world heritage by UNESCO. Évora's very rich historic soundscape results from the intense musical activity in churches, squares, theatres as well as other social events that have taken place over the centuries.

The main goal of the project is to chart historical sound events in the city, between 1540 (creation of Évora's Archbishopric) and 1910 (beginning of the Republic in Portugal), in a digital platform that gathers information about Évora in several formats (image, 2D and 3D video and audio), associating these testimonies with points of interest in a map of the city.

PASEV aims to provide audio content related to the soundscapes of the relevant period, through various virtual interactive interfaces, as well as tools to enable visitors to create their own simplified soundscapes [5,9,10].

2   Related Work

Immersive audio has been used before in historical, cultural, entertainment, and tourism related contexts. Focused mainly on the use of spatialised audio for entertainment, Gomes et al. applied an audio immersion technique to be used in a virtual reality environment, to create an immersive reproduction of musical events [6]. The spatialised audio combined with image, in a mobile prototype, allows the user to move the device around and hear sound's direction changing. The Virtual St. Paul's Cathedral Project uses spatialised audio in a historical context to allow listeners to experience what might have been listening to musical and liturgical events, and some historic sermons, at the site [14]. In the MeSch project [8], multiple loudspeakers are used on location and sound is introduced into the exhibitions at key moments, when the visitor is sensed.

The creation of soundscapes and spatialised audio is known to be a complex process. Sound Generation Tools such as those in the SoDA[3] project are targeted towards sound designers and too complex to be used by inexperienced users [2].

---

[1] https://unity.com/.

[2] https://pasev.hcommons.org/.

[3] Sound Design Accelerator Project.

The ADAM [12] soundscape mobile platform, focuses on audio augmentation for museum contexts, enabling visitors to create soundscapes to enrich their visit. This tool targets Immerscape's audience, but without immersive characteristics. The INVISO Project [3] also provides support for novice users to create immersive sonic environments, but using 3D dynamic sound components as sound sources.

Finally, tools to support the creation of soundscapes in a cultural heritage context have been proposed, such as support for the conception of historically informed soundscapes [4]. Nonetheless, the support of history and music scholars in the creation of simple historically referenced immersive soundscapes is still not entirely covered.

3   An Immersive Soundscape Generating Tool: Immerscape

Immerscape was designed for supporting PASEV's researchers in the task of creating audio clips as simplified immersive soundscapes for Évora's visitors, but it can be used to generate soundscapes for various purposes. It also supports the generation of standard format audio files from the immersive auditory scenes created.

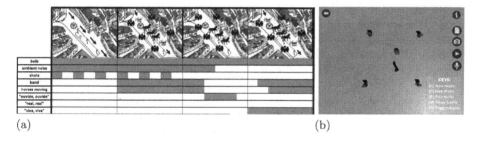

(a)   (b)

Fig. 1. (a) Soundscape storyboard with timeline of an historic event in Évora: King Afonso VI's acclamation ceremony (1656). (b) Immerscape GUI in up-view camera mode. Current elements include an audio object (the cube in the middle of the scene) and four mark points around it.

Figure 1.a illustrates the storyboard of a historical soundscape, created from existing descriptions in historical documentation. It describes one of Évora's historical events: the acclamation of the new King, Afonso VI in 1656 and was used as the basis to create a soundscape with Immerscape. Several audio tracks were collected to be used together in Immerscape, as defined in the storyboard. The orange bars in the bottom of the figure represent the audio tracks used in the soundscape, which start and stop playing at different times, and which were spatialised with Immerscape, to simulate the sound sources' movement and positioning.

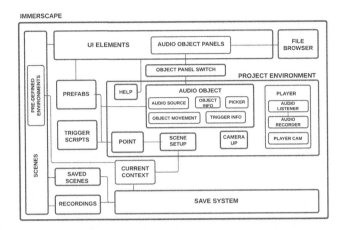

Fig. 2. Immerscape architecture

The user can populate the scene with audio objects (represented in Fig. 1.a by horses, people, musical instruments, etc.). They can then associate sounds to the audio objects and define temporal limits for them. The position of the audio objects in the scene defines their relative position to the listener. In addition, the audio objects can move in the scene and, As a result, the listeners hear the sounds moving in the 3D space around them. The soundscapes resulting from the application of this methodology can be used on location, to give the visitor a sense of reliving the scene by becoming immersed in the past event's audio. In PASEV's Map Interface , they have been associated to the geographical location where the event took place, and can be played by the visitor when they arrive at the site.

Immerscape was developed with Unity. Google's Resonance Audio Software Developer Kit was used to create the spatialised immersive audio with HRTFs [7]. At the heart of the Google Resonance Audio SDK are the SADIE (Spatial Audio For Domestic Interactive Entertainment) Project's HRTFs [7,13].

3.1   Immerscape Development

The set of requirements for Immerscape stems from the generalization of the mechanisms needed to create historical soundscapes of Évora. The core features of Immerscape are the following: (1) To have an immersive presence within the scene's environment; (2) To create audio sources; (3) To edit audio properties of each source; (4) To provide movement to the audio source; (5) To provide a mechanism of triggering sound events; (6) To play and save the soundscape associated with the scene. Figure 2 shows Immerscape's system organization, which takes advantage of the Unity Editor properties and its built-in assets: Scenes, Game Objects, Audio Components, its UI-tools, among others.

Immerscape's development environment supports the storage of multiple under development projects. Six predefined environments are available as base templates, which can be used to build soundscapes. Scenes can be populated by audio objects , each with an associated audio clip, and parameters such as volume, altitude from the ground, when it is played, among others. The final composed sound consists of the mixture of the sounds from all the audio objects present in the scene. The audio objects can be positioned in different locations of the scene, moved and rotated. These actions affect the sound associated to the audio components and affect the properties of the final sound composition.

The Audio objects movements can be set by the user as routes, which are defined by a series of spatially located mark Points (Fig. 1.b). The user indicates the speed and selects the order by which the audio object must reach, or pass, the selected mark points. In addition, audio objects can have action Triggers associated to the mark points in their routes.

The user is immersed into the scene in character form, represented by the Player (Fig. 2), and can move around the environment. The Player has, among other components, an Audio Listener component, which picks up the sounds emitted by the Audio Objects' audio sources with immersive spatial awareness. The engine can then simulate the effects of a source's distance and position from the listener and play it to the user accordingly. Then, the scripting component, the Audio Recorder, can be used to record the composed sound. When the recorder script is activated, it writes everything the Audio Listener picks up into a WAV file until the recorder is stopped.

4   User Study and Results

In order to assess Immerscape's functionalities, the quality of content generated, as well as the ease of use and acceptance, we conducted a preliminary user study with a total of 17 participants (9 men and 8 women). The participants were divided into two distinct groups: developers (with advanced technological skills) and non-developers. This latter profile, i.e. users that use technology from a user perspective, corresponds to the profile of the target audience for Immerscape. (mainly students and researchers related to the history and musicology areas).

Since this work was developed during the Covid-19 pandemic, the study was performed remotely over Zoom[4]. The tool ran in one of the authors' computer while the participants tested the tool using Zoom's remote control.

The study's protocol consisted of a set of eight small interrelated tasks that addressed the tool's most relevant features and that resulted in the creation of a simple soundscape. The tasks included: (task 1) creating a new project with a predefined sound environment and testing the player's movements; (task 2) setting up the scene, which includes positioning audio objects and mark points in the scene according to the layout presented Fig. 1.b ; (task 3) editing the scene, which includes defining the sound associated to objects in the scene; (task 4) testing the audio, which includes playing the scene and navigating around the environment to explore the spatial dimensions of the sound; (task 5) applying

---

[4] https://zoom.us.

movement to audio objects, as well as rearranging the objects' positions in the scene; (task 6) creating and manipulating trigger events; (task 7) recording the created soundscape; and (task 8) accessing the previously recorded audio.

All participants completed the tasks successfully. Although some tasks presented different difficulty levels, most were considered easy to complete.

The analysis of the results was separated by user profiles. Globally, all participants were successful in creating the soundscape and recorded it with relative ease. Most participants considered using Immerscape to create and record a soundscape easy (24%) or very easy (64%). Only 12% of all participants considered of average difficulty using Immerscape to generate immersive audio.

The study shows different results for the two groups of participants: in general, Developers found using the tool easier and more intuitive than Non-Developers. The large majority of Developer participants (90%) considered using Immerscape very easy, and 10%, simply easy. On the other hand, while the results from Non-Developer participants are also good, it is clear that these results are lower than for the Developers group. Only 29% of all Non-Developer participants found Immerscape very easy to use, while 42% considered it easy and 29% considered it of medium difficulty.

In order to further explore the different results between the two groups, we conducted a two-sample t-test. An unpaired t-test was conducted, since it is used when comparing two independent or unrelated groups (Developers vs Non Developers). For each one of the tasks, we calculated the average easiness for both Developers and Non-Developers. The results of the unpaired t-test considered the difference between the two groups to be very statistically significant.

The contrast in the Developer vs Non-Developer results is noticeable in the different tasks' results and it can be explained by the differences in the participant groups. While the Developer participants present a narrow age range and similar education backgrounds, the Non-Developer participants represent more heterogeneous profiles. They represent a wider range of ages with different education backgrounds and different levels of experience working with software. It can be argued that the age and experience with simulated environments are the two most significant factors that influence the results. However, due to the small number of participants, further research is needed to determine this.

When questioned about the level of immersion and the quality of the audio clip generated by the tool, the results show, overall, a good or very good sense of immersion. According to the results, 53% of all participants consider the audio to provide a very good sense of immersion, while 41% of all participants consider it good, and 6% of all participants consider it only somewhat immersive.

It is worth noting that the immersion testing conditions were not ideal as the audio was shared over Zoom. In particular, one of the participants reported that the result from reproducing the scene was not the expected one. They considered that the spatial dimension of the sound was not as evident as they expected. Yet, when this participant heard the resulting audio file locally in their computer, they stated to be satisfied with the result, concluding that the testing conditions were not ideal to listen to the immersive audio in full quality.

Additionally, the participants were queried on the level of satisfaction using Immerscape. According to the results, 35% of all participants were satisfied using the tool's functionalities to create sounds, whereas 65% claimed to be very satisfied while using the tool. 70% of all Developer participants reported being very satisfied, while only 57% of all Non-Developer participants said the same.

When asked about how useful they considered Immerscape to compose auditory scenes and generate immersive audio clips, the results show that the large majority of all participants (88%) recognizes the tool as very useful. While all Developer participants considered Immerscape very useful to generate immersive audio scenes, 29% of the Non-Developer participants considered it simply useful.

With the exception of one, the participants had never used a similar tool to generate immersive audio content. The participant that reported having used a similar application was a musicology PhD student. He reported having used MAX/MSP, which is a visual programming language for music. He used it for an eight-channels composition.

5   Conclusions and Future Work

While there are existing solutions for creating immersive soundscapes, non developers and non audio professionals may experience difficulties to create these sounds. Here, we propose a tool that can easily be used by inexperienced users to interactively create immersive soundscapes.

The proposed tool focuses on providing a set of simple-to-use functionalities to create spatially-aware immersive soundscapes, using monaural or stereo audio clips. The audio clips can be uploaded to one of the available environments, adjusted and edited to compose a scene through sound. The proposed technique gives the audio recording a spatial dimension, due to the use of HRTFs on each of the uploaded audio clips.

The preliminary user study conducted showed that the tool is accessible to inexperienced users and includes the essential functionalities for creating simple immersive soundscapes. The audio produced in the process has a reported satisfactory quality, providing the desired audio immersion , when playing the composed scene through headphones. It was concluded that a future user study should address tasks of higher complexity. The results also show that although the tool performed well , there is room for improvement (e.g. by making the player's capabilities easier to understand) and some functionalities need to be extended to offer a wider range of options when composing scenes.

As future work, we will take the feedback provided by the study's participants and the observed interaction notes, to improve the design of some aspects of the tool, and implement some of the suggestions provided, including: offering additional confirmation feedback, improving the player's controls in the different camera modes and the interface's layout.

Acknowledgments. PASEV is funded by national funds through FCT/MCTES and co-financed by the European Regional Development Fund (ERDF) through Compete 2020 - Competitiveness and Internationalization Operational Program (POCI). Reference: PTDC/ART-PER/28584/2017 Grant Number: ALT20-03-0145-FEDER-028584/LISBOA-01-0145-FEDER-028584.

References

1. Ardissono, L., Petrelli, D., Kuflik, K.: Personalization in cultural heritage: the road travelled and the one ahead. User Model. User-Adap. Inter. **22**, 73–99 (2012)
2. Casu, M., Koutsomichalis, M., Valle, A.: Imaginary soundscapes: the SoDA project. In: Proceedings of the 9th Audio Mostly: A Conference on Interaction With Sound (AM), pp. 1–8 (2014)
3. Çamcı, A., Lee, K., Roberts, C.J., Forbes, A.G.: INVISO: a cross-platform user interface for creating virtual sonic environments. In: Proceedings of the 30th Annual ACM Symposium on User Interface Software and Technology, pp. 507–518. UIST 2017, ACM, New York, NY, USA (2017). https://doi.org/10.1145/3126594.3126644
4. Dedousis, G., Katsantonis, K., Georgaki, A., Andreopoulou, A.: Designing historically informed soundscapes for the augmentation of modern travel-guides: challenges and compromises. In: The 26th International Conference on Auditory Display (ICAD 2021) (2021). https://doi.org/10.21785/icad2021.036
5. Ferreira, A., Wohlmuth, C., Rodrigues, A., Correia, N.: Plataforma multimédia interativa: Experiência imersiva da paisagem sonora histórica de Évora. In: de Sá, V., de Paula, R., Conde, A.F., Gouveia, A. (eds.) Sonoridades Eborenses, pp. 313–335. húmus (2022), https://research.unl.pt/ws/portalfiles/portal/44478809/Sonoridades_Eborenses.pdf
6. Gomes, D., Magalhães, J., Cavaco, S.: Exploring audio immersion using user-generated recordings. In: International Conference on Digital Audio Effects (DAFx) (2019)
7. Kearney, G.: Binaural audio for virtual and augmented reality (2021). https://www.york.ac.uk/research/impact/binaural-sound/. Accessed Jan 2021
8. meSch: Project mesch - About (2019). https://www.mesch-project.eu/about/. Accessed Oct 2021
9. Rodrigues, A., Correia, N.: Using technology in digital humanities for learning and knowledge dissemination. EducaOnline **15**(2), 27–44 (2021)
10. Rosário, J., Rodrigues, A., Correia, N.: A responsive platform for the auditory atlas of Évora. Paisagens sonoras históricas : Anatomia dos sons nas cidades. Évora : Publicações do Cidehus. (2021)
11. Rumsey, F.: Spatial Audio. Focal Press (2001)
12. Salo, K., Bauters, M., Mikkonen, T.: User generated soundscapes activating museum visitors. In: SAC 20117: Proceedings of the ACM Symposium on Applied Computing, pp. 220–227 (2017). https://doi.org/10.1145/3019612.3019691
13. University of York: SADIE — Spatial Audio For Domestic Interactive Entertainment (2021). https://www.york.ac.uk/sadie-project/about.html. Accessed Oct 2021
14. Wall, J.: Recovering Lost Acoustic Spaces: St. Pàul's Cathedral and Paul's Churchyard in 1622. Digital Studies/le Champ Numérique **3**(3) (2014). https://www.digitalstudies.org/articles/10.16995/dscn.58/

Author Index

A
Anh, N. T. 50

B
Bang, L. K. 50
Bang, N. H. 50
Bao, Q. T. 50
Ben Jmaa, Ahmed Baha 159
Berrezueta-Guzman, Jonnathan 104
Boudko, Svetlana 57

C
Cavaco, Sofia 179
Correia, Nuno 179

F
Ferreira, Carolina 179
Findling, Rainhard Dieter 35

G
Gotoh, Yusuke 144

H
Hien, Q. N. 50
Hieu, M. D. 50
Hofer, Philipp 129

K
Khanh, V. H. 50
Khiem, H. G. 50
Khoa, T. D. 50
Kirinoe, Kota 93
Kobiela, Jaroslaw 20
Koyama, Takashi 144
Krusche, Stephan 104
Kurata, Naoki 173

L
Loc, V. C. P. 50
Luong, H. H. 50

M
Mayrhofer, René 3, 129
Miyajima, Yusuke 77
Mizuno, Goro 173
Montalvo, Melissa 104
Murao, Kazuya 173

N
Ngan, N. T. K. 50

O
Ohnishi, Ayumi 93, 120

P
Phuc, N. T. 50

Q
Quy, T. L. 50

R
Rass, Stefan 3
Rodrigues, Armanda 179
Roland, Michael 129

S
Sato, Hiroki 120
Schwarz, Philipp 129
Sebai, Dorsaf 159
Sedlak, David 35

Son, H.   50
Sonntag, Michael   3

T
Terada, Tsutomu   65, 77, 93, 120
Triet, M. N.   50
Trong, D. P. N.   50
Tsukamoto, Masahiko   65, 77, 93, 120

U
Uchida, Junpei   65
Urbaniec, Piotr   20

Y
Yoshida, Kazuki   173

Printed in the United States
by Baker & Taylor Publisher Services